Rural
Resource
Management

■ PROBLEM SOLVING

Rural Resource Management

FOR THE LONG TERM

Sandra E. Miller

Craig W. Shinn

William R. Bentley

IOWA STATE UNIVERSITY PRESS / AMES

Sandra E. Miller is the director of the Arkansas Rural Enterprise Center of Winrock International at Morrilton, Arkansas. The center assists small, rural manufacturers to compete effectively in the global economy. She has worked with nonprofit development organizations and voluntary groups in the South and the Upper Midwest in the United States and with groups in Africa to design effective rural development programs. She earned a Master of Science degree in agricultural economics from the University of Wisconsin–Madison.

Craig W. Shinn is an assistant professor of public administration at Lewis and Clark College at Portland, Oregon. He has dealt with resource-management issues as a forestry researcher with Crown Zellerbach, as the manager of an apple orchard, and as a land-use planning commissioner in his local community. He holds a Ph.D. in forestry from the University of Washington, and a Master of Public Administration degree from Lewis and Clark College.

William R. Bentley is a senior research scientist in the Yale University School of Forestry and Environmental Studies and senior program officer for Winrock International. He has conducted forest-management research and developed forestry programs for Crown Zellerbach, the Ford Foundation, and several universities, including University of Michigan, University of Wisconsin, and Iowa State University. He has addressed forest-management problems in the West, the Upper Midwest, the South, and across Asia. He holds a Ph.D. in agricultural economics from the University of California–Berkeley and a Master's of Forestry from the University of Michigan.

© 1994 Winrock International Institute for Agricultural Development, Morrilton, Arkansas 72110
All rights reserved

Authorization to photocopy items for internal or personal use, or the internal or personal use of specific clients, is granted by Iowa State University Press, provided that the base fee of $.10 per copy is paid directly to the Copyright Clearance Center, 27 Congress Street, Salem, MA 01970. For those organizations that have been granted a photocopy license by CCC, a separate system of payments has been arranged. The fee code for users of the Transactional Reporting Service is 0-8138-0686-0/94 $.10.

♾ Printed on acid-free paper in the United States of America

First edition, 1994
Second printing, 1995

Library of Congress Cataloging-in-Publication Data

Miller, Sandra
    Rural resource management: problem solving for the long term / Sandra E. Miller,
Craig W. Shinn, William R. Bentley.—1st ed.
      p.   cm.
    Includes index.
    ISBN 0-8138-0686-0
    1. Natural resources—United States—Management.   I. Shinn, Craig W.   II. Bentley,
William R. (William Ross). III. Title.
    HC103.7.M56   1994
    333.7'0973—dc20   93-38131

■ Contents

4

MAKING DECISIONS   *83*

5

MAKING DECISIONS WHEN YOU ARE IN CHARGE   *123*

6

MAKING DECISIONS WHEN NO ONE IS IN CHARGE   *165*

7

TAKING ACTION   *217*

8

TAKING ACTION WHEN NO ONE IS IN CHARGE   *251*

9

UNDERSTANDING CAUSE AND EFFECT   *267*

10

CHALLENGING OURSELVES TO ACTION   *303*

■ Preface

Over the past 15 to 20 years, each of us has worked on frameworks and group process steps for solving problems of individuals and organizations. Our experiences collectively were far ranging. They included line agencies, corporations, associations, cooperatives, church and other volunteer groups, a wide variety of rural development interventions in Asia, Africa, the United States, and an assortment of academic research and teaching situations. Each of us had different sets of experiences, and each of us digested them differently. As we came together, became better acquainted, and began sharing our perceptions of rural resource development, our excitement with common ground was often frustrated by our differences. We are reminded of George Bernard Shaw's observation on the United States and the United Kingdom—"England and America are two countries separated by the same language"—as a description of our situation.

The strength of the book comes from our talking, writing, ranting, and upon occasion raving; it draws together three different perspectives. The essential task of identifying and solving problems is to agree on some common frameworks and process steps. These enable each participant to share their perspectives—their understanding—with one another and, with this sharing, develop a mutual yet more complete knowledge.

The tools described and developed in *Rural Resource Management* are a means for gathering data and converting it into knowledge. This is a very applied and pragmatic definition of knowledge but one appropriate to our intended audience of rural resource managers. Useful knowledge is, in this sense, defined by the clientele, the individuals, and organizations who perceive themselves to have a rural resource problem. It may be a problem of organizing how to achieve a desired result; it may be a problem of deciding which among several alternative means is best; it may be one of understanding why a particular symptom occurs.

Some relevant data—the numbers and qualities pertinent to identifying or solving the problem—usually is available. The process steps required to select which data is useful and which additional data is desired and to structure this into useful knowledge for the client, in essence, generates information. The steps give form to data in terms of client needs. While a bit "bookish" in character, this definition describes what *Rural Resource Management* is about: the frameworks and processes that enable groups concerned with the management of rural resources to gather data, generate information, and create knowledge that is understood in terms of the problems at hand.

Some groups will be well structured, and some will be made up of the lone individual who manages particular resources. More and more frequently, however, groups are formed by individuals, representatives, or organizations that perceive themselves as stakeholders in an often vague but burning resource issue. Fewer rural issues are clearly the province of a given person or organization. Participation by a mix of individuals and groups is often called for by law or precedent. Increasingly, however, we recognize that better results arise from integration of different perceptions followed by broader participation in implementation and ongoing analysis and discussion.

Over the course of developing this book, we have benefitted from the support of the Pew Charitable Trusts for writing the initial draft and testing our ideas in Arkansas, the Ford and Rockefeller Foundations for material development and testing in India, the U.S. Agency for International Development for testing in context of multiple-purpose tree species research and practice in Asia, and Winrock International and Yale's School of Forestry and Environmental Studies for support while we finished the text. To these organizations and the individuals who supported our general efforts on rural development, we offer much appreciation and thanks.

Books grow from kernels of ideas into final publication because many people take the time and care to help often disorganized and disoriented authors. We can never acknowledge all the people who have helped us, but among the most important people are Barbara Scott and Karen Seckler, who once again handled a Winrock book with competence and patience; Bob Havener, Enrique Ospina, Fee Busby, and Doug Henderson, who gave us advice and support when needed; Cheryl Parks and Conrad and Jennifer Shumaker, who edited early drafts; Chris Nunn, who contributed so much to the reorganization of the first draft; and the many reviewers at Winrock

International, Yale University, University of Washington, Texas A&M University, India's forestry institutions, and others, who suggested innumerable improvements while encouraging us to continue on to the final product. To each one and all we offer thanks without implicating you in the flaws that still remain.

Sandra E. Miller

Craig W. Shinn

William R. Bentley

■ Introduction

PEOPLE CAN BUILD A FUTURE THAT IS
MORE PROSPEROUS, more just and more secure.
Our[s] . . . is not a prediction of ever increasing
environmental decay, poverty, and hardship in an
ever more polluted world among ever decreasing
resources. We see instead the possibility of a new era
of economic growth, one that must be based on
policies that sustain and expand the environmental
resource base. And we believe such growth to be
absolutely essential to relieve the great poverty that
is deepening in much of the developing world.
But . . . hope for the future is conditional on
decisive . . . action now to begin managing environmental resources to ensure both sustainable human
progress and human survival.

OUR COMMON FUTURE,
United Nations' World Commission on
Environment and Development

The Challenge to Resource Professionals

Professionals who influence how resources are managed face a paradox that can paralyze the will to act. At one level, we know something must be done to address the interdependent ecological, social, and economic problems that confront us; and we acknowledge that we each are responsible. But at another level, we know everything is related to everything else. Each of us is but one among 5 billion people, and the resources we command are minuscule compared to a world economy in the trillions of dollars. Anything we do is inconsequential compared to the immensity of the effort required.

We know the environmental problems our world confronts. At the global level, desertification, deforestation, acid rain, ozone depletion, and global warming threaten. Closer to home, chemical residues contaminate water supplies; pollution defiles the air; groundwater is being depleted and wetlands destroyed; wind and water carry away precious soil; and solid waste continues to grow at an unprecedented rate.

As a nation, we are quick to explain why our actions fall short. We degrade, deplete, and pollute in the course of producing, consuming, and disposing the products and services that fuel our economic growth, generate jobs, and support our lifestyles. We continue to demand ever more, despite the widening resource gap between industrial and developing nations—between rich and poor.

At the same time, the world's population will grow from 5 billion to between 8 and 14 billion in the next century, straining human interaction and placing ever greater demands on our already stressed natural resources. Most will be born in developing countries. Most will be born in poverty. Without jobs, the developing nations' poor have no alternative but to cultivate increasingly fragile lands to survive. In the process, hillsides are eroded, forests cut, and permanent wastelands created.

In a global community, the fates of individuals worldwide are inextricably tied together. My actions affect others' options; others' actions affect mine. We are interdependent. Despite the crises that challenge our interdependent future, the very interlocking of these crises through our interdependencies is cause for hope. Guided by the philosophy often summarized by "Think globally, act locally!" we can influence and affect each other's actions for the good, not just the bad.

The Challenge to the Individual

What can one person do to move the world toward more productive, more equitable, and more sustainable ways of managing resources? Change occurs when people act. The changes that occur are sometimes planned; more often change is an unforeseen result—the fateful accumulation of many small, seemingly insignificant deeds. What one person can do may seem limited in the face of global problems. Yet, individuals working toward similar goals, acting on similar values, and working across the multiple faces of inseparable environmental and economic problems can make a perceptible difference. Even our smallest acts are not insignificant.

Problems—no matter how big or small—represent an opportunity for action. Our action can make a situation better or worse. In this case, the adage "If you're not part of the solution, you're part of the problem" is true. Being part of the solution hinges on accepting responsibility. But accepting responsibility is not enough; being an agent of change requires intentional and well-thought-out action. Even the smallest act may be important if we desire to produce food, fuel, and fiber for all people without jeopardizing the ability of future generations to do the same.

Rural Resource Management will help you do what you can to solve the resource management problems over which you have some control—as an individual, a group member, a leader, or an advisor. The book presents practical techniques to help resource managers solve problems and reconcile tradeoffs between productivity, equity, and sustainability. It is written for

- Professionals in industry, government, nonprofit organizations, extension, and the academic community who address resource degradation, pollution, and depletion problems

- People who are trained as disciplinary specialists yet must address resource-management problems that transcend disciplinary boundaries

- Managers, consultants, advisors, community leaders, extension agents, and others who are concerned with finding balance between productivity, equity, and sustainability

- Leaders who must generate trust, develop a shared understanding, and establish a common purpose among diverse individuals and groups in order to address the intricate, unsettled questions that face us all in a world of growing economic, social, and environmental interdependence

- Students who are preparing to make a difference in the world

Frameworks and Process Steps

The book introduces four sets of questions, or *frameworks*. Answering a framework's questions will reveal information needed to solve a problem effectively. Each set of questions has a different purpose. The frameworks will help you

1. define a problem that calls for action
2. make a decision
3. plan effectively
4. understand cause and effect

Each framework is presented with corresponding *process steps* to help you order and guide your thought processes as you answer its questions. These steps separate creative thought, which is inventive and original, from critical thinking, which is discriminating and rational. Similarly, the process steps separate the expression of legitimately subjective values and preferences from objective facts.

An illustration helps explain the relationship between a framework's questions and the process steps. Assume a framework includes the following questions: What do you want to achieve? What actions are required? Who will carry out each action? When? Answering these questions constitutes a plan that will lead you to achieve your objective—for example, planning your day at the office.

Your objective is to clear your desk before you go home. As you ask, "What actions are required to clear off my desk today?" your eye catches a letter that has been sitting in your waiting-action file for three weeks. You ask, "When should I respond to this letter?" You think, "Right now." It takes 20 minutes. Your eye catches another letter in the waiting-action file. You make a phone call in response to it and talk for one-half hour. Your eye catches a stack of periodicals you put aside to read when time permitted. You start reading. Two hours later you're still reading. At the end of the day, your desk is as messy as ever.

Looking back, you realize you asked the first and second questions and immediately moved to the fourth. You never had a chance to ask, "Who will carry out the action?" that caused you to make the erroneous assumption that only you could deal with the mess on your desk. In contrast, you could have generated a mental list of all the actions you could take to clear off your desk, ranging from filing to lighting a fire under the whole mess. Coming up with this list draws on your creative thinking skills. Don't assume creative thought won't help. You can't take actions you don't consider, and creativity may be exactly what you need to make sure the situation doesn't recur.

With a mental list in hand, critical thinking is needed to differentiate between actions that truly will clear your desk by 5:00 p.m. and those that are unrealistic. Your critical analysis will use two kinds of information: legitimately subjective preferences and objective facts. Your preferences flow out of what you think is important—filing or answering phone calls, for example. You want to be home by 5:00 to have supper with your family. In contrast, facts are objective statements that your critical analysis must take into account: The board of directors meets tomorrow, and your boss said clear the mess off your desk—no matter what; the stack of periodicals on the corner of your desk has been accumulating for six months; next week you have to write a progress report, and the information you will need is scattered throughout your office. The process steps help you separate creative and critical thinking, improving the results of both. They also help you differentiate between subjective and objective information and use both wisely.

The frameworks and process steps can be applied to straightforward problems with simple cause-and-effect relationships or to problems involving complex biophysical, socioeconomic, and political interactions. The frameworks' questions increase the range and relevance of information you consider when solving a problem. The process steps improve the quality of your answers. Used in groups, the process steps improve group effectiveness. The frameworks and process steps make problem solving more systematic, generating more effective actions and results consistent with your short-run objectives and long-run goals. They do not provide a formula for finding easy solutions to tough problems.

The Importance of Context

The frameworks and group processes are only useful when applied to solving problems in their context. For example, you have a flat tire. You have to decide what needs to be done. The answer is obvious, right? Not necessarily! What if it's pouring down rain? What if you're alone, it's after midnight, and you don't have a spare in the trunk? What if you're dressed in your best suit on the way to a job interview?

To demonstrate the importance of context to problem solving, this book explains the frameworks and process steps in the context of four resource management problems. Chapters 1, 2, 5, and 6 deal with sedimentation of a river in the Pacific Northwest. Chapters 4, 7, and 8 address pesticide use on an Upper Midwest apple orchard. Chapter 9 considers environmentally damaged pines in the Northeast, and chapter 10 deals with solid waste disposal in a poultry-producing area of the South.

Of all the contextual factors, who the problem solver is—an individual or a group—has greater implications for the outcome than any other. To illustrate the effects of this contextual factor, the cases we chose have different kinds of problem solvers. Chapter 4 deals with decision making by an individual farmer, chapter 5 with decision making within a corporate department, and chapter 6 with decision making in a voluntary group of citizens who come together solely for the purpose of solving the problem at hand. In chapter 7, an individual farmer plans how he will reduce his pesticide usage. In chapter 8, the action-planning framework is used by a group that is just organizing and has characteristics of both voluntary and structured groups. In chapter 9, a voluntary interagency work team uses causal analysis to figure out what is causing yellowing pines.

The Book's Themes

Every book has one or more themes that flow through its content, and this book is no exception. Five themes underlie *Rural Resource Management:*

- Resource degradation, pollution, and depletion problems represent the accumulated consequences of individual choices over time. The problems will be solved in the same way they were created—one step at a time. Progress depends on improving the quality of our daily choices.

- The analytic frameworks presented in this book help identify solutions that reconcile value tradeoffs and improve the effectiveness of our actions.

- Values energize the search for more productive, more sustainable, and more equitable ways of managing resources. Stating our values explicitly helps us better understand how values direct our actions.

- The group process steps presented in this book promote greater understanding and trust among individuals and groups with diverse perspectives and conflicting objectives.

- Progressing from our present resource management practices toward more productive, more sustainable, and more equitable practices is a process of discovery. The path is not laid out, nor can we know with certainty all of the ramifications of our choices. We must make the best choices possible with the time, information, and resources at hand.

Rural
Resource
Management

1

■ What Is a Problem?

The word *problem* means different things to different people. Problems can be frustrating situations beyond our control or mathematical propositions to be solved. Problems can be intricate, unsettled questions that seemingly defy understanding or questions that call for action.

Two Kinds of Problems

This chapter deals with the latter two kinds of problems: intricate, unsettled problems and problems that call for action. It also examines how an individual moves from awareness of an intricate, unsettled situation to defining a problem that calls for action. Chapter 2 explains how to phrase a call for action that is likely to yield the desired result in a given context.

Problems that call for action

Some problems are readily defined; they call for action. These problems are precipitated by an unwanted or unexpected deviation from what is expected or desired, caused by a change of one kind or another. Generally the deviation is something to be corrected or removed. However, it can be a positive deviation, signaling an opportunity to improve. A flat tire is a negative deviation from the expected; it calls for immediate action. A car that gets 20 miles per gallon more than the Environmental Protection Agency average is a positive deviation that beckons the curious to ask why.

An example that is familiar to anyone who has ever used a computer illustrates a problem that calls for action. You're working on a computer. The screen goes blank, the lights overhead go out, and the ventilation system stops. Experience tells you that these symptoms mean that the problem is not with the computer itself; rather, the power has been shut off. You quickly look for clues that will help you figure out what caused the electricity to be shut off. Do neighboring buildings have power? Is power to the whole building out or only some parts of the building? In moments, you discover that only your section of the building is affected, which leads you to believe that a breaker switch is the source of the problem. You check the switch box, find the tripped switch, reset it, and the power comes back on. This is a problem that calls for action. You diagnosed the problem by identifying and analyzing the problem's symptoms, determined the likely cause, and took action.

Intricate, unsettled situations

Intricate, unsettled situations are more difficult to understand. We don't recognize a distinct problem that calls for action; rather, we sense a vague gap between what we want and what is, although we may be unsure of what we want and may be unable even to define the situation as it is. Poverty and environmental degradation are intricate, unsettled situations—problems only to the extent that they make us feel troubled. How we define these intricate, unsettled situations that trouble us depends on our attitudes and what we think is important, or our values.

The first step in solving an intricate, overwhelmingly large problem is to define it. Often this means splitting it into smaller issues, sharpening the vague standards of our "discomfort gap" to focus on those aspects over which we have control.

Action or Thoughtful Consideration

Sid Riedel, an inspector in a state agency responsible for water quality, is confronted with a problem situation.

■   Ray Green farms 320 acres. The farm extends from the Cascade foothills to the banks of the Powder River. The farm's alluvial soils along the river are deep and rich and have been planted in corn and green beans under contract to a cannery for the last few years. Some years, Ray plants the lower lands along the riverbank as well, even though this land is often under water in spring. In the low foothills, he sows grasses and sometimes grain. Ray is now planning for the spring planting season.

Above Green's farm, Northwest Forest Products owns 22,000 acres. The state owns forestland adjacent to Northwest's land at the lower elevations. The United States Forest Service controls the hilltops. Betsy Tomlin, a forester for Northwest Forest Products, is checking a recently reforested area. Several sites planted in Douglas fir have shown poor survival rates—some as low as 30 percent. Paul Hartner, her boss, asked her to evaluate the sites and figure out what is wrong before they place seedling orders for this year's planting.

Betsy stops her pickup; a mudslide has carried away part of the road. There is only a 9-inch drop now, but she can see a 20- or 30-foot-long area that is going to slide sooner or later. She gets out her map and locates the site. She will have to tell the forest engineer about this. "Too bad," she thinks, "the slide will fill the stream when it goes."

Downstream, Sid Riedel gets out of his pickup at the Red Ridge town water intake. As the inspection officer for the state's Department of Environmental Quality, Sid knows he will find the water just the way the public works supervisor told him he would. Elevated turbidity isn't surprising after the rain they have had the last few days. They always have more silt after heavy rain. The water plant can usually handle the added particulate matter, but this year is different. There is more silt.

Sid stands for a minute and looks at the branch stream. He can see the washed-out road that is causing the heavy sedimentation today. He shakes his head as he looks across the inundated fields between the road and the Powder River. Most of the river-bottom farms have the lower fields in pasture. But some, like Ray Green's, plant the bottomland in annual crops. Sid thinks to himself, "There's no telling how much sediment Ray's plowed fields contribute each year." Sid slides into the pickup and heads back down the valley.

The Powder River has been targeted by the Fish and Wildlife Service as a salmon-bearing stream. Research funded by the service and carried out by Pacific North State University identified turbidity and temperature levels that limit fish run. Based on their research, the state's Department of Environmental Quality put regulations in place last year that set standards establishing the minimum tolerable limits for temperature and turbidity. The regulations are clear: Turbidity at the Red Ridge town water intake is higher than allowable.

In the Powder River illustration, Ray Green, Betsy Tomlin, Paul Hartner, and Sid Riedel all are related to a problem and, through it, to each other. However, the relationship ends there. No one knows yet that they share the problem. Each one acts independently of the others, motivated by individual objectives and priorities. Each is aware to one degree or another that soil erosion, sedimentation, and declining salmon populations are issues, if not problems. Yet each sees these issues from a different perspective. Each has a different understanding of the issues, causes and consequences, and of who is responsible.

Ray Green is primarily concerned with his immediate problems: What will he plant, where, and how much? While erosion is a concern to him, it is not an immediate concern. Similarly, Betsy Tomlin is primarily occupied with her immediate problem: Why are the Douglas fir seedlings dying? Erosion is related to reforestation issues, but it is not her primary concern. Paul Hartner, Betsy's boss, is responsible for both reforestation and keeping soil erosion within bounds on company lands. However, right now he is preoccupied with more pressing issues.

Sid is the only one who sees an urgent need to deal with the situation. Moreover, he understands the relationship between erosion, sedimentation, and salmon runs more fully than the others. But even though Sid understands the relationship among these factors, he is in an ambiguous situation that calls for careful consideration.

Sid could go to Northwest Forest Products, issue a citation for the washed-out road, and be done with it. In other words, he could treat this situation as a problem that calls for immediate action. Alternatively, he can treat this as a troublesome, intricate, unsettled situation, which requires careful thought before taking action. What he decides will depend on his attitudes toward problems and his values—what he thinks is important. His thinking will also be influenced by the context—the biophysical needs of salmon; his relationship to a wide group of constituents, colleagues, friends, and associates; and the resources of his employer, the state Department of Environmental Quality. How much responsibility he feels for addressing the root causes of the situation versus doing his job is another important factor. He has to look at all the dimensions of the situation.

How Sid defines the problem will influence his own and other people's choices. When he has defined the problem and knows what he wants to achieve, then he can proceed.

Attitudes influencing our response to intricate, unsettled situations

Some individuals' life experiences cause them to believe that intricate, unsettled situations, no matter how troublesome, are beyond their influence. These people may talk about their troubled feelings, but the message is nearly always "isn't it awful." They see themselves as victims of a world over which they have no control when, in fact, they are imprisoned by their own inability to accept responsibility for what they can do.

Others have a vague sense that there is something they should be doing to address the problem but feel unequipped to understand the problem well enough to take action. Their feelings of inadequacy stymie constructive thinking that could narrow the problem and enable constructive action. Others believe that every problem calls for immediate action—a belief that leads to motion without direction.

Our scientific and technical education also influences our attitudes towards problems and their solutions. The training we receive encourages us to shape complex problems to fit our own discipline's paradigms and to ignore factors that do not neatly fit. Our training also can condition us to reduce questions that call for action to mathematical-like propositions, leading us to ignore or oversimplify those factors that are difficult to measure. We come to expect problems to have a solution in the same way that mathematical propositions have a solution. Both of these attitudes pose danger for the problem solver. Fitting complex problems into narrowly defined paradigms leads to misunderstanding and misdirected action. The search for one solution can blind us to the small, cumulative steps that move us toward more productive, more equitable, and more sustainable ways of managing resources.

Still other people look at a complex situation and see problems that call for action. They define the problem in a way that acknowledges their responsibility and makes action possible. Often this means splitting a big problem into smaller, more manageable parts, focusing on those aspects of the problem over which we—whoever we are—have control. The environmental problem is not one problem but many. It includes global warming, acid rain, soil erosion, nitrate runoff, overgrazing of rangelands, and waste disposal. Each of these problems can be broken down into smaller problems. Waste disposal issues include seepage of hazardous waste into water supplies, the ever-expanding stream of solid waste, and other problems. Each of these can be broken down into still smaller problems.

Most people who see problems that call for action see the world in terms of questions rather than statements. When someone says, "The ever-expanding stream of solid waste is a problem," it is reasonable to ask: "So what? What can I do about it? Why is the solid waste stream of concern to me?" While the statement leaves us hanging, the questions are more likely to produce action.

People who ask good questions are more likely to get good results. Broad, unfocused questions lead to broad, unfocused answers. As questions become more focused, the answers are more likely to generate the results we value. "What is the environmental problem?" is not a question that calls for action. In contrast, "Why is the waste stream growing in my community?

What is the best way for us to reduce it? How can our community begin recycling soft plastics?" are questions that do.

Of course, there is no single right question. Phrasing a question that calls for action casts the problem in a mold that gives shape and form to the problem and direction to the problem solver. The question Sid asks himself will put him on a path that leads to some more or less predictable result. The question "How much should I fine Northwest Forest Products so that they will be more careful in the future?" will lead Sid to much different actions and results than the question "What is the best way to reduce sedimentation on the Powder River?" Both are legitimate questions. Both call for action. Both have the potential to result in actions that reduce the sedimentation problem at hand.

However, following one path often precludes following others in the short run. Sid has to choose a path that makes sense given who he is and the context in which he will invest his time. His path should produce results that are consistent with his and his employer's short-run objectives and long-run goals. Despite its importance, phrasing the question that calls for action is one of the most frequently overlooked and misunderstood choices a problem solver makes.

The context influencing how we respond

When confronted with a problem situation, we do not often know all of the factors that affect the situation, particularly when the situation involves complex biophysical and socioeconomic interactions. Our response to even the most simple problems is context specific. Consider the thought process of a woman faced with a flat tire on a rainy night. She asks herself,

What is the problem? I have a flat tire *and* it's raining. I want to fix the tire *and* avoid getting soaked.

In what context will I solve this problem? I was on my way to the grocery store three miles from my home. We live just beyond the city limits of a small town. I know most of the people in these parts. The closest house is a half mile from here. My husband is at home taking care of the kids. He might worry if I'm late, but I've been late before. He will understand. The kids might drive him crazy if he waits for me to make supper, but that's his problem. There's no telling how long the rain might last. It's been like this for hours. It might not be practical to wait until it stops. On the other hand, the sky seems to be clearing in the west. It's cool outside; the temperature is only 40. I'm safely off the road, and I have my hazard lights on. I have the tools, and I know how to change a flat tire. I have an umbrella, but it won't keep me dry. And I've been sick with the flu the last two weeks. I sure don't want to get wet and cold now when I'm just starting to recover. I have money in my purse. I have a half hour before dark.

What is the problem that calls for action? How can I avoid getting soaked so that I don't have a relapse of the flu and get off the road before dark so that my husband is not worried and I am safe?

What is my response? I'm not in a rush. I'll wait ten minutes. Either the rain will slow or someone will come by and stop to help me. If that doesn't work, I'll take my umbrella and walk to the nearest house and call home for help. That way I won't get as soaked as I would if I tried to change the flat tire in the driving rain. In the meantime, I'll catch the news.

The woman only spent a moment thinking about the context and defining the problem. But in that moment, she considered a lot of context-specific information and tailored the question that calls for action to the situation at hand. If the context had been different, she would have defined the problem and acted differently.

No matter how straightforward the situation, the context continuously evolves. The woman knows that in ten minutes the rain could stop or a passerby could give her a lift home. The nature of a problem changes over time. Consequently, each question that we answer raises new questions. In chapter 2, Sid will evaluate the context and phrase a question that calls for action. Others who have a stake in the problem will do the same. The questions each one asks will differ in their detail yet answer the same broad questions: Who else is involved in the problem? What is their stake? What are the problem's biophysical and socioeconomic dimensions? What resources are needed?

These questions rarely have right or wrong answers. Rather, the answers will lead to more or less effective action. The quality of the answers depends on the quality of the questions and how the answers were obtained. Sid and the woman with the flat tire will seek the best possible answers given the context—answers leading to workable, effective solutions that go beyond their minimum acceptable requirements. Sid's and the woman's questions are effective if they lead them closer to achieving their short-run objectives and long-run goals. Their answers may not produce the best available solutions; instead, they will lead to the best possible solutions given the context.

There are no once-and-for-all solutions. There is only an accumulation of outcomes, each of which presents new questions. Our questions provide the thread that links the situation at this moment to the past and future.

Progress and how we apply our values

Our estimation of progress—that is, movement toward long-term
depends on our values. Values effect not only our choices as w
problems but also our standards for measuring progress. Values anc
vision of the future. Our vision influences the questions we choi
answers we discover, the actions we take, and the results we get. Wh
author has a vision that is unique, we agree on three broad unc
values: productivity, equity, and sustainability. Our shared vision is c
by the quotation in the Introduction of the United Nations'
Commission on Environment and Development report, *Our Common*
It is worth quoting again.

> People can build a future that is more prosperous, more just and m
> secure. Our[s] . . . is not a prediction of ever increasing environmer
> decay, poverty, and hardship in an ever more polluted world among e
> decreasing resources. We see instead the possibility of a new era
> economic growth, one that must be based on policies that sustain ¿
> expand the environmental resource base. And we believe such growth to
> absolutely essential to relieve the great poverty that is deepening in mt
> of the developing world. But . . . hope for the future is conditional
> decisive . . . action now to begin managing environmental resources
> ensure both sustainable human progress and human survival. (1987, p

Values are subjective. But as scientists, technicians, and manage
have been taught to prefer the objective; this makes us reluctant to i
our values explicitly. We focus on measures as quantitative expressi
values, unable or unwilling to acknowledge that these measures are j
for more elusive values. When we explicitly recognize our values,
reminded that our measures do not embody all that is important, ¿
refocus our attention on what is important as opposed to what is meas
Workable, effective solutions to complex natural resource manaɡ
problems depends on making values explicit. So here are our values ex
defined:

Productivity is efficient use of resources for constructive purpos
itself, productivity assumes each action is independent of others. Its c
is with the amount of profit, bushels, security, satisfaction, or aestheti
can be derived from a set of inputs in the short term.

Equity encompasses fairness, justice, and equal opportunity. Each
feels responsible to different degrees and for different people ranging

our own immediate family to the global community. Equity assumes interdependence among actions and deals with how we ensure people living in the present have opportunities to meet their own needs.

Sustainability assumes people are interdependent through time—that actions taken today affect present and future generations. Sustainability is concerned with our ability to maintain productivity through time, to provide intergenerational equity, and to ensure a future in which people have opportunities to meet their material and nonmaterial needs.

If we assume our actions are independent—that what we do does not affect anyone else—productivity will be the only value that forms our vision. If, on the other hand, we acknowledge our interdependence—that what we do affects other people living in the present—our vision will include equity values. If we acknowledge that present and future are interdependent, our vision also will be concerned with sustainability.

Issues and Problems That Call for Action

Sid was hired to enforce state water quality regulations. His textbook understanding of the biophysical factors that influence water quality was broadened as he became aware of how human and biophysical factors interact in the real world. As time passed, he noticed that although he was enforcing the regulations, water quality was actually getting worse. He becomes increasingly troubled about stream sedimentation and its effect on salmon. He knows something has to change, but he's not sure what or how. There are three significant stages of understanding:

1. Becoming aware of a situation's complexity
2. Recognizing that the situation contains within it a problem that needs to be addressed
3. Sorting through the complexity to identify something that an individual can do

The sections that follow describe these stages in greater detail.

Becoming aware of an intricate, unsettled situation

Awareness is the first step on the path that leads to action. Many people are only vaguely aware of resource degradation, pollution, and depletion. For these people, the resource problem is just one among many issues competing for their attention. An individual's initial awareness is often abstract. You read a journal article, hear a news report or people talking, and think, "Isn't that interesting?" At this stage, you aren't sure that the issue represents a problem—much less a problem that calls for action—and don't feel any personal responsibility to learn more about the issue. Moving from awareness to problem recognition is often a slow process, taking years. Some people may never move beyond a superficial awareness of resource problems. People sometimes move from awareness to problem recognition abruptly, when an event provides the catalyst to rapidly expand someone's understanding.

A child with leukemia provided the catalyst for the people affected by toxic waste at Love Canal to move from awareness to action. The nuclear accident at Chernobyl made people aware of nuclear power's real danger. The murder of Chico Mendes in Brazil focused attention on deforestation in the Amazon. Rachel Carson's book *A Silent Spring* turned a vague awareness of DDT's effects into action that eventually banned the pesticide and legitimized a role for nonscientists in recognizing and defining resource problems.

For Sid, problem recognition includes expanding his awareness of the problem. Sid was trained to observe and manipulate the biophysical factors influencing stream sedimentation and salmon runs when he started his job. However, he could not effectively address the problem until he became aware of the human dimensions as well.

Recognizing a problem

When awareness gives way to problem recognition, we realize the situation can be improved. At this stage, people tend to think about the situation in terms of how it "should" be. We think, "People shouldn't pollute," "Crime shouldn't exist," or "Poor people should do what I do—work for a living." At one level, these thoughts are unrealistic. At another level, however, they enable us to visualize a situation that is better than the present one.

Many people get stuck at this stage; they never move beyond thinking about how they feel things should be to discover how they can help bring about improvements. Three pitfalls stall people at this stage:

- blaming others for the problem
- confusing problems with solutions

• focusing on what we can't do

Blaming others. When "shoulds" give way to accusations, we fail to see what we can do and we get stuck. How often do you hear people say, "If government had been doing its job, we wouldn't have water quality problems" or "If businesses weren't so greedy, we wouldn't have so much pollution"? Whether or not our accusations are valid, we cannot move forward until we are willing to accept the situation as it is and do what we can to improve it. The unwillingness to examine our own relationship to the situation stalls many people in this stage indefinitely. We recognize the problem but continually blame someone else for not solving it.

Confusing problems and solutions. A minister says, "The problem is, we need to build a new sanctuary." The problem isn't that the church needs a new sanctuary, the problem is that the 10:30 service is overcrowded. Building a new sanctuary is one alternative. However, there may be others. Perhaps the church could add another service or expand the existing sanctuary or buy new pews that take up less space. Whenever you hear someone say, "The problem is, we need x or we need y," be aware that the speaker may have confused the problem with a solution. In doing so, he or she excludes all other alternatives from consideration. More importantly, the underlying problem may go unrecognized and unaddressed.

Focusing on what we can't do. Many problems cannot be solved by individuals working alone, including acid rain, ozone depletion, global warming, hunger, and poverty. These problems involve complex interactions among biophysical, social, economic, and political processes through time. In the face of these large and complex problems, we can easily be overwhelmed and focus on what we can't do. However, moving from problem recognition to problem definition depends on believing that all big problems are made up of many small, related problems—and focusing on what we can do.

Defining a problem that calls for action

Unacceptably high turbidity at the Red Ridge municipal water intake is the catalyst that will move Sid beyond problem recognition. During this stage, he will define the boundaries of the problem, explore the context, examine his role relative to the problem, and define his short-run objectives and long-run goals. Armed with this information, he will phrase a question that calls for action and decide how to answer it.

Sid, like most of us, will mull over what he knows. His thoughts may wander. He may daydream about what a respected colleague might do. He may try to envision what impact he can have. He may think through alternatives the way he would try on a new suit, going through all the "what ifs?" and "yes, buts," trying to envision what the follow-through will feel like. He may conjure up images of success and failure. In the process, he will reject some questions, leave his options open on others, and focus his attention on the question that seems most likely to meet his and his employer's needs.

Framework, Process Steps, and Problem Solving

Sid will define a problem and move forward even if he does so unsystematically. However, *Rural Resource Management*'s frameworks and process steps can improve the quality of his questions and answers, increasing the likelihood that his actions will yield the results he desires. In chapter 2, Sid uses the problem-definition framework and process steps to phrase a question that calls for action and to determine how to answer the question.

Before moving on to problem definition, however, this section briefly describes the frameworks and process steps, thereby providing a conceptual basis for the chapters that follow. There are four frameworks, or sets of questions.

- *Defining a problem.* What is the problem? Is this my problem? In what context will I address the problem? What is the first step?

- *Making a decision.* What decision do you need to make? What do you want to achieve? What are the short-run objectives? What are the long-run goals? On what values will the decision be based? What criteria flow out of these values? What alternative solutions exist? What are the consequences of each alternative relative to each criterion? Which alternative will most effectively achieve your objectives consistent with your long-run goals?

- *Planning action.* What needs to be done? By whom? When? After each step is acted on, what was done? By whom? When? Did the actions taken achieve the intended objective? If not, why not?

- *Understanding cause and effect.* What are the symptoms? What are not symptoms? What is the difference? What could be causing the symptoms? Does the cause adequately explain the symptoms?

The relationships among these frameworks, our problem situation, and our values is schematically represented in figure 1.1.

These frameworks form the basis of most sophisticated problem-solving tools used by businesses, government, and the academic community. These include CPM, PERT, and other planning devices; spreadsheets; program and capital budgets; linear programming; statistical analysis; hypothesis testing; and quality control. An understanding of these simple frameworks will improve your ability to use the more sophisticated tools effectively. These simple tools can provide a valuable source of understanding when time and information are limited or the more sophisticated tools are unavailable or inappropriate.

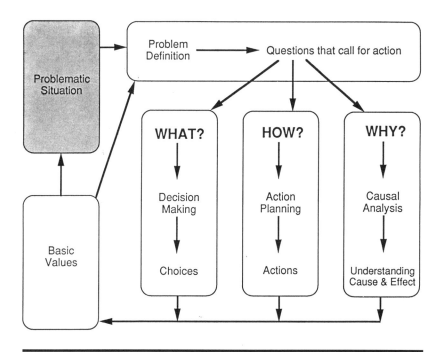

Figure 1.1. Problem-solving framework.

Applying the frameworks to the Powder River illustration

Returning to the Powder River illustration, Ray Green, Betsy Tomlin, and Sid Riedel all have problems they can address systematically using these frameworks. Each may begin with a different framework and move from one framework to another depending on the way each defines his or her problem.

Ray Green will use the decision-making questions to decide what, where, and how much to plant. As an independent farmer, he will consider short- and long-run economic and biophysical factors in making his decisions. Once he makes his decisions, he will use the action-planning framework to arrange delivery of seed and chemicals with the farm supply cooperative, negotiate forward sales contracts with the cannery, and schedule a time when his neighbor can plow the fields.

Betsy Tomlin will use the cause-and-effect questions to figure out what caused the Douglas fir seedlings to die. Searching for patterns, she will compare the seedlings that died with those that survived. She will also compare air, soil, water, and other conditions in areas with high and low survival rates. When she understands the cause and effect, she will pose decision questions to identify her criteria and alternatives and to choose a course of action. She then will use the action questions to identify what steps must be taken to improve seedling survival.

Sid Riedel must determine what course of action to take to deal with the "river" problem. He could use the cause-and-effect questions to get a clearer view of what is raising the stream's turbidity levels. The decision-making questions will help him identify his and the agency's values. However, the problem is complex. Biological and physical processes interact to limit salmon runs. A wide range of factors influence temperature and turbidity. The problem is also socially complex. Many individuals, businesses, groups, and public agencies are involved. Their perspectives and interests differ widely. In many cases, livelihoods depend on how the problem is resolved. Almost inevitably, some will gain and others lose. Understanding the problem's complexity is a first step. At this point, Sid's problem is too ill-defined and too poorly understood for him to decide with any confidence what the first step should be, so he will use the problem-definition framework.

Choosing the best framework for the situation

It's pretty clear in Sid's case that he needs help figuring out what to do, and the problem-definition framework is what he needs. Unlike Sid, Ray and Betsy do not need the systematic structure of the problem-definition framework to phrase a question that calls for action. They answer this framework's questions unconsciously, just as the woman with the flat tire did.

Once a problem is defined, whether consciously or unconsciously, choosing a framework may not be as self-evident as it would seem. However, there are clues that will help you select the next appropriate framework. In nearly every case, you can determine which framework you need by asking yourself the next logical question.

If the next logical question starts with *how?*—How can I get *x* and *y* done?—planning is the next step. You know what you want to achieve and you have identified the best way to do it. Use the planning framework.

If the question that logically follows starts with *what?*—What is the best way to achieve *a* or *b* objectives?—you need to make one or more decisions. The decision-making framework helps you choose among competing alternatives—or different ways of achieving your objective. You know what you want to achieve, but you're not sure what is the best way to do it.

If the next logical question starts with *why?*—Why is this situation occurring?—turn to the cause-and-effect framework. This framework will help you understand what caused the situation to occur and what can be done to improve it. Understanding cause and effect helps ensure that when you intervene to change the situation, your actions are more likely to lead to the desired result.

Process steps and answering a framework's questions

As you will recall from the introduction, each framework has corresponding process steps that order and guide your thoughts as you answer a framework's questions. The man in the earlier illustration had every intention of clearing his desk. He needed a practical plan to organize his work day. He asked the planning framework's questions but failed to answer them systematically. As a result, he failed to achieve the day's objectives. The process steps tell you how to answer the framework's questions to find the best possible answers. They tell you in what order to answer the questions.

When groups set out to answer a framework's questions, the process steps become even more important. Individual group members have subjective tastes and preferences. Each one filters information through his or her own unique perspective, formed through training, life experience, and disposition. Each one has different strengths and weaknesses. Each holds different values. Each one asks and answers different questions. The best possible solution for one person may not be acceptable to another.

Using the process steps helps a group discover answers that are best for the group. The steps help group members understand and accept each other, promote trust, and reduce conflicts. They also encourage constructive discussion of differences and respect for all ideas.

The process steps differ from one framework to another and vary depending on who is involved. However, there are similarities. In response to many questions, you will see sequences of two process steps.

- List all possible answers, but do not discuss them.
- Refine your answers. Add, subtract, or combine responses.

Listing all the possible answers requires creative thought, which is inventive and original, but refining the answers calls for critical thinking, which is rational and discriminating. In addition, the frameworks use both subjective criteria and objective analysis of factual information. The process steps separate creative generation of ideas from critical evaluation of ideas. The process steps lead group members to answer questions that use subjective information separately from those that require objective facts. This separation helps groups be more creative when creativity is needed and more analytic when critical thinking is required. This separation also allows groups to differentiate subjective values from objective facts, which helps them use objective information and apply values to problem solving more effectively. While counterintuitive, groups use critical thinking skills to evaluate subjective criteria and creative thinking skills to list facts. An illustration shows the value of process steps.

The board of a rural water association is meeting. The board often quarrels, so a facilitator has been hired to help avoid conflict. The facilitator, Susan Anderson, introduces herself and says, "I understand your purpose this evening is to decide whom to interview for general manager. On what basis will you choose?" Louise Matillo, a retired schoolteacher, answers, "The best ones, of course." Susan responds, saying, "Tell me what you mean by best." Louise answers, "Competent, of course." Susan probes further, "What do you mean by competent?" "We want someone who has experience managing a rural water system!" Louise answers a bit testily. "Thank you, Mrs. Matillo. That's the level of detail I'm looking for. What else are you looking for in a candidate?" Other board members add their criteria. After everyone has had a chance to speak, Susan reads the list.

The group's list includes experience managing a rural water system, ability to do routine maintenance on the system, experience in billing, knowledge of drinking water laws, ability to work with state regulatory people, engineering experience, ability to use a computer, and skill at managing time. They also want someone who is responsible and bondable. Before moving on, Susan asks if there are any more criteria that should be included on the list.

Jane Hunter adds one last criterion, "I think we should hire a woman." Art Wold, another board member, says, "Yah, one with pretty legs. This community needs some new blood—if you get my drift." Susan thanks Jane for her contribution. She turns to Art and asks, "Do you want me to add pretty legs to the list of qualifications?" The board erupts in laughter, and Art sheepishly declines.

While the decision criteria are subjective, listing them uses creative faculties. No discussion of criteria is allowed until all group members have expressed their views about what is important—what criteria should influence the choice. This ensures that each group member has the opportunity to participate.

After all possible criteria have been listed, Susan asks for discussion, explaining that the group should critically look at the list and combine repetitive criteria, reword confusing criteria, split apart criteria that express more than one idea, and eliminate trivial criteria.

A lively discussion ensues about whether or not it is important to hire a woman. After ten minutes Susan asks, "Is it likely that this will be one of your most important criteria? If not, you may want to look at other criteria on the list as well." Jane explains, "While I would like to see a woman as general manager, the candidate's qualifications and experience are more important." The discussion turns to other criteria. The group decides it is unrealistic to expect the general manager to have engineering skills and drops it from the list. They combine ability to use a computer and billing experience. They delete skill at managing time and insert ability to follow through without direct supervision.

While subjective criteria are at the center of the discussion, group members have drawn on their critical thinking skills to determine what revisions are needed.

Group membership

The process steps differ depending on who is involved in answering a framework's questions and their relationship to each other. *Rural Resource Management* considers problem solving in three situations:

- An individual has sole responsibility for answering the framework's questions.

- A group, in which members have clearly defined roles and agree on their responsibilities to each other, is answering the questions. Staff who work together regularly or an established committee of a community group are examples.

- A voluntary group, in which group members must establish roles and responsibilities as they answer a framework's questions, is making a decision. This might be a community group that meets to solve a common problem or an interdepartmental work team that comes together to carry out a special project.

At its core, problem solving is a process of asking and answering questions. Our questions must penetrate the murk of complexity to find the truth that determines progress toward our vision. Our questions must embody our most deeply held values—or our values won't be found in the answers. We cannot answer lightly; rather, we must reflect on how we will answer. Our questions must release our finest creative energies to generate alternatives and our sharpest critical faculties to choose among them. Problem solving is an art and a craft; at once, subjective and objective, creative and critical. At this level, problem solving becomes a process of discovery, fertile ground for both intuitive and analytic processes.

2

■ Defining a
Complex Problem

In this chapter, we continue exploring the complex Powder River situation introduced in chapter 1. Sid Riedel, state inspector for the Department of Environmental Quality, is confronted with a problem: a road washed out, partially blocking a branch creek and increasing turbidity levels above state standards on the Powder River. The Powder River has been designated as a salmon stream, and when turbidity levels exceed a certain level, Sid's agency has authority to issue fines and take legal action. It is Sid's responsibility to deal with the problem.

In this chapter, Sid struggles to figure out how he should define the problem. Figure 2.1 shows where he is in the problem-solving process. He will decide whether to simply issue fines—and be done with it until the next road washes out—or to search for a way to get at the root of the problem. As he does this, he will examine his role and what his responsibility is for the problem. He will consider the context and what can be done practically. And he will determine whether there are any practical steps he can take to address the problem as he has defined it.

The Complex Problem

Sid's situation is complex. The state standards were enacted less than a

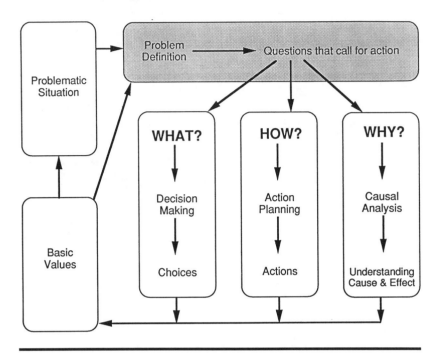

Figure 2.1. Problem-solving framework—questions that call for answers.

year ago. This is the first time the state agency has enforced the standard, so it is important to think the problem through before taking action. This problem involves many people with diverse perspectives, complex biophysical processes, and a relatively unknown political and legal environment. Because people's livelihoods may be affected, emotions run high.

As Sid heads back to the office, he thinks about how to deal with the situation. He can fine Northwest for the road slide and call it quits. That's all his job obligates him to do. "Besides," he thinks, "why stir up more trouble than necessary? Local people will get hopping mad, call legislators, and stir up the community. They will say we're meddling." Sid can't blame them too much. He'd probably get mad too. He knows they are just trying to make an honest living.

Sid grew up along the Powder. His friends accuse him of being nostalgic for the old days. "Maybe, I am," he thinks. "The river wouldn't be the same without the salmon runs." Then he thinks about the Native Americans downstream who make their living from the salmon runs. "There's more to this than nostalgia and I have a job to do." If he has to get tough, he will. He could get a court order to force Northwest to take care of the washed-out road. He might even have to cite a few farmers to get this thing under control.

However, Sid questions the value of court orders and citations. "They pay the fines and go about their business," he thinks. "Nothing is solved in the long run." He searches his mind for a better approach.

What is the problem anyway? To get the turbidity levels down to standard? Sid is too good a hydrologist to believe that is the issue. The problem is soil erosion. The only way to bring down turbidity levels is to get people along the stream corridor to change their farm and forest management practices.

While seemingly directionless, Sid's thoughts serve an important purpose—they will help him define the boundaries of the problem. Once he is comfortable with his definition of the problem that calls for action, he can tell if there is a practical way to address that problem. So far, Sid is going through the analysis unconsciously. He can enhance its value by making his analysis systematic and conscious.

The Problem-Definition Framework

Problem definition is an iterative process. The objective is to reconcile the fact situation and our own situation with the context of the problem and formulate a question that calls for action. When we have been successful, that question will direct our efforts toward an outcome that is important to us. Until we are satisfied that we have reached this objective, we continue to rephrase the question that calls for action and to use the problem-definition framework to test it. The problem-definition framework leads the problem solver through a series of questions:

1. What is the problem that calls for action?
2. Is this my problem?
3. In what context will I address the problem?
4. What is the first step?

In this iterative process, we build on the initial way we see the fact situation, exploring how that version of the problem fits, and what it implies. As adjustments are needed, we rephrase the fact situation and proceed again.

The later questions in the framework probably will reveal that the first answer to the first question—What is the problem?—has some deficiencies. Perhaps this problem doesn't belong to us. Or it may be that in the context of the problem as we have expressed it, there are no resources available to address it. That is, the approach that flows from the way we have expressed the problem may not be realistic, given who we are or the context of the problem.

If this happens—and it usually will—we restate the problem and move through the framework again, exploring the modified problem. The problem-definition framework allows us to study our initial one-dimensional response to an event in the many-dimensional context of our own roles, values, and responsibilities and the physical, social, and institutional world in which the problem exists. Because the framework is very general, it helps to break each of these big questions down into smaller questions that develop the specific features of the problem situation we are facing. Beginning with the first question in the framework, let us examine each by subdividing it into more narrowly focused questions.

1. What is the problem that calls for action?

Problem-Definition Framework

1. **What is the problem that calls for action?**
   - What event, change, or symptom signals that a problem exists?
   - How do you want the situation to change or improve?
   - What is the question that calls for action?
   - What approach flows out of the question?
   - Is there a practical way to address this problem?

2. Is this my problem?

3. In what context will I address the problem?

4. What is the first step?

What event, change, or symptom signals that a problem exists?

Begin by describing the situation. As you explore the dimensions of the problem, the way you see or express this event may change, but don't worry about that at this stage. Just express the event in the simplest and most natural way. "The board of directors is meeting tomorrow, and I have to clear my desk by this afternoon," or "I have a flat tire and it is raining."

For Sid, the event that signaled a problem was the increase in particulate levels at the Red Ridge water treatment intake when a section of road washed out, dumping sediment into the river. But particulate levels are not the problem; they describe the problem. Particulate is a measure of turbidity, which is a symptom. So he asks, "A symptom of what?" And furthermore, "So what? Who cares? Does the measurement reflect a problem or not? What problem?" He proceeds.

How do you want the situation to change or improve?

This question requires you to compare the facts as they exist with your objectives and goals. "I want to be able to see the surface of my desk, but I don't want to lose track of messages that need a response by putting them out of sight" or "I want to fix the tire and avoid getting soaked."

When you face bigger problems than a disorderly desk or a flat tire, you often find that the changes you really want are so large that you can't relate them to any specific action. Major changes are the result of many incremental actions taken over a long time. So you need to answer this question at two levels: your long-term goals and the more readily achievable short-term objectives that make up the incremental steps to the long-term goals.

Long-term goals and short-term objectives. Overemphasis on short-run, narrow objectives does not lead us where we want to go. Short-run objectives often deal with symptoms rather than problems. An extension specialist is concerned because county agents are not using his training materials in their programs. He focuses on his immediate objective: getting agents to use his materials. There is no doubt that this objective reflects his immediate desire. However, this objective assumes that the symptom—agents not using the materials—is the problem. If he honestly tries to figure out what is causing the symptom, he may find that the materials do not meet the agents' needs. How different the outcome will be if he asks, "How can I better meet the agents' needs?" Ironically, the specialist is more likely to meet his immediate objective (getting agents to use his materials) if he focuses on his broad goal (meeting agents' needs).

On the other hand, if we state our goals and objectives too broadly, the range of alternatives is so wide that our actions are not sufficiently directed. The vision that directs our actions is not focused. As a result, our actions may appear hit-and-miss or misdirected. Our goals must be broad enough to lead us where we want to go but narrow enough to direct our actions.

The right balance between broad definition of goals and narrow definition of objectives depends on our role, responsibility, authority, and the context in which the problem will be solved. Consequently, identifying balanced goals and objectives is part of the iterative process of problem definition. We may restate our goals and objectives several times as we analyze our own strengths and weaknesses and the context's opportunities and threats.

Usually we have multiple goals or objectives. It is important to lay them all out. The woman with the flat tire in chapter 1 had two objectives: She wanted a functional tire and she didn't want to get soaked in the rain. Adding the second objective eliminated the routine solution—replacing the flat tire with the spare immediately. Whenever we include more goals and objectives, we reduce the range of alternative solutions. If we have too many objectives, we may be left with no alternative that can meet our expectations. Conversely, if we fail to specify all of our goals, even a successful outcome will disappoint us.

Sid looks at his goals and objectives. The Department of Environmental Quality has a mandated objective to keep the level of turbidity, as measured by particulate levels, within regulatory standards. Research on the Power River has demonstrated that increased turbidity and other factors limit salmon runs, which inhibits reproduction, which reduces salmon populations. Salmon are important to Native Americans who depend on them for their livelihood, to sports enthusiasts who get recreational value from salmon fishing, and to other people of the Northwest whose regional identity is, in part, defined by the annual salmon runs. To protect these interests, the state set turbidity standards a year ago.

However, turbidity is not the true objective, even in the short run. The state's turbidity standards provide a benchmark for performance—they define how much turbidity is too much. Deviation from the standard signals a problem but still does not tell us what needs to be changed. Turbidity is caused by excessive soil runoff into the river. Runoff is caused by soil erosion. Soil erosion is caused by natural processes and exacerbated by farmers' and foresters' management practices.

As we will see, Sid can define his objectives and goals in a number of different ways. Which he chooses depends on how he sees his relationship to the problem and on his own creativity. These, in turn, depend on what he thinks is important—his values.

What is the question that calls for action?

Phrasing the question is an iterative process. At the outset, you may identify several questions that call for action. The list of questions need not be exhaustive. It must be sufficient to generate a single question that makes sense. For simple problems, the question that calls for action may be pretty obvious: "How can I clear my desk without burying messages I need to respond to and still get home by 5:00?" or "How can I fix my tire without getting soaked?" For more complex problems, there will be many alternative ways of putting the question that calls for action, each of which suggests a very different way to proceed.

For each question you ask, "Is this my problem? Is this a problem that I have the authority and responsibility to solve? Can my actions make a difference?" If the answer to these questions is yes, you continue: "Does this question make sense given the context? Where will this question lead me?" As your understanding grows, you refine the phrasing of the question. Even in the action stage, you anticipate and respond to changes in your role and the underlying context. As the context evolves—and new information becomes available, as new people and groups enter the situation—you refine the question and make corresponding shifts in your approach.

How Sid puts the question depends on how he sees his role. Sid can phrase the question that calls for action in several ways. His approach to the problem will depend on how he phrases the question. Since Sid is a complex person, he has a number of alternative roles in his job. We will look at Sid, the good old boy; Sid, the bureaucrat; Sid, the technician; and Sid, the problem solver.

Sid, the good old boy, says: "I have a problem. There's more sedimentation than I can overlook. How can I do my job and create the least fuss possible?" While the farmers and employees of Northwest Forest Products are not close friends and neighbors, Sid, the good old boy, wants to be liked by everyone. Though he feels obligated to write up Northwest Forest Products, he's going to fine them the minimum and let them know that he understands their problems. The solution will meet his obligation to his employer.

Sid, the bureaucrat, says: "I have a problem. Agency rules say turbidity levels are not supposed to exceed 125 parts per million. Levels at the Red Ridge intake are over 125 parts per million. How should I enforce the regulation?" He is concerned with compliance. He works for the state, and the state says that when particulate levels exceed the standard, the individual or firm responsible will pay. Sid, the bureaucrat, is going to make sure that the rule is enforced.

The agency gave Sid one primary means of enforcement under the administrative rule: fines ranging from $50 to $5,000 per violation. Sid uses the remedy prescribed under the statute. He fines Northwest Forest Products the maximum.

Sid, the technician, says: "I have a problem. Particulate levels above 125 parts per million affect salmon runs. How can I bring particulate levels down to acceptable levels?" He knows that high particulate levels are a symptom of excessive soil runoff into the river. He decides to fine both the farmers that contribute to soil runoff as well as Northwest Forest Products. He fines the farmers $100 each as a warning. As for Northwest Forest Products, Sid warned them about excessive runoff last year. So he fines them $5,000 and warns them that he will get a court order forcing them to shore up the logging road if they do not fix the problem immediately.

Sid, the problem solver, starts with what he knows. High particulate levels are a symptom of what?—a washed-out logging road in the short run, soil erosion in the long run. Sid cannot ignore the immediate problem. He levies fines and makes sure that the logging road gets fixed immediately. Sid, the problem solver, will explore the long-term problem. He asks, "What's wrong with soil erosion?" Research demonstrates that excessive soil runoff into the river limits salmon runs. In response to the research, the state established standards for turbidity measured by particulate levels. The intent of the regulation is to protect salmon runs.

Based on the rule's intent, Sid says, "I have a problem. Excessive soil erosion is leading to sedimentation that may limit salmon runs." The problem is further complicated because the regulation has generated tension in the community. He phrases the question that calls for action, "How can I protect salmon runs now and in the future *and* minimize conflict today?"

Most complex problems are not solved once and for all. We take incremental steps that move us from the present situation toward our long-term goals. Problems are solved most effectively when we set short-run incremental objectives while keeping in mind our broader long-run goals.

What approach flows out of the question?

Sid is comfortable with the statement of the fact situation and of his objectives and goals. The question, "How can I protect salmon runs now and in the future *and* minimize conflict?" feels right to him as a motivator for taking the next step in solving the problem. He is disturbed, however, that he doesn't know of a practical way to respond to this question.

The *how* in this question seems to indicate that the way to approach this problem will involve planning. The research that led to the current understanding of the cause-and-effect relationships between turbidity and salmon runs has already been done. The decision that salmon runs should be protected has already been made. What is needed is a *plan* for reducing soil erosion to protect salmon runs now and in the future with minimum conflict. Planning is the approach that flows from the question. Yet planning at this stage of problem definition is premature because many decisions remain to be made to identify what is the best way to protect salmon runs. The conundrum is typical during the problem-definition process.

Is there a practical way to address this problem?

A question that calls for action doesn't make sense if there is no practical action to take in response to the question. Sid's question calls for a planning action, but a plan for protecting salmon runs while minimizing conflict will involve more than issuing citations. Sid cannot plan without deciding what is the best way to protect salmon. And he is stuck for alternatives.

At this point, Sid could say, "This may be a problem, but it's somebody else's problem. No solution available to me will solve it." Then he would go back to the fact situation to find another way of phrasing a question that calls for action, one he does know how to deal with. But he does not give up because protecting salmon is important to him. Sid realizes that his decision to protect salmon runs cannot lead directly to planning. Rather, it leads to a broader search for alternatives and more decisions. He expands his search for a practical response.

Sid is a professional. He knows that the rule is intended to protect salmon, not to put a band-aid over symptoms. He decides to talk to his boss. Maybe she can suggest a strategy that is more likely to protect salmon in the long run and reduce conflict over the issue in the community.

It has taken a fieldhand like Sid some time to adapt to his boss, Jill Baker-Schofield. She is bright and political, and the agency is grooming her for promotion. At first, Sid questioned her grasp of the technical issues, but over time he has come to respect her in spite of her inexperience. Even he has to admit she is well trained and committed. And he is impressed by her sensitivity to people's feelings when emotions are running high—as they soon might be along the Powder River. For her part, Jill has come to like this crusty but capable fellow from the old school. She can tell he's troubled.

Sid starts, "I checked out the Red Ridge water intake. Particulates are high." Jill waits as Sid gathers his thoughts. "I can get a court order or write citations, but that won't protect the salmon in the long run. I'm here because I want to find a lasting solution, but I don't know what options we have besides citations and court orders. The situation is complicated. Folks along the Powder are still fired up from those hearings last year when we got public input on the new salmon regulations. Paul Hartner, the operations manager at Northwest Forest Products, got into a shouting match with Ron Banks from the reservation downstream. People took sides, and . . . you get the picture. Whatever we do, we have to avoid polarizing the community any further."

Jill likes the way Sid approaches the problem. She wants to find a lasting solution too. "What's the cause?" she asks. Sid describes what he saw. "There's a washed-out logging road—Northwest's, I think—silting a stream. There are a few farmers who have plowed the flood plain. They're part of the problem too."

Jill has been waiting for a "stick" with which to push people to try out the basin-planning option in the state's Forest Practices Act. The act gives the agency a chance to do more than issue after-the-fact fines for noncompliance. If people in the basin agree on a management plan, it becomes the basis for regulatory control. They sign a contract agreeing to follow the plan for 10 years. The act gives people living and working in the basin freedom to develop a plan that meets their needs; this is the "carrot."

The planning option is relatively new. A couple of groups have used the approach to develop plans for forested basins. Jill is convinced that the upper Powder River is a good place to test the option's applicability in multiple-use basins. The Powder River basin is a narrow agricultural valley that gives way to industrial and federal forestlands. The threat of citations and court orders gives the agency a "stick" for pushing the forest and agricultural interests to develop a management plan together.

Jill explains the idea to Sid. He raises a number of red flags—things could go wrong. People might not be willing to work together. Even if they are willing, they might not agree on a plan. He cautions against making this a test case. "If we proceed, it has to be locals only." He continues, "You might get agreement but not if you air local problems all over the state."

Impatient to proceed, Jill says, "Talk to the mayor of Red Ridge—Glenn Hoffmann. See how he feels about the idea. Then get back to me."

In spite of his discomfort, Sid calls Glenn. They schedule a meeting for the next day to talk about Jill's idea.

Based on his discussion with Jill, Sid tentatively phrases the question that calls for action and settles on an approach.

Fact situation:	Agricultural and forest-management practices are causing soil erosion, leading to higher than acceptable turbidity in the Powder River.
Question that calls for action:	How can I influence farmers' and foresters' management practices?
Immediate objective:	to reduce soil erosion and to decrease turbidity to acceptable levels

Long-term goals:	to protect the salmon runs and not further polarize the community
Practical response:	I will explore the feasibility of using the basin-planning option in the Forest Practices Act.

Before calling Glenn Hoffmann, the mayor of Red Ridge, Sid will evaluate the tentative question and his approach in light of his authority, responsibility, and stake in the outcome by asking, "Does this approach make sense given my strengths and weaknesses and my stake in the outcome?" If he decides to proceed, he will explore the context's opportunities and threats with Glenn, giving him ownership in the problem and involving him in the problem-solving process.

2. Is this my problem?

Reinhold Niebuhr's serenity prayer, "God, give me serenity to accept what cannot be changed, the courage to change what should be changed, and the wisdom to distinguish the one from the other," eloquently describes the two parts of the decision every problem solver faces. What *can* I do about this situation? What *can't* I do about this situation? The problem-definition framework helps us to sort these out, to move toward having the wisdom to know the difference. The question, "Is this my problem?" clarifies what I *can* do; the next question, "In what context will I address the problem?" clarifies what I *can't* do.

A sign in a Chicago Sunday school reads "Make someone happy. Mind your own business." What wisdom! The difficulty lies in understanding the boundaries of problem ownership. A problem can be mine, theirs, or ours. Our role changes in each setting. Identifying our relationship to the problem is a crucial step in problem definition and is essential in understanding our role in problem solving.

We are now at the second question of the problem-definition framework, and we need to define it in terms of specific subquestions.

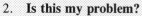

Problem-Definition Framework

1. What is the problem?

2. **Is this my problem?**
    *   Do I have any responsibility for addressing this problem? Why? How much? To whom am I responsible? For what?
    *   Do I have authority to address this problem? Do I share authority? With whom? For what?
    *   What is my role in relation to this problem?
    *   What are my strengths to address this problem? My weaknesses?
    *   What is my stake in the outcome?
    *   Does it make sense to proceed?

3. In what context will I address the problem?

4. What is the first step?

As these subquestions show, our relationship to the problem is determined by our responsibilities, our authority, what we have to offer—our strengths and weaknesses—and what we have at stake. A systematic inventory of this relationship often clarifies the problem more than all the external data gathering we can accomplish.

Do I have any responsibility for addressing this problem?

Here we look at whether our own actions contributed to the problem, whether there are actions we can take that would contribute to a solution, whether our jobs or positions in the community require us to respond to the problem, and whether we have special information regarding the problem that is needed to find a workable solution.

Answers to these questions are objective. Anyone evaluating our responsibility should answer the questions the same way. If the answer to all of these questions is no, our relationship to the problem is not well defined. If we are still determined to make this our problem, we will have to develop a relationship to it.

It will also be important to evaluate how much responsibility we have, to whom we are responsible, and what we are responsible for. Often the most practical way of responding to a problem takes us outside the realm of our defined responsibilities. When this happens, we need to be aware that we are developing new roles and new relationships. This is what is happening for Sid in the Powder River situation.

Sid's responsibility. Responsibility for the Powder River situation clearly falls within Sid's job description. He is responsible for enforcing turbidity standards, and turbidity exceeds standards. Protecting salmon is clearly within his job description. However, the basin-planning option is not identified as a remedy in the salmon regulations.

Basin planning is an option in the new Forest Practices Act to promote long-term sustainability of land and water resources. Clearly, soil erosion from forestlands adversely affects forest soils and the watershed, and thus downstream water quality. To make the link between long-term quality and turbidity levels on the Powder River today, a professional like Sid will have to reach beyond his job description. He will have to decide whether or not he wants to accept responsibility for basin planning as a means to protect salmon and avoid community conflicts.

The basin-planning option is intended for forest owners. If Sid and the Department of Environmental Quality promote the planning option, they are crossing administrative boundaries in ways that can threaten other departments. Farmers are serviced by the state Department of Agriculture, and the Forest Practices Act is the responsibility of the Division of Forestry. Most farmers own some woodlands, so they technically fall under the Forest Practices Act for harvesting consequences, but Sid is concerned that he and his agency not get too far out on political turf claimed by other agencies.

We have to act on some problems. Our responsibility is clear; we have no choice. But often our responsibility is not so clear. Many problems fall through the cracks of organizational and institutional authority and responsibility. Then we have to use our judgment to decide whether or not we are responsible. That is Sid's dilemma.

Do I have authority to address this problem?

As a professional, your authority is defined broadly in relationship to others inside and outside the organization. Power is the ability to direct resources, especially other people, to get a job done. Authority is legitimate power—power others see as appropriate to the position we hold, our expertise, or our life experiences. Each of us has formal and informal authority. A chief executive officer or agency manager has formal authority derived from his or her position. Informal authority derives from attributes that move with us—who or what we know, how we act, and what others expect of us. Professionals enjoy particular authority associated with their specialized knowledge. Individuals can increase power by controlling critical resources: information, money, time, capital, equipment, technology, and other inputs.

Sid's authority. As an inspector, Sid is accustomed to clearly defined authority. When things get out of line, he can warn offenders. After repeated warnings or a blatant violation, he can write citations. If necessary, he can recommend legal action, but he has no authority to force the Powder River group to develop a plan.

He can influence how resources are used within the agency because of his seniority coupled with his demonstrated performance record. His boss and the agency's legal department trust his judgment. While he will have no explicit authority to force people along the Powder River to develop a plan, he will have some influence. Through Sid, the agency will offer the group the carrot of self-determination if they succeed—juxtaposed against the stick of stiff citations and court orders if they fail.

What is my role?

Agricultural, environmental, and natural resource professionals play a variety of roles—manager, producer, technician, advisor, consultant, researcher, and regulator. While professionals often play multiple roles, problem solving is improved if the problem solver acknowledges his or her role at each point in time. Other important roles in resource management problems are the roles of consumer, citizen, taxpayer, individuals exposed to environmental hazards, and policy maker. The way we define the problem will be influenced by our role, and our role, in turn, may be influenced by the way we define the problem.

Sid's role. If Sid and the department accept responsibility for basin planning, Sid's role could expand. If the department assigns him to the job, he will be an advisor and facilitator, in addition to his traditional roles of regulator and inspector. His decision to accept or reject responsibility depends, in part, on how capable he feels in these unfamiliar roles.

Generally, roles, authority, and responsibility are assigned by discipline, function, and task. But many problems transcend these narrow compartments, causing problem solvers such as Sid to test and expand the boundaries of their authority and responsibility to find the best possible solutions to problems.

What are my strengths and weaknesses to address this problem?

Next, Sid will critically evaluate his responsibilities, authority, and role, categorizing all the information available as a strength or weakness as it relates to carrying out the approach suggested by the problem that calls for action. Based on this analysis, he will determine whether or not he can positively influence the outcome (i.e., the probability of success). Then he will ask himself, "Does the question and my approach make sense in light of my strengths and weaknesses?"

As professionals, our roles, responsibility, and authority are generally defined in a job description and through the expectations of our supervisors and colleagues. Sid is looking for a question and approach that lead to the desired outcome. But the approach must be consistent with his authority and responsibility or it will be impractical.

After critically assessing his role, responsibility, and authority, Sid categorizes each piece of information (table 2.1). He evaluates whether it is a strength or weakness relative to the question that calls for action and the problem-solving approach he tentatively has selected.

Table 2.1.   Sid's strengths and weaknesses in addressing the Powder River problem

Strengths	Weaknesses
Responsibility	
Sid is explicitly responsible for turbidity levels. Protecting salmon runs is implicitly his responsibility.	Sid is not responsible for basin planning.
	Sid is not responsible for reducing soil erosion.
Sid is explicitly responsible for fining those who contribute to turbidity.	
	He is not responsible for the management practices of farmers and foresters except as runoff from operations contribute to turbidity.
Sid feels a moral responsibility to the foresters and the farmers causing the problem.	
Sid's boss and his agency feel a similar moral responsibility.	

Table 2.1. (*continued*)

Strengths	Weaknesses

Authority

Strengths	Weaknesses
Nothing in the salmon regulations explicitly precludes the agency from using the basin-planning option as a remedy.	Basin planning is not explicitly identified as a remedy in the salmon regulations.
Sid has explicit authority to enforce salmon regulations using fines and litigation.	Sid's boss will support him as long as everything is going well. Sid is unsure of her support if the basin-planning option fails.
Sid's boss has given him authority to test basin planning as a remedy.	Including farmers in the basin plan may cause the Department of Agriculture to question the agency's authority.
Sid can talk to the Department of Agriculture and other agencies with authority in advance to forestall turf battles.	

Role

Strengths	Weaknesses
The facilitator role comes naturally to Sid. He fills this role in his community service.	Sid is more familiar with the inspector/ regulator role in his work. People may distrust him in any other role.
His boss will support him in this role and has offered to assist him.	Facilitating and advising on the job are new roles. Sid may have to learn new interpersonal skills.

As Sid looks at his and the agency's strengths and weaknesses, he thinks to himself, "It's too bad. This would be a lot easier if the guys who wrote the salmon regulations had anticipated using the basin-planning option as a remedy for noncompliance. At least, nothing prevents us from using the basin-planning option."

What is my stake in the outcome?

Solving problems involves change. Ideally, change leaves everyone who has a stake in the problem better off. In many cases, everyone *is* eventually better off. When a flat tire is fixed, everyone is better off. The owner of the car can use it again. Other drivers are safer because the parked car is no longer a hazard along the road. The service station has profited from fixing the flat.

Environmental changes, social changes, and resource management changes are inevitably complex. People's interest and their stake in the problem vary. Often people gain and lose by the same change because of multiple stakes. Clean air may cost more, but we may breathe more easily. The time frame also complicates people's stakes. Someone who loses a job due to changing pollution control technology is worse off in the short run but may be better off in the long run because he or she enjoys a longer, healthier life. Sorting out who holds a stake in the problem is part of problem definition.

Sid evaluates his stake. Sid's stake in the outcome is his expectation of tangible and intangible gains and losses that could result from accepting responsibility for the problem both in the short and long run.

The agency has an obvious stake in the outcome—protecting salmon runs. Since Sid works for the agency, his stake is tied to the agency's stake. However, the basin-planning option increases both the agency's and Sid's stake in the outcome. No matter how much he objects, Sid knows this will be treated as a test case. If Sid pushes the basin-planning option and the group fails to agree—or agrees to a plan but fails to follow through—Sid and the agency could be criticized for extending their authority beyond legislative and regulatory intent.

Sid realizes that whoever takes the initiative is sure to be noticed, but he hopes to retire in a couple years so he doesn't care about getting noticed. On the one hand, Sid is willing to test the boundaries of his authority and responsibility for important issues. Protecting salmon runs is important to Sid. Yet, he isn't willing to test the boundaries if the agency won't support him. He doesn't fully trust his boss to support him if the process goes sour. He decides to think about this again after he and the mayor assess how the Powder River people might respond to the basin-planning option.

How we perceive our stake depends on our values. Each of us values our stake on the basis of how we are affected personally. We ask, "How much do I stand to lose or gain from the change?" That is not to say that people are necessarily self-centered. To varying degrees, individuals' values are based on how the collective is affected. Each defines the collective differently, ranging from family to group to local community to nation to global community. The extent to which individuals extend their stake is related to whether they assume their actions are independent or interdependent. This, in turn, corresponds to an underlying set of values, which will be treated at length in chapter 3.

An individual guided by *productivity values* is concerned primarily with how much the production unit stands to lose or gain. Depending on the problem at hand, the production unit may be the individual only, it may include family, or it may extend to other members of groups to which the individual belongs (i.e., farmers, wage workers). An individual guided by *equity values* extends his or her moral responsibility to others, seeking to provide equal opportunity, resource access, or fair distribution of resources to others. Each individual decides how far to extend moral responsibility. An individual guided by *sustainability values* accepts moral responsibilities through time. This explains why some people get involved in Greenpeace, Nature Conservancy, Sierra Club, and other environmental organizations.

Most people are *anthropocentric*—that is, people-centered—and their values are people-centered too. Most of us value the environment based on how it serves human purposes. Most of us restore, maintain, and enhance the environment not solely for its own sake but also for people's sake. Sid and the agency seek to protect salmon both for the sake of the salmon and because salmon serve (or may serve) people's purposes.

When we deal with problems of resource degradation, pollution, and depletion, we can avoid some unnecessary disappointment by recalling that most people are anthropocentric. If we define the problem on the assumption that people should value the environment for its own sake when they do not, our efforts are unlikely to change their behavior. People are much more willing to change their behavior to get a result that they value.

A stake is more than money. Gains and losses are not always monetary. Direct gains and losses affect

- *Livelihood.* Present, expected, and potential wages and salaries, profits, stock dividends, and income-generating options.
- *Physical well-being.* Present, expected, and potential health and safety.
- *Quality of life.* Present, expected, and potential aesthetic value, amenities, leisure, flexibility, participation, and other less-tangible attributes.

Public agencies and institutions have a more complex stake in the outcome.

- *Public good.* Public agencies and institutions seek to enhance, maintain, and restore livelihood, physical well-being, and quality of life for the public in aggregate. Some agencies play an advocacy role for a narrowly defined group. Other public institutions aim to balance competing interests, seeking the public good in a broader sense.
- *Maintaining order.* Public agencies seek to order our society and coordinate behavior among diverse individuals and groups for the public good.
- *Self-perpetuation.* Employees of public agencies seek to perpetuate

their jobs and protect their livelihood. Consequently, a positive public image, visibility, and other objectives are important.

Sid's stake is closely tied to that of his employer's. Professionals generally work for others. Sid's stake is even more complex than the agency's. Professionals protect their employers' stakes but, as breadwinners, also must protect their own personal stake. Career progress, promotions, and salary increases are important. These tangible rewards are affected by job performance, and problem solving is an integral part of most professionals' jobs. As a result, professionals take both their employers' and their own stakes into consideration when assessing "Is this my problem?" Betsy Tomlin, for example, is unlikely to see soil erosion as her problem until it becomes a concern of Paul Hartner's and the company that employs them both. Sid is unlikely to consider the basin-planning option without Jill's support. His hesitation is based on the well-founded fear that his agency's interests might diverge from his if the plan causes conflict.

Generally, the employer's and employee's stakes coincide. When they diverge, conscious awareness of the multiple and conflicting objectives that drive the search for solutions enables the professional to set priorities and act on objectives that are truly important. When conflicting objectives result in unresolvable ethical dilemmas, the professional may choose to accept responsibility for the employer's stake with unquestioning loyalty, voice his or her concerns, and accept whatever repercussions result or leave the organization.

Should I proceed?

Sid has looked at his strengths and weaknesses to address the problem as he has defined it, and he has made a realistic assessment of his stake in the outcome. Sid asks himself, "Given these, does it make sense to proceed?" He realizes that he is not committing himself to anything concrete at this point. He will come back to this question after he has learned more about who else has a stake in the outcome and the factors that influence what can be done (i.e., the context). Nevertheless, he has to decide whether to take the next step.

Sid is willing to take risks. He's nearing retirement and is not as concerned about promotions and raises as he once was. He determines the risk is worth it just on the principle of the issue and decides to proceed.

Sid's decision to accept or reject responsibility for the problem is based on two factors: the importance of his stake in the outcome to him and the probability that his efforts will make a difference. As the decision matrix in figure 2.2 illustrates, he is more likely to accept responsibility when the outcome is important to him and he has a high probability of achieving his goals. He is less likely to take action when the outcome is unimportant and he has a low probability of achieving his goals.

Between these extremes, each individual decides how important is important enough and what probability of success is high enough. Some people are more action oriented than others, and some people are more willing to take risks than others. These are individual characteristics that play a crucial, but poorly understood role in determining when and how people accept responsibility for problems.

Like the other stages of problem definition, assessing the importance and probability of success is an iterative process. Different ways of seeing the problem lead to different goals and approaches. Different goals are of more or less importance to us. Different approaches to the problem have different probabilities of achieving success.

We intuitively (and often unconsciously) analyze the probability of success based on what we know and what we think we know. We act on perceptions as though they were fact. We may choose not to act on problems that are important to us because we *know* our efforts would be futile. Our

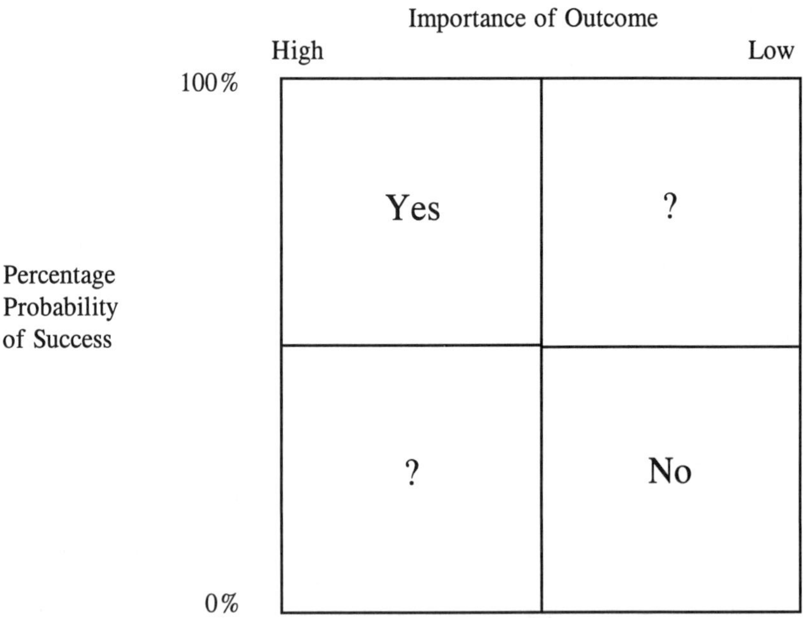

Figure 2.2. Evaluating a decision's importance and risk.

knowledge is based on fact. In contrast, we may fail to act on problems that are important to us because we mistakenly *think* our efforts would be futile.

We often perceive that we cannot successfully address a problem when we have phrased the question that calls for action too broadly. We have posed a big problem, and we envision correspondingly big and dramatic results. The probability of achieving big and dramatic results is low, however, so we end up rejecting all responsibility. This is like saying, "If I can't solve the solid waste problem, I'm going to keep on drinking coffee from foam cups and diapering my baby with disposable diapers." Usually, we can rephrase the question that calls for action, defining the problem's boundaries more narrowly in terms of the things we *can* change and setting more immediate and narrow objectives that move us toward our broad goals. Focusing on the things that we can change improves the probability of success and enables us to act when action at first seemed futile.

We tend to assign importance based on urgency and immediacy. Sid's first concern is to respond to the urgency of the washed-out road. He can write citations and get a court order if he has to, forcing Northwest to take measures to prevent another washout. The situation is urgent. More of the road could wash out at any time, dumping tons of soil into the already overburdened river. In this case, the short-term objectives are important. They are not always important. Too often, we equate urgency and importance. A short-sighted focus on urgent objectives may exclude important long-term considerations. Sid realizes that while urgent action is needed to reduce the immediate risk of further washouts, the long-term goals are of primary importance.

3. In what context will I address the problem?

Sid has come a long way in defining his problem. He has a working version of a question calling for action that clarifies his immediate objective and his long-term goals. He is exploring the potential of basin planning as a practical way to address the question. He has inventoried his strengths and weaknesses and his own stake in the problem. Based on this, he has decided that, at least at this stage, a solution is important to him and he has an acceptable chance of being successful. He wants to proceed. Before going much further, he will need to know more. Who else is affected by the problem? What are the legal, economic, biophysical, and political implications of the problem? He needs to ask, "In what context will I address this problem?"

Problem-Definition Framework

  1. What is the problem that calls for action?

  2. Is this my problem?

  3. **In what context will I address the problem?**
   - At what level are people affected by this problem? Local? State? National? Global?
   - Who has a stake in the outcome?
   - What do stakeholders stand to gain or lose?
   - What is the political context of this problem?
   - The economic context?
   - The biophysical context?
   - The legal context?
   - What resources are available to solve the problem? What additional resources are needed?
   - What opportunities and threats does the context present?
   - Who should be involved in solving the problem?
   - Does it make sense to proceed?

  4. What is the first step?

Problems are addressed in some unique context. Few problems are so generic that they can be solved out of context. The context of the problem determines the things we cannot change (though we may be able to affect the way they work). Every problem has stakeholders—people and groups who stand to gain or lose depending on how the problem is solved. The solution must be compatible with what these stakeholders will choose to do, given their values and alternatives. The way the stakeholders relate to each other is the political context of the problem. Every problem context also has economic, biophysical, and legal dimensions—factors that influence what can be done and what the outcome will be.

- To identify the *level* of the problem, ask: Which people will benefit if this situation improves? Are they defined by a physical region, a neighborhood, an economic class, a national boundary? Which people will have to change their behavior to improve this situation? Some local problems are so common that they seem national or global (like sedimentation). Some global problems have large local effects (like climate change). Confusion on these questions leads to inevitable failure.

- To identify *stakeholders,* ask: Who has a stake in the outcome? Who has contributed to the problem? Who is affected by the problem? (These may or may not be the same individuals or groups.) What public agencies and institutions have a stake in the outcome? What special interest groups and trade associations might have an interest in the outcome? Others? Who stands to lose? to gain? How much?

- To identify the *political and economic contexts,* ask: How are the stakeholders related to the problem? To each other economically and politically? How much influence does each group have relative to each other? What economic relationships are involved? What political forces could promote or hinder problem solving?

- To identify the *biophysical context,* ask: What is known about the cause-and-effect relationships? What is not known? What is assumed? On what basis do we know it?

- To identify the *legal context,* ask: What policies, programs, rules, standards, taxes, or subsidies exist that condition people's response to this problem? Do they encourage creative approaches or constrain them?

- To determine what *resources* are available, ask: What resources are needed? What resources are available? What resources can be obtained? At what cost? Does the benefit exceed the cost? What needed resources are unavailable? How will their unavailability affect the outcome? Resources include time, information, people, capital, natural resources, equipment, supplies, and technology.

- When we have a good picture of the context of the problem, we can begin to inventory the *threats and opportunities* inherent in the economic, political, biophysical, and legal environment. Then we can ask ourselves again: Does it make sense to proceed?

Sid has identified his alternative approaches based on his own perspective as an employee, a professional, and an individual. Now he will look at the potential usefulness of the basin-planning approach in light of the context. As his understanding of the context evolves, he is continuously asking, "Is this approach likely to achieve my goals and objectives given the context as it exists now?"

Sid enlists Glenn's help to explore the context. Sid realizes the Powder River situation is complex. Many people with widely different perspectives have a stake in the outcome. The relationships between soil erosion and dying salmon aren't obvious. Basin planning is a new and unfamiliar process. So Sid goes to Glenn Hoffmann, the mayor of Red Ridge, for help in understanding the context. By involving Glenn, Sid is also expanding ownership in the problem, implicitly asking Glenn to share responsibility for bringing the problem to the community's attention and facilitating the problem-solving process.

Sid meets with Glenn early the next day and explains the problem. He concludes by saying, "The department has two options. We can go in and write citations or we can try to get folks to work together to develop a basin-management plan."

Glenn says, "Now let me get this straight. Are you telling me that one way or the other the department is going to push the people along the Powder River to comply with those regulations to protect salmon? They've been on the books for a year. Why start pushing people now? Why use us to make an example? Go write citations over on the Black River. They have more of a problem than we do!"

Glenn continues, "Sid, you know how people here feel about those regulations. We told you at the hearings. Don't you remember how many of our people turned out to testify against them? You guys sure have a short memory! Don't you realize what enforcing those rules will do to us? You're talking about our jobs and income. We're not high rollers here. We work for a living. Go use somebody else's town to make your example."

Sid didn't expect Glenn's anger and realizes he will have to be careful. "Glenn, I understand your concerns," Sid starts. "We're not making an example of the Powder. The department will be enforcing the rules on all of the salmon rivers. The Powder River just happens to be first. Besides," Sid continues, "you only heard half of what I said. We have *two* options. We can write citations *or* we can get folks along the river to try the basin-planning option." He pauses, hoping Glenn is listening.

"This basin-planning option," Glenn answers, "what is it? And don't sell me a line now. I want it straight." Sid explains that the basin-planning option was defined in the Forest Practices Act. It offers citizens an alternative to state regulation. "How?" Glenn asks skeptically. Sid continues, "People get together and develop their own forest-management plan. When everyone agrees, they sign

a contract with the state binding them to the terms of the plan for ten years."
Sid explains the option in detail while Glenn asks questions. He is interested, but not convinced. "What about the farmers along our section of the Powder? Can we bring them into the planning process? No plan will work without them." Sid acknowledges that farmers aren't explicitly mentioned in the Forest Practices Act but notes that "all forestlands are," which include farm forests and gives the flexibility to include farm owners when necessary.

Sid looks at his watch. They have been talking for two hours. He says, "Listen, Glenn. I have questions myself. I'll call a friend who worked with a group at Vine City that used the basin-planning option last year just after the governor signed the legislation. I'll arrange for us to talk with them. What do you say?" Glenn likes the idea.

A few days later, Glenn and Sid drive to Vine City to meet with Sid's friend, the mayor, a couple members of the town council, and several of the people who developed the basin plan. Nearly everyone they talk to is excited about the basin-planning option and offers advice and encouragement. They excitedly explain what they would do differently if they could start over. Because Sid knows that people aren't as open when a state inspector is present, he makes sure that Glenn gets time to talk to people on his own. He wants Glenn to come away satisfied that people have stated their feelings honestly.

Vine City citizens who participated in the process seem positive about the future. They have new-found confidence in the town's ability to deal with problems. Several talk about "being in control for the first time." By the time they leave Vine City, Glenn is sold on basin planning.

Glenn has wondered for a long time how to get people in Red Ridge to take charge of their future. "Maybe," he thinks, "this is it." Sid and Glenn schedule a meeting for the next day to plan their approach.

Without Glenn, the basin-planning option won't work, so his support is essential. Glenn knows the people. He knows the community. As a local leader, he understands the social dynamics of the community probably better than any other person. He knows what motivates people—and what irritates them. By involving Glenn, Sid hopes to understand better what he is getting into, and he is trying to expand ownership in the problem.

Glenn did not recognize a problem until Sid brought it to his attention. Like Sid, Glenn will have to define the problem based on his role, responsibility, and authority. He will have to determine how much responsibility, if any, he is willing to accept and phrase a question that calls for action. He might think, "I have a problem. The state has chosen to enforce turbidity standards on the Powder River, and the citizens of Red Ridge are likely to be upset. How can I help the state carry out its responsibility in the least disruptive manner possible? Better yet, how can I transform this problem into an opportunity to bring the community together?" His question differs from Sid's because he comes to the problem from a different perspective. Despite their different questions, Sid's and Glenn's goals and objectives are complementary.

At what level are people affected by this problem?

For many problems, especially environmental and resource problems, both effects and responsibility are experienced at many levels. Global warming is a planetwide consequence of the actions of individuals everywhere. American firms complain that environmental regulations put them at a cost disadvantage relative to foreign producers. Federal groundwater protection regulations may require states to restrict landfill sites, leaving municipalities with the dilemma of more solid waste than there is space to dispose it in, requiring households to find ways to reduce their solid waste or develop alternative means of disposal. The level at which people are affected depends on how we define the problem—how we phrase the question that calls for action.

The level at which people are affected is important because it is only the people who "own" the problem who will be able to change it. They must recognize it as *their* problem. If we want to approach the solid waste problem by reducing the waste stream rather than by increasing disposal capacity, we must find a way to give ownership of the problem to the households, packagers, manufacturers, and recyclers that affect the size of the solid waste stream.

Sid's problem doesn't fit into a neat category. The Powder River problem is a landowner's problem. Landowners are not the only stakeholders, however. All of Red Ridge's citizens are stakeholders. More importantly, it is a river basin problem. The Native Americans who depend on salmon runs for income live downstream from Red Ridge, and their community has little direct social or economic contact with the citizens of Red Ridge. Finally, the problem is a statewide problem. The Forest Practices Act containing the basin-planning option is a state law enacted for the public good.

Who has a stake in the outcome?

When solving a problem involves change on the part of many people with different stakes in the outcome, each person ultimately decides individually whether or not to make the change. The best possible solutions are tailored so that gains are distributed equitably and losses are minimized. This requires an understanding of the people who stand to gain or lose from the proposed changes. Sid and Glenn must identify those who have a stake in the outcome and evaluate the nature of what is at stake.

- Who has a stake in the outcome? Those who contribute to the problem, those affected by the problem, those who represent these individuals and groups, and those who work for public agencies are involved.

- What is at stake? Will they gain, lose, or remain the same if my objectives are achieved?

Sid and Glenn identify stakeholders. Feelings for and against the salmon regulations run high. To realize a plan, Sid and Glenn will appeal to reason rather than emotion. However, even reasonable arguments are filtered through perspective. A solid understanding of the objectives and perspectives that drive everyone with a stake in the outcome will enable Sid and Glenn to make their appeal more effective.

Sid and Glenn meet the next day to plan their approach. Sid starts, "The plan must be a local initiative. I want to take a back seat on this one, but I'll help in any way I can." Glenn nods. He had already come to a similar conclusion. He responds, "The people involved have to feel they own the plan. It can't be yours or mine. I'll get the process started, but I hope a member of the group emerges as leader before we get too far into planning."

Sid changes the subject. "It seems to me," he says, "that the most important step right now is to figure out who has a stake in the problem. We need to include everyone with a stake." Glenn starts naming people.

Sid interrupts. "Before you go too far, let's figure out what kinds of people have a stake in the problem, then name individuals." Glenn begins, "There are the forestry firms like Northwest Forest Products and the farmers along the river. A few independent landowners sell wood on the side. And the U.S. Forest Service has land on the higher elevations. We'll have to bring them into the process. And we can't forget the Indian reservation downstream. They make a good share of their income on the salmon catch."

Glenn stops for a moment. "Unfortunately, Ron Banks from the reservation faced off with Paul Hartner at the hearings. The conflict polarized the community. Neither was willing to listen or give ground in public. Fortunately, they're both reasonable people in private. I believe they will both come around in time. Meanwhile, we need to be sensitive to feelings on both sides." Glenn continues, "I hate to ask, but what about that environmental group that has been all fired up about the salmon runs? And that canoe group out of Capitol City? And what about the resorts upriver? They've all got a stake in this. Tourism and recreation are big business around here, and salmon are an important draw."

Sid writes as Glenn lists the groups (table 2.2). "Slow down, I can't keep up with you," Sid says. "Let's take them one by one. What's their stake in the outcome?"

Table 2.2. Sid's notes—stakeholders

Those contributing to the problem
Forestry companies
Farmers
Other landowners
U.S. Forest Service and state forest service

Those immediately affected by the problem and its solution
Salmon fishers on reservation
Recreational salmon fishers
Environmental groups concerned with species protection
Recreation groups concerned with aesthetics
Tourist industry concerned with aesthetics
Independent log cutters and sawmills whose income could be affected if Northwest were
    ordered to stop clear cutting on steep slopes along the river

Intermediary groups concerned with public good
Red Ridge community
Department of Environmental Quality

Stakeholder analysis identifies individuals and groups with something to gain or lose. The analysis may be cursory if the groups with a stake in the outcome have a similar perspective and complementary objectives. When people with diverse perspectives and conflicting objectives have a stake in the outcome, it is important to understand their relationships to the problem and each other. Answers to the following questions provide the information needed.

- How are stakeholders related to the problem? Do those who have a stake in the outcome recognize that a problem exists? At what stage of problem awareness/recognition/definition/action are they? From what perspective do they approach the problem? Why?

- What do they stand to gain or lose in the short run? The long run? How important is their stake? How urgent is solving the problem to them?

- What are their relationships to each other and to you? What role, responsibility, authority, power, or influence do they have over the outcome? Have they worked together in the past? What successes/failures did they have? Why?

- Are they likely to have a common understanding of the problem? What common ground might they have?

With what point of view will stakeholders start? Perception, objective fact, and reality differ. Individuals approach a problem through their own unique perspective. Individuals' perspectives are determined by their relationship to the problem, who they are, how they think, what they value, how they relate to other people, their training, and their life experiences. Even the most objective problem solver filters information and ideas through his or her perspective.

In contrast, objective facts are true statements that can be substantiated with evidence. All reasonable people will agree with an objective statement of fact when the evidence is laid out. Reality is the middle ground where objective facts and subjective perspectives meet. In reality, people act on a mix of facts and impressions only partially supported by facts filtered through their perspective. Let's look at Sid's and Glenn's perspectives.

Sid is a professional. He works for a state regulatory agency, charged with protecting the environment and the public good. He takes his job and the agency's mission seriously. His approach is technical. He likes clear, lucid arguments supported by facts and figures. He's a hydrologist by training. While he's not swayed by emotional arguments, he likes and respects nearly everyone he meets. His life experience has led him to believe that all problems can be solved through persistence. He prefers action to talk. He's practical. While he takes his job and protecting salmon very seriously, he's emotionally detached from the problem at hand. He won't be directly affected by the outcome. He will get his paycheck however the problem is solved.

As the mayor of Red Ridge, Glenn is charged with protecting the interests of his constituency. As an elected official, he is constantly balancing competing interests. Glenn listens to technical and emotional arguments. He prefers compromises rather than winner-take-all solutions. He believes that impressions—whether accurate or inaccurate—strongly influence people's behavior and accepts that this perception often becomes reality. As mayor, Glenn is ever aware of how his actions will affect his next bid for reelection. Life has treated him well. While he's inclined to question new ideas at first, he's an enthusiastic and committed team player once he's convinced an idea has merit. He conveys genuine concern for people and can motivate and excite people when necessary.

Perspectives aren't right or wrong. Individuals come to the problem with their own equally valid and unique perspectives. Sid's and Glenn's perspectives differ from those of others with a stake in the outcome.

The operations manager of Northwest Forest Products, Paul Hartner, will approach the problem from the perspective of his employer. In fact, his employer has contributed substantially to the sedimentation problem at hand. Paul has moved up the ladder by intuiting senior management's priorities and putting their priorities ahead of all others. Now he is a senior manager. Like all industrial firms, Northwest is concerned with productivity—producing the most from given resources. Paul scrutinizes any action that will increase costs. He knows through experience not to agree readily to anything, particularly things that appear to increase costs, without generating corresponding benefits in some reasonable time frame. And Paul is keenly aware that the chief executive officer's time frame is short—too short for Paul's liking. At the same time, Paul is a professional. As a professional, he considers facts objectively. If he can be convinced that something is in the firm's best interests, he will make the recommendation.

Ray Green approaches the problem from a different perspective. He owns his farm. His livelihood depends on producing grain and livestock for market. If he doesn't produce, he can't pay his bills. Unlike Paul Hartner, he doesn't get a monthly salary check. When his costs go up, his income goes down. It's that simple. Ray is skeptical of professionals telling him what to do and how to farm. They don't have to pay the bills if their recommendations don't work. Because his production loans will have to be paid off at harvest, he doesn't have the luxury of looking at the long run. If his production goes down or his costs go up, Ray will be even more cash-short than usual through the winter months.

Ron Banks lives on the reservation downstream. Salmon are an important source of income for him and many others. He doesn't have many income-generating alternatives, and jobs are scarce on the reservation. The local community has never shown much sympathy for tribal people, and many are openly hostile. Non-Indians resent the protected Native American fishing rights. While Ron understands that farmers like Ray Green are just trying to make a living, he's unsympathetic. He's even less sympathetic to highly paid company people like Paul Hartner and the forestry firms they represent. As far as Ron is concerned, the forestry industry can afford to clean up after itself. While Ron's life experience has provided him with adequate cause to be suspicious of outsiders, he tries to give others the benefit of the doubt on first meeting.

The perspectives of these five people are very different, yet they share a common problem. Asked to phrase the question that calls for action, each would phrase a different question based on his own perspective.

Paul Hartner might define the problem and phrase the question this way:

"I have a problem. A state inspector is asking about the washed-out road Betsy Tomlin reported last week. What should I do to get him off the company's back until we have more time to deal with the road situation? We have all we can handle planting seedlings right now."

Ron Banks might define and phrase the question like this: "I have a problem. The state doesn't appear to be doing anything about that washed-out road that's silting up the river—much less the underlying problems. What should I do to push the state to move faster?"

Their questions cannot be judged "right" or "wrong" or even "better" or "worse." A question's value can only be judged from the perspective that spawned it. From Paul's perspective, his question makes sense. From Ron's perspective, his question makes sense. The two approach the problem from radically different perspectives.

However, perspectives are not set in stone. They evolve as people are exposed to new experiences and information. Individuals don't change their perspectives and accept someone else's, but people can learn to understand and appreciate other perspectives. They can learn to view the problem from a historic perspective. In the process, they may learn that they share a common problem. Their perceptual differences will remain no matter how great their understanding. If either Paul Hartner or Ron Banks had more information, he might rephrase the question in a way that is more responsive to other perspectives but still consistent with his own.

Paul could say, "I have a problem. The state wants us to shore up the high-risk area of the road now to prevent further washout. They also want us to deal with the broader soil erosion problem. Our crews are overburdened with spring planting. How can I meet the company's immediate needs and the state's immediate needs so that we can deal with the underlying soil erosion problems at a more convenient time?"

Ron could say, "I have a problem. The state is not moving as quickly as my neighbors and I would like to ensure that Northwest Forest Products' road does not wash out further this spring. No action is being taken on the underlying problem. How can I help reduce the risk of another washout and encourage the state to deal with the broader issues?" With their rephrased questions, it is possible that Ron Banks could provide a work crew to Northwest to shore up the high-risk area of the road until more permanent measures can be taken.

Perspectives are problem specific. Ray Green may side with Paul Hartner on this issue because their interests coincide to some degree. But if Northwest Forest Products proposed building a paper mill upstream from Ray's farm, Ray might side with Ron Banks in opposing the idea.

An individual's perspective isn't always consistent or fully revealed. Ray Green feels strongly about protecting his bottoms from erosion. Yet he cannot ignore his immediate cash needs. He can't see any middle ground, so the perspective he presents *in public* appears to be uncooperative and uncaring. Ron Banks is willing to give people the benefit of the doubt to a point, but he is cautious. His life experience suggests that others may not give him the same benefit.

What do stakeholders stand to gain or lose?

Sid and Glenn continue. "What economic stake does each group have in the outcome?" Glenn asks. "They'll all benefit from erosion control. Nobody loses," states Sid. "Sure, but in what time frame?" Glenn continues, "If the time frame doesn't make sense, Northwest or Ray Green could go out of business before they benefit from erosion-control measures. The people who will have to pay the costs of putting in erosion controls won't even come to the table to talk if we don't acknowledge that they have a lot at stake in the short run. If Ray has to quit planting his bottomland in crops, he may as well quit farming. And Northwest—this could really add to their costs. I don't know what kind of financial position they're in, but I've heard rumors about problems. They have a lot to protect in the short run." As Glenn talks, Sid takes notes (table 2.3).

In addition to representing the interests of their employers, professionals involved in problem solving have a personal stake in the outcome. Expectations of career progress are part of the context in which the problem will be solved. If, for example, Jill Baker-Schofield has immediate political ambitions, she might use the Powder River situation to gain visibility. Her personal objectives could conflict with the objectives of those involved in the planning process. An awareness of professionals' personal stake can improve understanding of the context.

What is the political context of the problem?

Webster's dictionary defines *politics* as "competition between competing interest groups or individuals for power and leadership in a government or other group." The political context describes the balance of power that exists at any point in time among competing interest groups. A group's power is measured by the ability of its members to influence decisions. Their power is derived from access to key decision makers, the resources they command, their ability to attract the attention of the mass media, and the number of constituents they can influence.

Many of the stakeholders live in or near Red Ridge. They are individuals with a history of social and economic interaction that will influence the outcome of the planning process. Most know or know of each other. Some respect each other; some have contempt for each other. They will bring all of this social baggage to the basin-planning process.

Other stakeholders are organized groups. These include the environmental and recreation groups. While a few of their members live in Red Ridge, the groups themselves have no social ties to the community. Residents of Red Ridge view these groups as "outsiders." These groups' primary relationships to the other stakeholders are political.

Of the contextual dimensions, the political arena is the most difficult to define and evaluate, partly because it is so fluid. Individuals organize to gain power. Groups form coalitions to increase their political clout. Groups may ally on one issue and oppose each other on another. Groups compromise to form coalitions, horse-trading until each group's key concerns are allayed. Power is as much an issue within organizations and among organizations as it is in government.

Together, Sid and Glenn go down the list of stakeholders. Glenn shares his impressions about their positions, who they influence, and how much clout they have. Glenn is careful not to stereotype people. He tells how Paul Hartner's and Ron Banks' positions have evolved over the years. On a few names he says, "I'm just guessing but . . ."

Declining to characterize the positions of the environmental and recreational groups, Glenn comments, "Anything I say will be based on hearsay. I really don't understand their concerns very well."

There is great danger in knee-jerk analysis of the political context. To be sure, political realities exist and must be considered. However, we rarely understand fully what other people think or why. Moreover, people's positions change over time. We have a tendency to stereotype the opposition based on what we know of them at one point in time. We set ourselves up as the good guys and them as the bad guys. When we relate to the opposition based on our good-guy/bad-guy stereotypes, positions harden and common ground is more difficult to find. Over time, the issue becomes increasingly emotional and stakeholders increasingly polarized.

Americans have tended to address resource degradation, pollution, and depletion problems through an adversarial legal system that promotes good-guy/bad-guy stereotypes. All sides see themselves as *the* good guys. Many have erroneously come to believe an inevitable tradeoff exists between environmental protection and economic growth—between "timber beasts" and "tree huggers," between developers who "pillage" the land and "preservationists" who would fence it to prevent all uses. Artificial battle lines have

Table 2.3. Sid's notes on stakeholder analysis

Group	Perceived Stake	Potential Impact
Those contributing to the problem		
Forestry firms	Profits/cost	Short-term loss
	Erosion control	Long-term gain
Farmers	Profits/cost	Short-term loss
	Erosion control	Long-term gain
Independent landowners	Livelihood/cost	Short-term loss
	Erosion control	Long-term gain
U.S. Forest Service	Costs/credibility	Short-term loss/gain
	Erosion control	Long-term gain
Those affected by the problem		
Environmental groups	To maintain biodiversity	Long-term gain
Indians	To maintain economic returns	Maintain status quo
	To increase salmon stock	Long-term gain
Recreation groups	To maintain quality of life	Maintain/improve status quo
Tourist industry	To maintain profits	Maintain/improve status quo
Intermediary Groups		
Red Ridge community	Trust/participation	*
Department of Environmental Quality	Compliance/trust	*

Professionals	Personal Stake	Representing
Glenn Hoffmann	Stature/reelection	Red Ridge
Sid Riedel	Stature	State Agency
Jill Baker-Schofield	Stature/career future	State Agency
Paul Hartner	Career progress	Northwest Forest

* The basin-planning process could increase trust, participation, and compliance with state regulations and concern about the problem. If mishandled, it could generate distrust and contempt.

been drawn. These have limited our vision and stymied our search for solutions that reconcile tradeoffs. As we will discuss further in the next chapter, productivity, equity, and sustainability values are not mutually exclusive. In fact, they are closely related.

While we must take political realities into account, we have to be careful not to stereotype stakeholders who don't share our perspective. Rather than condemning perspectives other than our own, we need to try to understand them. A better understanding of why people choose the position they do enables us to find solutions in which everyone can participate.

What is the economic context of the problem?

Much is written about the economic factors that affect resource management, particularly productivity of resource use. The most critical economic factor in the Powder River case is the classical problem of who pays and who benefits, which often is referred to as a market externality. The farmers and forest owners feel they are being asked to incur costs and pay for benefits that accrue to other people, such as those who harvest salmon. But the salmon fishers and other downstream users see the landowners as benefiting by not paying all their costs of production, while those downstream believe they are losing their rightful benefits from the river. While less well understood, whether people feel hopeful or pessimistic about the future affects their willingness to consider changes that might affect their costs or returns. A community experiencing rapid growth often is more willing to try new approaches than one experiencing economic and population declines. Similarly, if real values are rising, additional costs are more easily incorporated into new decisions than if real prices are falling.

What is the biophysical context of the problem?

Sid is confronted with two separate but related issues. The immediate issue is primarily biophysical—the imminent threat that another section could wash out with the next heavy rain. Sid defined and took action on this problem quickly. He talked to Paul Hartner about shoring up the logging road within hours after he discovered the high turbidity levels. While Paul was not very responsive, Sid wasn't too worried as long as the rain held off. He would, if necessary, get a court order forcing Paul to shore up the weakest section of the logging road. If Paul still didn't respond, Sid could use the state's powers of eminent domain and have the work done at Northwest's expense.

Sid is more concerned about the long-term biophysical issues. Research has demonstrated the relationships illustrated in figure 2.3. Based on these relationships, Sid realizes the only way to protect salmon in the long run is to change farm- and forest-management practices in the short run. He also realizes that farmers and foresters will be unwilling to change their management practices if short-term productivity and profits are reduced demonstrably.

Research shows that high temperatures also contribute to the problem. Unless water temperatures are lowered, reduction of turbidity might not be sufficient to protect salmon runs. Sid knows this but decides to deal with the issues separately because different causal factors, such as waste water

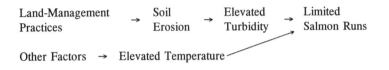

Figure 2.3. Biophysical relationships leading to limited salmon runs.

discharge from industry, contribute to the temperature problem, and another division of the Department of Environmental Quality is responsible for monitoring industrial discharges.

Sid believes that farmers and foresters oppose the salmon regulations, in part, because they don't understand the biophysical relationships between their management practices and preserving salmon runs. He is convinced that their opposition would lessen if they understood how their actions threaten the salmon.

▮   Sid looks at his watch. "Before we quit for the day, there are a couple more things we need to discuss. We're going to get a lot of questions about why this thing is so important. I'll see if I can get a fisheries expert to work with us. He'll be able to explain how soil erosion affects turbidity—and how turbidity limits the salmon runs."

Glenn interrupts. "But there will be even more interest in technical aspects of erosion control. I'll arrange to have someone from the Soil Conservation Service available to answer technical questions."

Biophysical relationships often are not well understood, making problem recognition and definition far more difficult than our present illustration would indicate. Objective researchers legitimately disagree about the relative importance of different economic and biophysical causal factors. Chapter 9 deals with this issue.

What is the legal context of the problem?

The legal context includes local, state, and national legislation; private property rights; regulation; and the forum in which a person with a legally recognized grievance can seek recourse. Like the political, economic, and biophysical context, the legal context is continuously changing. Indeed, causing a change in the legal context may be part of the solution to the problem. The conditions for changing the legal context are an important part of the legal context itself. The questions we will want to ask will include

How are decisions made? The decision-making process describes who has access to the policy-making process that generates laws, administrative rules, case law, and so forth. It also describes when one has access and how. *Who is legally responsible for the problem and its solution?* While the process determines who has access to the bureaucratic process, individual bureaucrats bring their own priorities and understanding to the process. One person may administer the process or interpret a rule differently than another.

What laws, administrative rules, case law, programs, taxes, or subsidies will influence the outcome? These can direct behavior by requiring or prohibiting certain actions or encourage or discourage certain choices through incentives and penalties.

In the Powder River case, state legislation, the Forest Practices Act, provides for the basin-planning option. A state administrative agency promulgates the standards for turbidity levels. The federal Internal Revenue Service and the State Revenue Department establish tax structure that influences landowners' choices. The U.S. Forest Service and Soil Conservation Service may have programs that encourage soil conservation on forest- and farmlands. There may exist case law, established through state and federal courts, that further refines application of rules, standards, programs, and policies.

Sid continues. "I want to dig further into the Forest Practices Act before we call a meeting. I want to be sure that I understand all of the nuances of the basin-planning option. Should I invite a resource person who is more familiar with the act to describe it and answer questions? When you talk to SCS, will you get a list of federal programs to encourage soil conservation? I will check with the national forest supervisor. Maybe he is aware of federal assistance for forest firms. Should we contact anyone else?"

Glenn asks, "Are there tax implications when you agree to a plan? What about legal consequences if someone who signs an agreement withdraws before the end of ten years? I'll arrange to have a CPA and attorney at the meeting to answer questions."

The legal context of this case is relatively well defined. Sometimes, the legal context in which sustainability problems are solved is not well defined; that is, legislation, rules, case law, and programs do not address the specific problem. At other times, the legal context structures incentives in a way that encourages a short-run perspective and discourages sustainable solutions. In these cases, the most effective approach may be to push government institutions to clarify and further define the legal context through civil suits in the courts and public pressure on the legislative and administrative branches at the appropriate level of government.

What resources are available?

When Sid and Glenn finish talking about the political context, they move to the next element of the context: What resources are available? The best approach won't work if the resources are not available to follow through. Resources include the following:

Time. How much time is available? Minutes, hours, weeks, months, years? What else could I be doing with my time? Do the benefits justify the time compared to other things I could be doing?

People. How many people are needed? With what training and skills? When are they needed? For how long? Are they in place? Are they available? How much will they cost? Do the benefits justify the cost in the time available?

Natural resources. What natural resources are needed? Are they in place? Are they available? At what cost? What impact will the activity have on the resource in the short run? In the long run? If there will be negative consequences, are they reversible? Do the benefits justify the monetary and nonmonetary costs in the present? In the future?

Capital. How much capital will be needed? Working capital? Investment capital? When will it be needed? Where? At what cost? Is it available? Do the returns justify the cost in the time available?

Information. What information is needed? How accurate must it be? How precise must it be? How will it be analyzed? How will it be used? When is it needed? Where is it needed? Who will collect it? Who will analyze it? Do they have the skills/training needed? What will it cost? Do the benefits justify the cost in the time available?

Technology. Is the technology in place? Can it be acquired? Can it be developed? How much does it cost? Are there people who know how to use it? What equipment is needed to use it? Do the benefits justify the cost in the time available?

Equipment. Is the equipment in place? Is it available? How much does it cost? Are there people trained to use it? Do the benefits justify the cost in the time available?

Supplies and other inputs. What raw materials, supplies, and services will be needed? How much? How often? What quality? Where? Are they available? How much will they cost? Do the returns justify the cost in the time available?

Sid continues, "Do you have money in your budget to pay for a CPA and a lawyer? I don't! Maybe we had better figure out what resources we're going to need and how we're going to get them."

They start a list. They will need professional help (accountants, lawyers, maybe others), postage, photocopying, and clerical support. Glenn asks, "What about your time? Will your boss let you work with us? It might take a lot of meetings."

Sid remarks that he will ask Jill how much support the state agency can provide. He will recommend that the department provide his time, clerical support, postage, and photocopying. Sid adds, "We'll also need someone to collect information and write the plan. There might be other things as we go along. We may need to buy land to take it out of farm production. But we'll have to deal with some of these issues as they arise. Otherwise, we'll get bogged down before we start."

Sid reminds Glenn that they still have to figure out how to pay for the CPA and an attorney. After a long silence, Glenn offers to twist a few arms and get someone to do the work for free. Sid agrees but he cautions Glenn about getting a general practice lawyer. "We're breaking new ground here. We need the best." Glenn explains he might be able to get an attorney from Capitol City to help. "And we have one of the best CPAs in the state right here in Red Ridge. Just retired. I'd stake my reputation on him."

Sid and Glenn evaluate what resources they will need to address the problem compared to what resources are available. The primary resource they need is time to work with the people involved to develop a plan.

Time is a significant resource. For the planning process to succeed, Sid and Glenn will have to invest substantial blocks of time for meetings, collecting information, and perhaps even writing the plan. Ray Green, Paul Hartner, and the others will as well. If all of the key people are not willing or able to commit their time, the planning process will fail because success depends on stakeholders taking ownership in the plan and ownership depends on participation. Participation can be achieved through emotional or physical involvement. Not every person must attend every meeting.

In this case, the other resources required are not substantial. However, many problems require substantial resources to be solved. While the absence of resources constrains solutions, too many fail to try because the resources might not be available.

What are the opportunities and threats presented by the context?

Sid and Glenn feel that they understand the context as well as they can with the time and information available. Next, using the form in figure 2.4, they evaluate the context, categorizing the parts of the context that present opportunities or threats. They ask themselves, "Given the question that calls for action, what opportunities or threats does the basin-planning approach provide?"

This step requires critical analysis to make subjective choices. Whether something is an opportunity or threat depends on how it is perceived. For example, Glenn could view the Forest Practices Act as an opportunity or a threat. It's an opportunity if Glenn sees it as a chance to build greater trust and cooperation in the community. It's a threat if he feels that the state is forcing it on Red Ridge against his will.

Who should be involved in solving the problem?

This is an important strategic question. One approach is to involve everyone who has a significant interest, positive or negative, in the problem situation. The rationale for this approach is that if everyone who will be affected has an opportunity to represent their interests and their particular circumstances, the solution is more likely to be equitable. The other is to

	Opportunities	Threats
Stakeholders		
Socioeconomic context		
Biophysical context		
Legal context		
Availability of needed resources		

Figure 2.4. Opportunities and threats.

involve only those people who must be convinced to change their actions voluntarily, reducing the decision-making costs and time lags as well as the possibility that the process will be stalled in irresolvable conflict. With either approach, one must have the meaningful involvement of any stakeholder who will be called on to change behaviors.

Sid asks, "Where do we go from here?" Glenn responds, "Getting agreement to a plan depends on getting people to feel a shared responsibility for the problem. They need to feel like 'We're in this together.'" Glenn continues, "I think we should meet with the key people individually before we set up a public meeting. If we can get Paul, Ron, and a couple of others to agree to the process in private, they're a whole lot more likely to be reasonable in public. If we catch them off guard, they are likely to reject the idea as out of hand or, worse, get in a shouting match again. After we have their private commitment, we'll set up a small meeting with the landowners who will have to change their management practices first. If we can get them to commit to the planning process in a small public meeting, then we can open the process up for broader participation. Then we'll be ready to start the real work of planning."

Glenn offers to call key people. Sid agrees to send a meeting announcement after Glenn gets verbal commitments to attend the meeting. They summarize what each has agreed to do and when. Before they part, Sid reminds Glenn that he needs to get final approval to participate in the planning process from Jill before proceeding further. Recognizing that Sid's participation is essential for success, Glenn agrees to wait to begin calling people.

Does it make sense to proceed?

On the way back to the office, Sid reviews the events of the last few days. He returns to the statement of the problem and asks himself if it still makes sense to proceed.

Fact situation:	Agricultural and forest-management practices are causing soil erosion, which is leading to higher than acceptable turbidity in the Powder River.
Question that calls for action:	How can I influence farmers' and foresters' management practices?
Immediate objective:	to reduce soil erosion and decrease turbidity to acceptable levels

Long-term goals:	to protect the salmon runs and not further polarize the community
Practical response:	I will explore the feasibility of using the basin-planning option in the Forest Practices Act.

This general response has been made more specific in the course of his interaction with Glenn. The steps they plan are

1. Talk to key people in private. Obtain a private commitment to cooperate in the planning process from farmers and businesspeople who would have the most to lose in the short run by agreeing to a basin-management plan.
2. Evaluate.
3. Organize a small public meeting, inviting key people with the most to lose in the short run. Let the group *decide* what is the best way to reduce erosion and how to proceed.

Is this an approach that makes sense? Sid is pleased with the progress. Glenn has accepted responsibility for initiating the process and seems to have a good grasp of what the basin-planning option entails—both the technical issues as well as the people issues. They have defined a common problem and phrased a question that calls for action. They identified those with a stake in the problem.

Sid is confident that Glenn and he have laid a firm foundation to solve the problem. They approached the problem systematically and analytically. Their expectations seem reasonable. Even so, he will feel more confident after he talks to Jill—and a lot more confident after the first meeting with Paul Hartner, Ray Green, and the others. He knows it won't be easy, but he is prepared to take the risk.

An ever-changing context

Context is dynamic. Whether it changes very quickly or evolves over years, it is always changing. New information becomes available, people change their minds, new people become involved, businesses sell out, laws change, technology improves or becomes less expensive, capital becomes available, interest rates go up or down, and natural processes alter the landscape.

Phrasing the question places the problem solver on *a* path that leads to *a* specific objective or set of objectives. The decision to follow one path precludes the option to follow other paths at any given point in time. If you follow a path only to discover that it does not lead to the desired outcome, you can go back and try another path. However, the set of paths from which you choose the second time may themselves have changed in the interim because the context in which problems exist is dynamic.

What if Sid had elected to take a wait-and-see approach? Next year, the context could be quite different. The Red Ridge mayor could lose his election. The new mayor might have a confrontational approach to the state's regulatory apparatus rather than Glenn's cooperative approach. Jill Baker-Schofield may accept a more lucrative job offer. Her replacement might be less willing to take risks or less supportive of testing the regulatory boundaries. Northwest Forest Products could be acquired by a larger firm that suspends production in the Powder River area, making the firm less likely to participate in a local basin-planning initiative. Ray Green may sell his farm to a real estate developer who would be unwilling to commit to anything for ten years. Heavy rains may cause a major slide that blocks the branch creek for good. These changes in the context would change Sid's assessment of the situation. Depending on the context, the basin-planning approach may be a more or less acceptable approach to solving the problem.

Looking Ahead

Subsequent chapters further develop the three frameworks that have already been introduced. These frameworks will structure your analysis for

- *Decision making.* Sid, Glenn, and the Powder River group will use this framework to decide how to proceed.

- *Taking action.* When the Powder River group has decided on the elements of the plan, they will use this framework to plan and control implementation so that their actions lead in the direction they want to go.

- *Understanding cause and effect.* If Sid and Glenn had not understood why turbidity was high, they would have used this framework to determine the cause before defining the question that calls for action.

Each framework is presented with group process steps. Process steps are presented for an individual like Ray Green working independently, a structured group like Paul Hartner's department, and a voluntary group like the Powder River stakeholders. Group process steps may be applied to any one of the frameworks, including problem definition.

Before developing the frameworks further, however, it is necessary to look explicitly at an issue that has been implicit in every step we have examined so far: values. We recognize, define, and solve problems based on what we value. In a sense, a problem is a situation that threatens our values; a solution is the removal of that threat. Becoming conscious of what we value and how that affects problem definition is central to being a good problem solver.

3

■ Values and Searching for Answers

Our values define what is important to us. All of us talk about what is important to us, but what we say rarely is entirely consistent with what we do. We reveal our true values in the choices we make and the actions we take. Each of us is faced with options every day compelling us to choose among things we think are important. Sometimes we choose the easiest path; at other times, we decide to stand for what is truly important to us; and on occasion, we search for a different approach that reconciles our perceived tradeoffs. This is what Sid did in chapter 2 when he looked at his various roles.

Our choices reflect what our values are and what order of importance we give them. In turn, our values influence the problems we recognize, the way we define them, the decisions we make, how we implement our plans, and even our understanding of cause and effect (figure 3.1). Progress—movement toward our long-run goals—depends on our values. By examining our values—that is, what motivates our actions—we affect each area of problem solving in ways that move us and others toward our goals.

In this chapter, we examine more closely the three groups of values important to rural resource management introduced in chapter 1: productivity, equity, and sustainability. As we shall see, these three are closely

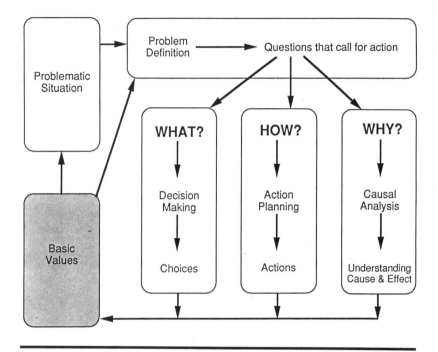

Figure 3.1. Problem-solving framework—basic values.

related. We shall also see that each one of us is likely to define them differently depending on how we view interdependence and how we define our responsibility for ourselves and others.

Three Groups of Values

We do not believe that there is some optimum level of productivity, a perfect balance of equitable distribution, or holy grail of long-term sustainability. Our problems rarely are like mathematical questions that lead to one optimum, let alone "correct," solution—not even to a set of more or less equal "best" answers. Instead, we look for the best answer, given the information and the time we have, to each question we face, knowing we will have new questions tomorrow as the situation changes.

Just as values are revealed in behavior, values can only be discussed meaningfully in the context of problem solving. Consequently, values, both implicit and explicit, are an important part of the discussion in every chapter of this book. We discuss them briefly here to establish a general understanding of the principles involved in our approach to resolving the problems of rural resource management.

Productivity values deal with how we provide for ourselves in terms of production, consumption, income, profit, security, satisfaction, aesthetics, and others. By themselves, productivity values assume that the actions of each individual or small group are independent. In the extreme, I assume my actions do not affect other people's options and that I am responsible only for myself. To the extent that my actions impinge on others, productivity values assume that the marketplace and legal system will constrain me or compensate those I affect.

Equity values define how we fulfill our responsibility to others living in the present. Equity encompasses notions of fairness, justice, equal opportunity, and fundamental human rights. Equity values encompass productivity values, the idea that people are responsible for their own welfare. But those who hold equity values also assume people are interdependent. What one person does affects others. As a result, those who consider equity values believe people share some degree of responsibility for each other.

Sustainability values define how we fulfill our responsibility for the future. "Sustainability" is the current term for what previously was called "conservation." By either name, it means shifting resource use toward the future. This is most easily understood as maintaining resource productivity through time, for example, yields per acre per year. The premise underlying our inclusion of sustainability in the set of values is that production at one point in time affects potential production at later points in time. Consequently, sustainability also encompasses considerations of intergenerational equity. Choices we make about resource use today can negatively or positively affect choices about succeeding generations' use tomorrow.

everal Qualifications

Values are elusive, abstract descriptions of what we think is important. Consequently, it is important to keep in mind several key points.

- While we agree that productivity, equity, and sustainability are important values, this agreement breaks down on specifics. Each individual defines responsibility, measures progress, and weighs the importance of each value differently. Individuals also may weigh these values differently in different circumstances.

- There is a natural tension between what we want for ourselves and what we want for our community—however we define it—and between what we want in the present and in the future. Value conflicts arise out of these tensions.

- We reveal our values through our choices, our reactions to specific problems in specific situations. Statements of values reflect what we would like to think is important to us. While few of us apply our stated values consistently, we can strive to do so.

- While we often treat productivity, equity, and sustainability as separate values, they are inextricably intertwined. We cannot value equity and sustainability without also being concerned about productivity. Equitable distribution assumes that there are benefits of production to distribute. Sustainability is based on notions of intergenerational equity. While the links are not as obvious, maintaining productivity into the future depends on people believing that the benefits of production are distributed more or less fairly in the present.

Interdependence both today and over the long term is a fact. It is not a value or an assumption, and assuming we are not interdependent will not make interdependence disappear. How one views this fact is a value judgment. We believe that it is best to adopt a sense of shared responsibility and move in incremental steps toward living by our values, accepting responsibility for the consequences of our actions today and into the future.

Let us look at each of these three values in more depth.

Productivity and Independence

Productivity focuses on efficient use of resources for constructive purposes, and it assumes that each action, each person, each resource, and each process is independent of others in the present and through time. It is our concern for productivity that leads us to try to get the most out of the resources we have. Productivity is not concerned with equity or sustainability, but it is concerned with efficiency, the boundaries of each action, and the question of purpose.

Efficiency

Definitions of efficiency differ from discipline to discipline. Most scientists express efficiency as a ratio of input to output; for example, bushels per acre per year, cubic feet of timber per acre per year, bushels of wheat per pound of fertilizer, bushels of cotton per acre-foot of water per year, yield per person-hour or machine hour. Using this notion of efficiency, Northwest Forest Products is most efficient when it harvests as many board-feet of lumber as possible for each hour of labor or for each acre of land.

Many people confuse efficiency, a relationship of input to output, with the value "productivity." They mistakenly assume the input-output relationship is the only thing that is important and use "efficiency" as though it were a value. Used by itself, the efficiency criterion leads to numerous value conflicts. Farmer Ray Green, in striving to increase labor efficiency, may decrease fertilizer efficiency. Further, a process may be efficient over one cycle or two but inefficient over longer time periods.

Ray is concerned with both short- and long-term productivity. His first priority is to maximize production in the short run so he can convert his crops to cash to pay his bills. Even when monetary values are applied to these physical relationships, input and output prices do not include all environmental costs. So in a tight financial situation, Ray Green may make short-run efficiency decisions that affect his long-run income. He may not invest in soil conservation practices that would slow soil erosion even though over time erosion will result in decreased productivity.

Boundaries of each action

We also have the problem of locating the boundaries around each action, person, resource, or process because of this assumed independence. Each subprocess on Ray Green's farm can be reviewed for efficiency. Ray Green's whole farm can be reviewed for efficient water use. And the Colorado River basin can be reviewed for efficient water use. We obviously run into the problem of overlapping boundaries where efficiency in one situation or use adversely affects efficiency in another. Market forces mediate some but not all of these conflicts.

For economists, this is the problem of externalities—determining which costs not included by market forces should be included in the price to reflect true social costs. Here efficiency is expanded toward productivity by how we define the boundaries of the input-transformation-output system we are considering. If you buy chicken at the supermarket, the price does not include all of the social costs. Growing concentration of broiler production over the past 40 years has resulted in water quality problems in the Chesapeake Bay area. These social costs are not included in the supermarket price consumers pay for chicken.

Constructive purpose

Productivity assumes purpose—that each action has goals, each person has intent, each resource has value, and each process has direction. Purpose captures this aspect of productivity at both the individual and societal levels. Productivity expands on the notion of efficiency by including the assumption that the output produced has some social merit. Producing coca leaves for use as a local anesthetic is constructive in this sense; producing coca leaves to make cocaine for illegal sale is not. One cures; the other debilitates.

Although the law is silent in many areas, people often assume that anything legal is constructive. The absence of legal sanctions gives legitimacy that may not be warranted. This legitimacy can become a barrier to legislation that would limit or prohibit unconstructive activities. Farmers have legally buried waste in hazardous herbicide and pesticide containers for years. Few questioned whether or not it was a constructive way to dispose of the waste containers because the law was silent. The fact that this means of disposal had been practiced for so long made it politically difficult to regulate when the environmental consequences became better understood.

Constructive purpose is not clearly delineated for many activities. Different people place different conditions on their definition of what is and isn't constructive. While many people used to think that producing tobacco was constructive, a growing number now question its social merit. While most would agree that producing cotton is constructive, others would say so only if production doesn't deplete groundwater. This definition would shift production from the west where water is scarce to another region where water is more plentiful.

Equity and Interdependence

In the Powder River illustration, it is clear that Sid Riedel cannot solve the broader problem if productivity is the only set of values important to him. The individuals and groups along the river all value productivity, but their interdependence ensures that one person's actions will affect others' opportunities. The road that Paul Hartner built to make logging more efficient causes erosion that will reduce the number of salmon and the ability of Ron Banks' tribe to take care of themselves. If Sid makes the production of salmon his only criterion, Ray Green will be forced to use his bottomlands differently and his income might be reduced. When Sid defines one of his objectives as "minimizing conflict," he is really acknowledging the importance of fairness, or equity.

Of the three values, fairness is the most controversial, in part, because we say "equitable" but people hear "equal." All but the most utopian among us reject the notion that benefits should be divided equally. Rather, equity is concerned with how production is distributed. People who value fairness strive to make sure institutions and rules are established so that everyone has an equal chance and that the rewards are the same for the same level of effort no matter who you are. For most people, equity also deals with how society ensures that people's most basic needs are met.

Unlike productivity, equity is based on the premise of interdependence: people, processes, and resources are inextricably linked. One person's actions affect another person's options. Without doubt, people are interdependent. If I use water for irrigation, it is not available to my neighbor. Oil consumed by the industrialized nations is not available for consumption by developing countries. Capital invested to create jobs in Arkansas is not available to invest in Oklahoma. Research money used to develop biodegradable plastics is not available for developing new technologies to generate energy from biomass.

We avoid the reality of our interdependence using a "yes, but" argument. We explain, "Yes, but those resources are abundant enough that anyone can go out and get as much as they need without affecting anybody else's options. As long as the economy continues to grow—as long as there are enough salmon to support the tribe, as long as there are new oil fields to be discovered, as long as the federal budget continues to expand—what I do doesn't affect anyone but me." This argument enables us to acknowledge our interdependence yet avoid responsibility for the consequences of our actions on other people. We assume that economic growth, technological advances, and programmatic expansion will take care of all equity questions.

Productive use of resources is fundamental to equity. Productivity maintains and expands the size of the pie to be distributed. Waste, the inevitable result of unproductive resource use, reduces the amount to be distributed. However, the assumption of interdependence expands our understanding of constructive purpose and wise use. If we are interdependent, then constructive purpose suggests that resources should be used to meet the basic human needs of all people before they are used for other purposes. Wise use suggests that producers are responsible for unanticipated depletion, pollution, and degradation that affect other people. In addition, acknowledging interdependence leads to concerns about who has access to resources and the belief that access should be equal.

Responsibility to meet basic needs

Most of us can agree that some purposes are more constructive than others. However, few would agree about which ones. Even seemingly obvious rankings generate controversy. For example, consider these rankings: Growing tomatoes is more constructive than growing tobacco; using water for human consumption is more constructive than using it to fill swimming pools; providing grain for a malnourished child is more constructive than providing caviar for a dinner party. A tobacco farmer, a city recreation director, and a host of a charity banquet might well argue with these statements.

If we assume resources are infinitely available or that there is a substitute for every scarce resource, then it doesn't matter that one purpose is more constructive than another; there are no tradeoffs among purposes. Producers have no responsibility to consider whether one purpose is more constructive than another. Time and resources are invested wherever the return is greatest because people, processes, and resources are independent. However, if we acknowledge interdependence, then it does matter that one purpose is more constructive than another. Few resources are infinitely available. There are no substitutes for some scarce resources (e.g., potable water). If people, processes, and resources are interdependent, then there are tradeoffs among purposes. Allocating resources for one purpose may affect the availability of resources available for other purposes.

When we acknowledge interdependence, we become concerned with how our actions affect other people, and the nature of our responsibility changes. Responsibility stems from obligation and enlightened self-interest rather than charity. From a humanitarian viewpoint, most of us feel some degree of responsibility to ensure that the most basic needs of other people are met—that they have food, clothing, and shelter at a minimum. However, most of us limit our personal responsibility. We agree that the needs of others should be met, just so long as we are not adversely affected in the process.

Each of us defines differently the group to whom we feel responsibility. Most of us feel responsible for family and friends. If we are closely associated with a group, we may extend our responsibility to its members (e.g., company, church, voluntary organizations, community). Some feel responsibility to the community, the state, or nation. Others extend their responsibility to the entire global community.

Regardless of how far we feel our responsibility extends, the fact is our interdependence does extend worldwide. A look at conditions in developing countries makes this interdependence clearer. Without jobs, rapidly increasing numbers of impoverished people in these countries will meet their needs through the only means available to them: mining the natural resources of the global community by cultivating marginal lands, cutting forests, depleting groundwater resources, and grazing livestock on fragile, arid lands. In the process, they will contribute to erosion, deforestation, reduction of soil fertility, desertification, diminishment of habitat, and species loss. No one can expect them to do otherwise. Their survival must come first. Yet, the consequences of their actions affect us. We *are* interdependent.

Thus, solving the global problems of deforestation and desertification depends on meeting the basic needs of impoverished people. We must acknowledge that meeting basic needs is more constructive than other purposes and that our personal responsibility extends beyond national borders to the global community. Then we must act on our understanding, doing all that is within our personal power to ensure that everyone's basic needs are met. Some ways of meeting needs are more constructive than others. Providing a sustainable livelihood is more constructive than giving charity. However, charity is more constructive than ignoring basic needs altogether.

With the assumption of independence, the independent producer gets to decide within the limits of the law what is constructive. If we are interdependent, it follows that groups must take greater responsibility for defining on behalf of their members what is constructive. While government is the group that first comes to mind, other groups also define what is constructive— communities, churches, voluntary organizations, and businesses. Unless groups, including government, decide that meeting people's basic needs is a constructive use of resources, these needs will continue to go unmet.

Interdependence and responsibility for wise use

In a world of limited resources, we cannot equate freedom, a cherished value, with absolute independence. Freedom carries with it an obligation to avoid undermining the rights of others. Independence, on the other hand, assumes that nothing we do undermines other people's options, thus enabling us to abdicate the obligations that come with freedom and to legitimize irresponsibility.

Interdependence does not negate freedom. However, it underscores that the obligations of freedom are equal to its rights. Thus, the freedom to use resources carries with it an ethical responsibility to use them wisely—to avoid depleting, degrading, or polluting in a way that harms other people's health or affects their livelihood.

Interdependence as a call for equal access

Equity does not require equal division of resources, but it requires fairness in access to resources. Social and political institutions define the rules that encourage or limit access to resources. When we value fairness, rules are structured in a way that moves all people toward equal access to education, markets, jobs, land, information, water, capital, and other resources. In our own country, segregated schools, discriminatory lending practices, and poll taxes were rules that limited access to resources. As a result of the civil rights movement, we have changed the rules, restructured existing institutions, and established new institutions to improve access to resources. But now we are learning that changes in the legal system are not sufficient. To ensure equal access, groups and individuals must also accept personal responsibility to erase bigotry from their hearts and minds.

Equal access also can be applied to environmental concerns. Many people are concerned about preserving equal access to basic resources—air, water, the food supply, and wilderness areas, for example. Historically, we have taken for granted not only their supply but their quality. We assume that clean air, safe water, food free of harmful chemicals, and aesthetically pleasing wilderness areas will always be available.

In taking their quality for granted, we have ignored the fact that many poor people do not have equal access to these resources. Air and noise pollution have plagued the urban poor since the beginning of the industrial revolution. Access to safe drinking water is more of a problem for the rural poor than others. Creating parks and preserving wilderness areas has eliminated jobs in forest harvesting and processing, denying the rural poor access to a livelihood. The cost of getting to and using wilderness areas for hiking and other recreational activities often restrict the urban poor's access to them.

Now, when middle- and upper-income families are being affected by quality of life issues, we are beginning to question the institutions and rules that govern access to clean air, safe drinking water, food free of harmful chemical residues, and aesthetically pleasing wilderness areas. As we establish rules to preserve the resources that we have taken for granted, those who value equity will take care to ensure equal access for all people.

In developing countries, the consequences of rules that create barriers to resources are more apparent. Equal access is closely related to meeting basic needs. Farmers without access to land cannot produce food to feed their families, similarly, without access to credit, they cannot buy seed and fertilizer to grow crops. Marginal producers without access to transport and market information cannot sell the surplus crops for a good price. Children without access to education cannot hope to get a good job. Separated by institutional barriers from the resources they need to improve their well-being, the developing countries' poor turn to the only resource at hand—marginal arid lands and steep, easily eroded hillsides—for their sustenance.

Equity and meeting everyone's basic needs

For many people, equity requires more than ensuring fairness in access to resources. Equity also carries with it a responsibility to see that the basic needs of all people are met. However, individuals define *basic needs* differently. Some include only food, shelter, and clothing. Using this definition, we organize charities and service organizations to provide these most basic needs. Others define people's basic needs as the means to take care of themselves and their families. This definition makes education, health care, and a livelihood basic needs. This definition gives us responsibility to structure our institutions so that opportunities are equally available to all.

How we define basic needs is critically important. Even if we could feed and clothe all people, charity reinforces dependency. By using our resources and strengthening our institutions to create more jobs, provide more people with a higher-quality education, and improve people's health, impoverished people can become productive, self-sustaining members of a society. In America, our national definition of basic needs has shifted from the 1960s, when we tried to expand job and educational opportunities through the "war on poverty," to the 1980s, when we focused on feeding and clothing families in crisis. During the 1980s, our nation's policies led to greater concentration of wealth in the hands of a few, with a corresponding increase in poverty, and to corporate mergers in the name of efficiency, with a corresponding loss of jobs. The need for emergency food, clothing, and shelter grew—charitable efforts to provide these basic needs. If we are concerned about sustainability, this redefinition is a move in the wrong direction. As the next section points out, there can be no sustainability without greater social equity.

stainability and Interdependence through Time

In the Powder River illustration, Sid decides he will make Paul Hartner take care of the eroded logging road to protect other people's access to the river and what it provides. Sid knows, however, that such an action will preserve equitable access only for a short time. Unless sweeping actions are taken, soil erosion from several sources will lead to increased turbidity. The river eventually will no longer support salmon runs, denying future generations access to the river and its bounty. Sid wants a sustainable solution to the Powder River's turbidity problem, not just a "quick fix."

As professionals who influence how resources are managed, we have focused our hope on this "new" concept—sustainability. We have embraced the idea despite lack of agreement on a practical definition. To some, it is the current criterion of *wise use* or the "greatest good for the greatest number over the long run" that conservation has long represented. For others, it is a management strategy, like low-input "sustainable" agriculture. To yet others, it is a theoretical construct in need of greater definition. To a few, sustainability is a utopian vision of some future state in which people live and work in harmony with the biosphere.

To us, *sustainability* is a value that can guide and direct our day-to-day choices so that we "meet the needs of the present without compromising the ability of future generations to meet their own needs" (United Nations' World Commission on Environment and Development report, p. 8). It is a decision rule that gives direction and purpose to our daily choices. It forces us to ask, "Is this action productive? Is it equitable? Does it compromise the ability of future generations to meet their needs?"

As a value, sustainability encompasses all aspects of productivity and equity. Like equity, it is based on the premise of interdependence. However, sustainability links people, processes, and resources in the present and through time. Interdependence distinguishes productivity from equity and sustainability. "Through time" distinguishes equity from sustainability. Equity bridges the gap between productivity and sustainability. Unless we accept that people, resources, and processes are interdependent in the present, it is difficult to make the great leap of faith required to accept that they are interdependent through time.

Sustainability and our broadened perspective

"Until recently, the planet was a large world in which human activities and their effects were neatly compartmentalized within nations, within sectors (energy, agriculture, trade), and within broad areas of concern (environmental, economic, social)," explains the United Nations' World Commission on Environment and Development (p. 4). The complex and intertwined problems confronting us transcend arbitrary boundaries. The boundaries between sectors, nations, and broad concerns do not exist except in the mind.

Sustainability depends on recognizing interaction among biophysical, social, economic, and political forces—a transdisciplinary approach. It also depends on accepting the interdependence between rich and poor nations as well as present and future generations. If we cling to our narrow compartments for the false security they provide, any movement in the direction of sustainability will be chaotic and uneven. Our efforts will be characterized by the bandwagon calls of one false promise after another.

To find sustainable solutions, we must step out of our compartments and view the world from a new perspective, critically evaluating our goals, management strategies, and alternatives. Where they are inadequate, we must be willing to give up the security of the familiar and embark down a new path that leads in the direction of sustainability. Finding alternatives that meet both present and future needs is the only way to avoid tradeoffs between short-term productivity and long-term sustainability. We explore this strategy in chapter 4.

Sustainable does not mean stable or unchanging. Sustainable development hinges on flexibility to respond to changing biophysical, social, economic, political, and technological conditions. Sustainability challenges us to be forward looking, responsive, and flexible enough to evolve to meet changing human needs.

Interdependence through time and the meaning of efficiency

Sustainability is concerned with efficient use of resources *through time*. Acknowledging interdependence through time makes us personally responsible for the impact of today's production practices on resource productivity in the future. Because of the nature of forest production, foresters have addressed long-term efficiency issues perhaps more than any other profession. They use records of historical yields to estimate *sustained annual yields*, the optimum annual yield over time. While imperfect, these estimates are critical for forest management and planning. In many other areas of production, we do not have the tools to forecast or estimate sustainable yields. Rapidly evolving technologies and limited knowledge of cause and effect make it difficult to anticipate the consequences of today's production practices on productivity five or ten years from now, much less over a generation. Unless we consciously decide to focus on long-term efficiency, our bias for the concrete, measurable, and factual will continue to focus our attention on short-term efficiency.

Interdependence through time and expanded wise use

Interdependence through time expands responsibility for wise use further still. If my production activities are independent, then the responsibility to conserve scarce resources applies only to the extent that it affects *my* production. If our production activities are interdependent through time, we are responsible for depletion, degradation, and pollution as they affect this and future generations.

Many will argue over the extent of our responsibility. Are we responsible only for our own progeny or for future Americans, or are we also responsible for future generations of other countries? Are we responsible only to the next generation, the next five generations, or for all time? Are we responsible only for known consequences? Are we also responsible for consequences that we should have been able to anticipate? What about consequences that no one could reasonably anticipate?

Investment in the future and meeting basic needs now

When parents must worry about feeding their children today, the future has no reality. Every effort and every thought must be directed at survival today. They cannot worry about whether their farming practices used today will destroy the productive capacity of the land tomorrow. They cannot worry about whether a tree cut for fuelwood today will denude the hillside. Worrying about tomorrow is a luxury only the well fed and employed can afford.

Similarly, governments cannot easily invest in the future when their people face chronic and widespread hunger, malnutrition, homelessness, and unemployment in the present. Holding power depends on meeting the needs of today. Political willingness to invest in the future hinges on first meeting the needs of the present.

Interdependence and equal opportunity

If people, processes, and resources are interdependent through time, then sustainability depends on equal opportunity through time, which in turn depends on the reversibility of today's choices. The decision rule must be this: If I use this resource, can I reverse the consequences and restore the resource to its original state? Does this action permanently preclude other uses?

If a developer builds a shopping center on prime farmland, the land, for all practical purposes, is then unsuitable for farming for all time. If the snail darter's habitat is destroyed, the species is lost for all time—perhaps denying future generations of some unforeseen benefit. If tropical plant species are destroyed through clear cutting of rain forests for farmland, whatever medicinal, environmental, or commercial benefits that might be derived from their use is denied to future generations.

For some, equal opportunity is an absolute value. Regardless of the estimated future benefit, those people feel we must preserve the options of future generations. Others apply benefit-cost analysis, weighing the potential benefits and costs. Both approaches are flawed—the first because we cannot fully predict the consequences of our actions and the second because benefits and costs only have value in the context of the present and near future. Analysts cannot value uses that don't presently exist and can't be imagined.

We frequently don't know if consequences are reversible. We don't know if ozone that is depleted from the upper atmosphere can be restored. We don't know if the effects of acid rain can be reversed. Many biophysical systems have proven more resilient than expected. That we can clean up oil spills at all has surprised many. That the long-term consequences could be minimal startled most marine biologists. Yet we cannot assume that the effects are reversible. And even if they are, we often don't know how long it will take to reverse them.

Our understanding of long-term consequences and reversibility will always be imperfect. What level of risk is acceptable? What is the extent of our responsibility to preserve equal opportunity for future generations? Equal opportunity for what groups? Equal opportunity to what resources? Who gets to decide what risk is acceptable—individuals, groups, or government? Who is responsible for protecting opportunities for future generations?

Sustainability that is founded on flexibility

A colleague, Dick Harwood, says that *sustainable systems* have the capacity to "evolve indefinitely toward greater human utility, greater efficiency of resource use, and a balance with the environment that is favorable both to humans and to most other species." We like this definition for several reasons. It acknowledges that people and processes change through time. Human utility implies the need for equity. Yet the definition acknowledges that without efficient production, there is nothing to distribute. Sustainability does not require us to choose between people and the environment; it challenges us to find balance in an ever-changing world. Finally, and perhaps most importantly, Dick's definition tells us that sustainability is something that we have to strive for. It is not some rigid goal we will either achieve or fail to achieve.

For those who acknowledge their interdependence through time, sustainability encourages and nurtures changes that move us toward greater human utility, efficiency, and balance. When you hear someone say, "If it's not broken, don't fix it," that person is not considering sustainability. When someone explains their unwillingness to consider improvements, saying "this is the way we have always done it," you know that sustainability is not important to that person in this instance. Sustainability is founded on the flexibility required to seek better methods and results.

Measures for Efficiency

While selection of a measure is arbitrary, the choice is important because measures narrowly focus our attention. Yet we tend to measure things we can measure easily. We prefer low-cost, technically simple, quantitative measures over those that are more amorphous and less quantifiable. So we tend to measure things that are readily observed and measured. As a result, our measures focus on physical efficiency—one element of productivity—and on profit.

In our rush to embrace objectivity and facts, our underlying values have taken a back seat to the concrete and measurable. Because we can measure it, we have equated productivity with efficient use of resources and ignored equity and sustainability altogether. Confounding the situation, we often delude ourselves by acting as though profit measures economic efficiency and productivity. We carry the delusion further, assuming that gross national product per capita, or average income, measures individuals' well-being. The measures are not at fault; they provide useful information. What is at fault is the way we use them.

To deal with the intertwined environmental and development problems that confront us, we will have to make three fundamental changes in the way we think about our production activities. Otherwise, the solution set will come up empty.

- First, we must explicitly acknowledge that values underlie our measures and that measures are proxies for values. Focusing on values will improve our ability to find effective, workable solutions and empower us to seek creative solutions that lead us in the direction we want to go rather than mechanistic solutions that meet narrow objectives defined by imperfect measures.

- Second, we must acknowledge and accept that people, processes, and resources are interdependent through time. Many of us know this intellectually. Yet we don't accept it experientially or spiritually. We are unwilling to consider that what we do day in and day out may cause other people harm. If we did accept it, we would make different choices.

* Finally, it is not enough that isolated individuals acknowledge and act on our interdependence. As nations, we must come to grips with the fact that our world is interdependent—what we do affects others in the present and the future. As individuals and nations, we must seek alternatives that reconcile the tradeoffs between productivity, equity, and sustainability. These alternatives will enable us to meet the needs of the present without compromising the ability of this or future generations to meet their own needs.

id's Value Check

Sid took a risk when he decided to pursue the basin-planning option. As a public official and a good problem solver, he could see the importance of equity and sustainability. But he also knows that people become hostile when government standards are imposed from above, particularly standards that could potentially restrict short-term productivity.

In chapter 2, Sid examined his role. In effect, he examined his values, deciding whether equity and sustainability were important enough to risk his productivity as an employee, his effectiveness as a professional, and the goodwill he has built up among his neighbors. While Sid has clarified his own values, now it is up to the group as a whole to do the same. All the group members will have to acknowledge their interdependence through time and decide what priority they will give to each value in their own attempt to reconcile the three.

4

■ Making Decisions

We make decisions all the time. We decide what to wear in the morning, what to cook for dinner each evening, what to spend our time and money on. As professionals, managers, and specialists, we also get paid to make decisions or provide information to other decision makers. Decision making answers the question, "What is the best way?" As figure 4.1 shows, decision making involves making choices among competing alternatives.

Defining a Decision

An environmental engineer asks, "What is the *best* site for a solid waste landfill?" A research manager says, "I can only take on one new research project—what is *best*?" A forester questions, "What is the *best* stocktype of seedling to use for reforestation on a particular site?" A farmer thinks, "What is the *best* tillage system to save time and minimize soil loss?" A hydrologist asks, "What are the *best* sites to sink test wells to plot infiltration of groundwater contaminants?" These require decisions. Making a decision is choosing the best alternative available, given what the decision maker wants to accomplish and the context in which the decision will be implemented.

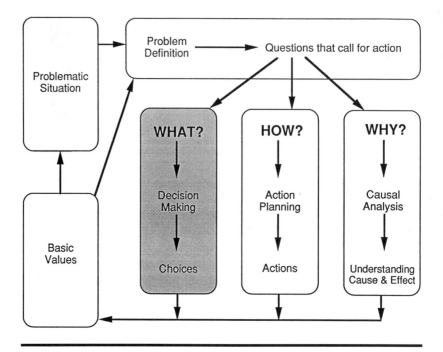

Figure 4.1. Problem-solving framework—choices.

The "best" decisions

Best is a relative term. We choose the best alternative by comparing the available alternatives. There must be at least two alternatives to compare, or there is no decision to make. There also must be a basis for comparison. We call the basis for comparison "criteria." Criteria explicitly state values that are important to the decision maker in terms that allow alternatives to be distinguished from one another. Since criteria reflect individuals' values and priorities, they differ from one person to the next.

If decisions are to reflect our values, our values must be expressed as criteria for the decisions. We can't evaluate the sustainability of our alternatives if we don't consciously include sustainability in our criteria. Nor can we choose a more sustainable option if we don't consider sustainable options among our alternatives.

We can become confused if we equate making the "best" decision with making the "right" decision. We make decisions in a world of ambiguity, risk, and uncertainty about the effect of one course of action compared to the alternatives. Most of the time we don't know what the "right" decision is—we have to make the best decision we can, given the time, information, and other resources available and our limited understanding of the context and of cause and effect.

The difference between the best decision and the right decision becomes especially important when we decide to include sustainability or equity values in our decision-making criteria. These values introduce more ambiguity into our prediction of effects. We don't know the consequences of our choices in the indefinite future. We often do not even know the consequences of our choices two to three years in the future. Yet we cannot let the difficulty of knowing the right choice get in the way of choosing the best. If we care about sustainability, a workable solution with a reasonable probability of being more sustainable is better than a course we know is neither sustainable nor equitable.

To choose an alternative that reflects *all* of the values important to us, our decision making must be conscious and systematic. The framework and process described in this chapter guide decision makers through a logical set of questions that can help them make better decisions.

Limits of Everyday Decision-making Processes

Often, we make decisions without even being aware we are doing so. If we can't identify the point at which decisions are made, we can't make the process more conscious and systematic. We can only evaluate the outcome after the fact. This section outlines some common approaches to decision making. Understanding their limitations makes the benefits of a systematic approach more apparent.

Impulsive choices

We frequently choose impulsively—selecting the familiar, the near at hand, or the most appealing because it feels right at the moment. In doing so, we give superficial consideration to competing alternatives and fail to consider many alternatives altogether. We decide unconsciously, unaware of the criteria on which we base our choice.

Yes/no choices

At other times, we phrase the choice as a yes/no question, which implies a choice between change and no change in the status quo. It also eliminates consideration of other alternatives. If I ask, "Should I buy a Honda Civic?" my choice is limited to buying the Honda or continuing with my current mode of transportation. It does not include some other make of car.

A yes/no choice focuses our attention on information gathering. We evaluate price, gas mileage, service record, and availability against our expectations. We may unconsciously seek information to support what we have already decided. The yes/no question eliminates consideration of other alternatives. Because this choice doesn't identify criteria, it fails to take into account our objectives.

Often we choose among multiple alternatives by making yes/no choices in sequence. We choose the alternative we intuitively guess will be best and ask, "Should I take this course of action—yes or no?" If the answer is yes, we've made a decision. If the answer is no, we move to the next alternative and ask if it is best—yes or no? We continue until we have chosen a course of action.

When we ask yes/no choices in sequence, we don't compare the relative merits of competing alternatives. We do not identify our criteria, so there is no explicit basis for evaluating the adequacy of alternatives. Our analysis is haphazard. We tend to gather and evaluate information that is close at hand, and we may miss out on information that points out the strengths and weaknesses of competing alternatives based on criteria that are important to us.

Either/or choices

We sometimes phrase the choice as either/or. "Should I buy a Honda Civic or a Ford Taurus?" We compare price, gas mileage, service record, and availability. We may list the pros and cons of each. This approach does not encourage us to search for other alternatives. Our unstated criteria may not reflect what is important to us. Our analysis is rarely systematic. Too often, we structure our either/or choice so that one alternative is clearly best. Then we collect information that supports our preconceived notions. By going through the motions, we justify and validate what we have already decided.

Decision rules

Sometimes we choose on the basis of conscious or unconscious rules of thumb. How many times have you heard . . .

"I'll take the usual. I've bought milk in disposable bottles ever since they were introduced into grocery stores. I'm not going to stop now." Never mind the disposal problem.

"Buy the cheapest. Powdered laundry detergents are cheaper than liquid. I'll buy powdered." Never mind that powdered laundry detergents often contain phosphates and liquids don't.

"I want nothing but the best. I'll buy a Cadillac." Never mind that smaller cars get twice the mileage per gallon of gasoline.

Tradition and intuition also can become decision rules.

"If it feels right, go for it." In the 1970s, we decided almost intuitively that gasohol was *the* solution to stretch scarce oil reserves. We spent little time evaluating the new and unanticipated problems ethanol-based fuels might cause. Preliminary studies in Brazil now show that ethanol-based fuels burned without catalytic converters create increased emissions of aldehydes, one of the so-called "greenhouse gases."

"We'll do it the way we've always done it. We've always applied herbicides at a higher rate than recommended. That way we make sure a weed problem won't arise." Never mind groundwater contamination.

"If it's not broke, don't fix it." This decision rule assumes that we live in an unchanging world and precludes the possibility of incremental improvements.

When we make these statements, we often take action without even being aware that we've made a decision. We assume our implicit decision rules embody all that is important. Most of our everyday behavior is automatic, based on tradition and intuition. Living would be even more complex than it is without automatic behavior. Think of all the decisions you would have to make if you had to decide every day whether to go to work, when to go to work, how to get to work; whether to eat, when to eat; whether to bathe, when to bathe; and so on. Routine, automatic behaviors save us time, freeing us to concentrate on important decisions.

On the other hand, automatic behavior keeps us from looking at how our actions relate to our values. When values change or conditions change, our implicit rules of thumb may keep us making choices that are no longer appropriate for us. To illustrate, consider where the term *rule of thumb* came from. In feudal England, a man was considered within his rights in beating his wife so long as the stick he used to hit her was thinner than his thumb. Values have changed since then, and few of us would accept the feudal rule of thumb as a good decision rule. Other decision rules become outmoded too. When this happens, we must be willing to reevaluate our decision rules and traditions to establish new automatic behaviors that better meet our needs. At these times, careful decision making can improve the chances that our automatic behaviors will lead to greater productivity, equity, and sustainability over time.

"Objective" choices

We often "let the data decide." We naively assume that collecting and examining data leads to an objective decision. Analyzing data is essential to sound decision making. But we must keep in mind that identifying alternatives, deciding which data are relevant, and defining the criteria on which our decision will be based are subjective, not objective, processes.

Defining criteria is a creative interpretation of our individually held values and priorities in the context of the kinds of alternatives we choose to consider. Identifying alternatives is also a creative step. Which facts are pertinent depends on the creative alternatives we choose to consider and on our subjective criteria. Data that seem irrelevant can become highly relevant if we identify a new alternative or if we redefine our criteria.

For example, benefit-cost analysis is often considered an "objective" decision process, but it is always based on implicit or explicit subjective values. Consider the benefit/cost analysis of a dam project that will flood a canyon. Is preserving the natural beauty of the canyon part of our criteria? How important is it? This has to be a subjective choice. Suppose the canyon is infested by a pesky bug. Is the elimination of the bug a benefit or a cost? What if the bug is on the endangered species list? How do we count the flood prevention benefits of the dam? This involves measuring both uncertainty and the loss of life. The subjective criteria for the benefit-cost analysis will determine what data are important and how to evaluate them. Simplistically adding up dollar benefits and subtracting dollar costs gives only very incomplete information on the desirability of the project. Few analysts would support a one-dimensional "net monetary benefits" criterion. Unfortunately, dollar values are easy to report and easy to relate to, while the analyst's summary of nonmonetary factors tends to be skipped over in our rush to the bottom line.

Weighing pros and cons

A more informative approach might be to list the pros and cons of each alternative. The limitations of this approach become clear if we look at a typical example.

Warren Olson grows McIntosh, Red Delicious, and Cortland apples on 90 acres of land in west central Wisconsin. Because of the humid climate, scab infections are a major problem. For years he has used traditional methods of scab control, spraying weekly with the fungicide Benomyl. Recently, however, the fungus has developed a resistance to Benomyl, making treatments less effective. Moreover, the federal government has threatened to ban the fungicides recommended as replacements for Benomyl because they break down into chemicals that have caused cancer and birth defects in laboratory tests.

Warren could use organic sprays such as Bordeaux (lime and copper sulphate), wettable sulphur, or lime-sulphur spray. These sprays, however, can kill beneficial organisms, such as predatory mites and spiders, that help control pests. Without careful application, the sprays also can damage leaves and cause russeting of the apple skins, which reduces their marketability. Since they wash off more easily than traditional fungicides, they must be applied often and regularly in humid weather, even if it means bringing spraying equipment into wet orchards and causing soil compaction.

Warren has heard of a new product, Nova, a sterol inhibitor that does not kill beneficial organisms or break down into carcinogenic byproducts. It also can control fungus infections up to 90 hours after they begin, which means he wouldn't have to spray when the soil is wet. But he doesn't know anyone who has used Nova. Faced with this complex situation, Warren lists pros and cons (table 4.1).

Table 4.1. Warren Olson's list of pros and cons

	Advantages	Disadvantages
Fungicide	Proven effectiveness	Possible cause of cancer
	Slower breakdown	Growing resistance
	No killing of beneficial bugs	Public concern about health
	Familiarity with product	
Organics	No carcinogens	More frequent applications
	No developed resistance	Soil damage
	Consumer acceptance of	Damaged appearance
	organic products	Killing of beneficial predator bugs
Nova	No carcinogens	Unfamiliarity
	Dry-ground application	Long-run effects (?)
	No resistance to date	

A list of pros and cons makes us conscious of the decision, and that's good. We make a different list of advantages and disadvantages for each alternative. The shortcoming of the list approach is that we have no basis for comparison. The list poses the question "Is this alternative acceptable?" instead of "Which alternative is best?" If more than one alternative is acceptable, the list of pros and cons doesn't make it much easier to choose among them. While there are implicit criteria in the pros and cons Warren lists, there is no explicit standard for choice. Comparing "proven effectiveness" with "possible cause of cancer" is like comparing apples and oranges. Which is more important? This depends on Warren's criteria, values, and priorities, which have not been explicitly stated. Without such information, Warren can't link comparable data or reject irrelevant data. Warren's list hasn't really enabled him to distinguish the legitimately subjective choice of criteria from the objective analysis of factual information. He can't analyze the information in terms of his desires or needs because he hasn't defined his desires and needs.

For simple choices, a decision maker may be able to mentally fill in the missing information in a list of pros and cons, but comparisons become increasingly impractical as the number of alternatives, criteria, and information increases.

Improving Decisions

When confronted with a complex and important decision, each of the decision-making strategies discussed before is deficient. The resulting decisions may or may not achieve the intended short- and long-run objectives. This chapter presents a systematic framework and process for individual decision making. Group decision making is discussed in chapters 5 and 6.

The *framework* asks a series of questions that separate the identification of criteria (what matters to us) from the identification of alternatives available. The *process* guides the sequences of answers, separating creative idea generation from critical evaluation and subjective exploration of criteria and values from objective analysis. Together, the framework and process lead the decision maker to answer the question, "Which alternative is best given how I define best?"

> **Decision-making Framework**
>
> 1. What is the decision to be made?
>
> 2. On what criteria will I base my decision?
>
> 3. What alternative courses of action exist?
>
> 4. What is the expected effect of each alternative on each criterion?
>
> 5. Which alternative is best?
>
> 6. How can this alternative be put into action?

The framework first asks us to phrase a question that calls for a particular kind of action—a choice. As in chapter 2, our long-run goals and short-run objectives should be part of the question. The second and third questions ask us to make lists of our criteria and our alternatives. We use these lists to build a decision matrix (table 4.2). Each row represents a criterion (low cost, safety, marketability) and each column represents an alternative (continued use of Benomyl-type fungicides, use of organic sprays, planting scab-resistant trees). We answer the fourth question as we fill in this matrix, using the best objective information we can gather in the time we have to estimate the probable consequences of each alternative for each criterion. Consequences are evaluated separately for each combination of criterion and alternative. Using Warren's decision to illustrate, in table 4.2,

Table 4.2. Decision-making matrix

	Alternatives		
Criteria	A Benomyl	B Organic sprays	C Scab-resistant trees
1. Low Cost	A1	B1	C1
2. Safety	A2	B2	C2
3. Marketability	A3	B3	C3

Warren would write the consequences of alternative B, say, using organic sprays, in terms of criterion 3, perhaps marketability. He might write "possible damage to appearance."

The process

The process steps that follow are a guide through the questions. The process separates questions with subjective answers from those with objective answers. They also separate creative thinking, which is inventive and original, and critical thinking, which is rational and objective.

Questions about criteria and alternatives call for subjective answers. Answers are based on what we think is important, our creativity in seeking innovative alternatives, and the range of alternatives we are willing to consider. Questions about consequences call for objective answers. "What is the probable effect?" asks for an objective prediction of an alternative's likely effect based on observation, theory, applied research, or informed opinion. Separating objective and subjective questions gives us the freedom to explore values and innovative alternatives more deeply and analyze the consequences of competing alternatives more rigorously, thus improving the quality of our decisions.

Creative thought lets us explore potentially better ways of doing things. There should be no censorship in these steps. Here we are looking for the new and unusual, unfettered by the familiar or what is acceptable. Even apparently silly alternatives may have a valuable kernel of insight. Recall the man with the messy desk who was described in the introduction. When he listed his alternatives, he included setting a match to the whole mess. A bonfire is probably not the answer, but some of his papers probably belong in the trash can.

In contrast, critical thinking helps us test our creative ideas against reality. Trashing is more realistic that torching. Recycling is an improvement on trashing that still removes the whole mess. Through critical thought, we evaluate and clarify ideas, seeking a fair assessment of their worth. Critical thought also helps us clarify and refine criteria, judge the feasibility of alternatives, and evaluate them.

Separating creative thinking from critical thinking gives us the freedom to examine and explore ideas unencumbered by the responsibility of being "reasonable." With all of our creative ideas on the table, we can apply our critical skills vigorously in evaluating, classifying, and modifying. Table 4.3 lists the sequence of steps in the decision-making framework, the kind of information, and the thought process used.

Table 4.3. Process steps

Question/Process Steps	Information	Thinking
What decision?		
State the decision as a choice	Subjective	Critical
What criteria?		
List but do not evaluate criteria	Subjective	Creative
Refine criteria	Subjective	Critical
Rank criteria in order of importance	Subjective	Critical
What alternatives?		
List but do not evaluate alternatives	Subjective	Creative
Refine alternatives	Subjective	Critical
Review the criteria and alternatives	Subjective	Critical
What effect?		
Gather cause-and-effect information	Objective	Critical
Evaluate consequences	Objective	Critical
What alternative is best?		
Choose	Combination	Critical

Using the framework and process together

Together, the framework and process lead to improved decision making because

• The framework allows a systematic consideration of multiple creative alternatives.

• The framework organizes information efficiently for comparing the relative objective strengths and weaknesses of competing alternatives.

• The framework highlights relevant information, while it sifts out irrelevant information. Information is relevant only if it describes the consequences of the alternatives considered on the criteria selected.

• The framework lets the decision maker consider a larger volume of relevant information.

• The framework helps the decision maker discriminate among alternatives in several dimensions, allowing for the many shades of gray that lie between the black and white of simple pros and cons.

• The process releases creativity in generating potential alternatives and exploring and affirming the values that underlie the criteria. At the same time, breaking evaluation and criticism into discrete steps lets us use information and analysis at a higher standard of objectivity.

1. What is the decision to be made?

Decision-making Framework

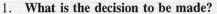 1. **What is the decision to be made?**
   • State the decision as a choice.
   • State long-term goals and short-term objectives.

2. On what criteria will I base my decision?

3. What alternative courses of action exist?

4. What is the expected effect of each alternative on each criterion?

5. Which alternative is best?

6. How can the alternative be put into action?

In chapter 2, Sid evaluated his situation, moving from an ill-defined problem to a question that called for action. He determined what he wanted to accomplish and settled on a strategy to move him forward. In this chapter, Warren Olson will go beyond defining a question that calls for action and decide what to do.

Warren phrases the question that calls for action based on his perspective and his values. He has always thought of himself as someone who cares about other people, and he is bothered by the possibility that a pesticide he uses may endanger family members, workers, or consumers. He also is concerned about the environment and feels that people should do their part to protect it. At the same time, as a grower he has to be concerned about his financial security. Like most people in agriculture, he has to keep production levels up and costs down or face losing everything he has worked for. He cannot consider any alternative that might threaten his ability to grow and sell apples and make a profit in the process.

Warren says, "I have a problem. Benomyl is no longer effectively controlling scab in my apple orchard, and the fungicide may be harmful to me and my workers. What can I do to maintain production and marketability, yet minimize harm to people and the environment?" He has analyzed the context, finding out about alternative approaches and considering his own stake in the outcome. Now he can see several possible ways of controlling scab, and he must make a decision.

State the decision as a choice.

From experience, Warren realizes that phrasing the decision question is something he will undoubtedly have to do more than once. As he gains a better understanding of his criteria and the available alternatives, he will continually rephrase the question to reflect the way this new information relates to his values, immediate objectives, and long-run goals. Like the problem in chapter 2, phrasing a decision question starts with a fact situation. The decision question that follows the fact situation includes three parts:

Fact situation: Benomyl is no longer controlling scab in my orchard, and the fungicide may be harmful to me, my workers, and consumers.

The decision as a choice: What fungus-control strategy should I use,

Immediate objective: to protect productivity and marketability, without harming my customers' and workers' health,

Long-term goal: and to assure my family's long-term financial security and health and protect the environment?

Just as phrasing the question that calls for action was the most critical step in defining a problem, phrasing the decision question is the most critical step in decision making. It is the step that sets us on a path. If we misstate our objectives or goals, our decision is less likely to accomplish our aim.

2. On what criteria will I base my decision?

Decision-making Framework

1. What is the decision to be made?

2. **On what criteria will I base my decision?**
    * List criteria.
    * Refine criteria.
    * Rank criteria in order of importance.

3. What alternative courses of action exist?

4. What is the expected effect of each alternative on each criterion?

5. Which alternative is best?

6. How can the alternative be put into action?

List but do not evaluate criteria.

When our objectives and goals are expressed in terms of the outcome of the decision, they become criteria. Criteria provide the basis for choice. Our criteria drive the decision-making process; they determine what information we need to make a sound choice.

First, we list our criteria and ask, "What is important to *me*? What do *I* want to achieve with this decision?" We don't weigh the importance of one criterion over another or think about how we will use criteria to analyze alternatives. We don't begin to analyze, we just make a list. This process is subjective and creative. We listen to our innermost feelings and list the criteria that are important to us. It is essential that we give ourselves permission to be honest. Criteria are not right or wrong.

Warren's criteria flow out of the goals and objectives he articulated in the decision question. The decision question and his criteria are based on his values. He lists his criteria as they occur to him without worrying about their relative importance, overlap, completeness, or other refinements.

Warren's Criteria
financial security
marketable fruit
cost effectiveness
reliability
no dangerous chemicals
demand on time
environmental safety
proven method

Whose criteria are they? Criteria are subjective. Consequently, whose criteria are used makes a difference. One executive told a group of subordinates that he didn't care who decided so long as they used his criteria. He could determine the outcome by setting the criteria. He was confident that his staff could competently handle the creative and critical steps that follow.

In this case, the criteria are clearly Warren's. As long as he doesn't violate federal or state regulations, Warren has the right to choose any fungus-management plan that satisfies him. Warren does turn to others for counsel. Though his wife died a few years ago, he relies on the advice of his son, Bill. Someday, Bill will inherit the orchard. Warren also values his foreman's advice. Jim has worked for Warren for years. He knows the operations as well as or better than Warren. But even so, the final decision is Warren's and no one else's.

In many cases, it isn't nearly so clear whose criteria count. We often make decisions based on what we think are our own criteria, only to find that we have really been acting on someone else's values. We all have known someone who chose a career only to discover that they were responding to pressures from a parent, spouse, or friend. One day, they discover that they really don't get much satisfaction from what they do. At this point, reexamining what one wants and needs from a career can be difficult. Many farmers in the 1970s made decisions about their farms based largely on Washington's desire to increase exports and enhance the position of the United States in world markets. Farmers put more land into production and accepted incentives that seemed to further their own objectives, only to find in the 1980s that they had become less able to achieve their long-term goal of financial security.

Warren realizes he will get a great deal of pressure and reassurance from the dealer who sells Benomyl and other fungicides. But he understands that the chemical company's criteria are not necessarily the same as his own. He will have to distinguish between what they want him to do and what he needs to do to achieve his own goals. This doesn't mean that the desire to please or cooperate with other people is an unacceptable criterion. By making our criteria explicit and examining them carefully, we can consciously weigh that desire against others.

At work, we often decide whose criteria to use. As professionals, we make decisions on behalf of our employer. Perceptions of the employer's criteria may differ among staff. The classic tension between marketing, production, and finance departments is ultimately a clash over whose version of the employer's criteria are more important. In the public sector, similar conflicts arise over whose criteria count between politicians and constituents, the executive and legislative branches, one special interest and another, and public agencies and beneficiaries of their programs. In nonprofit organizations, criteria conflicts arise between funding agencies, the organization itself, and program beneficiaries.

While it is important to recognize that criteria differ, conflicts over whose criteria count often divide groups unnecessarily. Some conflicts can be resolved by simply replacing the question, "Whose criteria count?" with the question, "What are *our* criteria?" given what is important to me and what is important to you. This topic is taken up in the next two chapters.

Refine criteria.

Our choice of criteria has the potential to dramatically alter the choice among alternatives. Critical review helps ensure that the criteria reflect our real priorities.

We ask the following questions: "Why is each criterion important? Is the list complete? Is this criterion too broad or too narrow? Is there overlap among criteria? What purpose does each criterion serve?" Now is the time to be critical and evaluate our answers. We don't include a criterion because it *should* be important to us; we include criteria that *are* important to us. Then we revise and refine our list, adding, deleting, or combining criteria as needed.

As Warren assesses the values that underlie his criteria, he realizes "financial security" is too broad. It will be helpful to break it down into more useful parts: sustaining productivity, producing marketable fruit, and minimizing costs. Since two of those are already on the list, he can substitute the more specific "sustained productivity" for the vague "financial security."

"Environmental safety" also seems vague to Warren. He wants to keep from damaging his soil, protect the predators that help control insect pests, and avoid chemicals that might damage harmless plants or animals when they run off into local streams. He deletes the broad criterion and adds the more specific ones. "No dangerous chemicals" is partly covered by his environmental concerns, but he decides to add a criterion addressing his concern for workers and consumers. Moreover, given the recent furor over Alar on apples, he realizes that using pest-control chemicals that are acceptable to consumers is an important factor in marketing his fruit. Warren refines and ranks his criteria.

What purpose does each criterion serve? Criteria may describe the minimum requirements that any alternative must satisfy to be feasible. Any alternative that doesn't meet these constraining criteria is rejected at the outset. However, we make decisions based on the differences among alternatives, not similarities. When all of our alternatives meet the minimum requirements set by our constraining criteria, we turn to other criteria to decide the relative strengths and weaknesses of each alternative. Thus, to be effective, Warren's list will include not only constraining criteria but other criteria that differentiate among alternatives.

Warren's Criteria Refined

First List	Refined List Ranked by Importance
financial security	maintain present level of production
marketable fruit	consumer acceptance/marketability
cost effectiveness	cost effectiveness
reliability	demand on time
no dangerous chemicals	minimize risk of cancer and
	other health-related consequences
demand on time	reliability to control scab
environmental safety	minimize soil compaction and
	chemical runoff
proven method	protection of beneficial predators
	time-tested method

"Cost effectiveness" differentiates among Warren's alternatives. Warren decides that cost is only important relative to benefits—the lower the cost relative to the benefits the better. Warren knows from experience that it is misleading to consider total cost alone. It's better to pay a little more to get the results you want than to take the cheapest way and find out it won't do the job.

In contrast, "minimize cancer risk" sets a minimum requirement that each alternative must meet. Warren is unwilling to accept a high risk of cancer even if the alternative promises higher production levels or more marketable, attractive fruit. He will not consider alternatives that will place his family and employees at a high risk of cancer. For Warren, this criterion constrains the alternatives he will consider. He will only consider those that meet his minimum standard. Of course, it is up to Warren to decide how much risk is too much. Beyond the minimum, increased safety will make an alternative more attractive.

If we make our list of criteria—especially constraining criteria—too detailed and specific, there may be no alternative that satisfies all criteria.

This is what happened to Dorothy Richards, an attorney who left her environmental advocacy practice five years ago to start a family. When her three children were still in preschool, she began looking for a job in environmental advocacy litigation at which she could work three days a week. She wanted to remain in the South Dakota town of 30,000 where she now lives. She didn't want to work in a large firm, and she wanted the flexibility to take off at her own discretion. Dorothy waited 18 months for work to appear that would meet her criteria. She eventually realized that she would have to relax either her criteria for quality of life or her criteria for professional achievement. She decided that though she would prefer to work in environmental advocacy, she was willing to practice general law. She was not willing to work more than three days a week, however; nor was she willing to leave her community. She set up a private practice and began building a clientele for a general law practice. Essentially, Dorothy made some of her constraining criteria into differentiating criteria.

On the other hand, if we leave criteria out altogether, the odds are we will be dissatisfied with our decision. If Dorothy begins with "I want a job at which I can work only three days a week," she is likely to wind up checking groceries at a local supermarket. Changing constraining criteria into differentiating criteria lets us consider all the criteria that are important to us, but it doesn't eliminate alternatives from consideration altogether.

Rank criteria in order of importance.

Now Warren will rank his criteria in order of importance to him, the decision maker. This may be hard to do since they are all important and some will be interrelated. Warren realizes, for example, that productivity and marketability have to go hand in hand—one means nothing without the other. Two of his criteria seem to be in conflict—safety and proven methods. Many of the seemingly safer methods are experimental.

Ranking is easier if we make the values underlying our criteria explicit. Values underlie all decision criteria. Values are a statement of what is important to you. Examining our values improves the chance that our decision will meet our short- and long-run criteria. Understanding the values that underlie criteria also makes it easier to assess tradeoffs among criteria.

■   Warren explores the linkage between his criteria and his values. "Productivity" is important because. . . . "Marketability" is important because. . . . "Cost" is important because. . . . He thinks about the values that underlie his criteria. Advocating consumer protection is one thing, acting on it is another. Warren realizes his values are not reflected in what he *says* is important—they are revealed in what he *does*.

To himself, Warren acknowledges that consumer protection is more important than he wants to admit. Consumer advocates who try to tell him what chemicals he can or can't use annoy him, but he is disturbed by recent studies that show the breakdown of pesticides into chemicals that can cause cancer. The people closest to him eat pesticide-treated fruit daily. Moreover, he can see that publicity about pesticides inevitably will affect the way people buy fruit. "Still, my family won't be helped if I go bankrupt, so I'll put criteria related to financial security first," he reasons.

Warren also has a difficult time deciding just how important it is to use a method that has been proven over time. Like most growers, he tends to be conservative when it comes to production decisions. He prefers to use proven products and methods. Still, he has confidence in his own ability to adapt and respond to problems. At worst, he can switch back to chemical sprays midseason and minimize his crop losses. If he has to choose between protecting the environment and using a well-tested method, he's willing to take a chance on the experimental method as long as he can find enough data to satisfy his concerns. "Besides," he reasons, "there may be more testing done on these new alternatives than I realize."

Notice that values are revealed in behavior.

It is not enough to say sustainability is important. Our values are revealed in the choices we make and what we do, not in what we say. While we often say equity and sustainability are important, our actions may not show it. The statement "sustainability is important" only rings true when it is made concrete and applied as a criterion in our daily choices. Our accumulated choices will not reflect our stated values, when we

- don't understand the long-run consequences of the choices we make
- are unaware of alternatives that would make our behavior more consistent with our values
- assume tradeoffs are inevitable and fail to search more widely for alternatives that reconcile tradeoffs
- state values that make us feel good, but that we do not expect to act on

Avoiding these pitfalls depends on

- understanding cause and effect as fully as possible
- searching widely for alternatives
- avoiding the assumption that tradeoffs are inevitable
- evaluating our own values critically

3. What alternative courses of action exist?

Decision-making Framework

1. What is the decision to be made?

2. On what criteria will I base my decision?

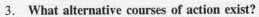

3. **What alternative courses of action exist?**
   • List alternatives but do not evaluate.
   • Refine alternatives.
   • Review the criteria and alternatives.

4. What is the expected effect of each alternative on each criterion?

5. Which alternative is best?

6. How can the alternative be put into action?

List but do not evaluate alternatives.

In this step, we generate a laundry list from which viable alternatives can be selected later. Generating alternatives is creative. We give free rein to our imaginations, giving ourselves the freedom to dream and brainstorm, unencumbered by tradition or the status quo. We don't evaluate or eliminate any alternatives at this point. Many effective technologies and solid ideas go ignored because they are never considered.

Choices can be improved by searching more widely for alternatives. Most of us tend to cut the list short to rationalize one alternative or another. When tempted to do this, we can remind ourselves that this decision is *our* choice. Including more options can't force us to choose something we don't want; it can only increase the possibility of finding an alternative that more effectively meets all of our criteria.

There is no right amount of time to spend generating alternatives. Nor is there a right number of alternatives. We want enough alternatives to minimize tradeoffs among criteria, but not so many that information gathering and comparison are impractical. At a minimum, two alternatives are needed or there is no choice.

The more he thinks about it, the less satisfied Warren is with his three alternatives. There seem to be too many tradeoffs, and each alternative has clear drawbacks. He keeps reading everything he can find on scab-control methods in the hope that new alternatives or new information on existing alternatives might appear. He learns that new varieties of pest-resistant apples are being developed.

Although Warren has heard that most resistant strains aren't very appealing to consumers, the New York State Agricultural Experiment Station and a cooperative breeding program run by universities in Indiana, New Jersey, and Illinois have developed several varieties that are more marketable and significantly reduce the need to spray. Obviously, Warren can't replace all his trees, but he files the information away as potentially helpful in the long run.

Warren also learns about a new twist to a relatively old approach to pest control called (IPM) integrated pest management. With this method, Warren would closely monitor the life cycles of pests and use a combination of methods to break that cycle instead of spraying regularly. IPM is based on new discoveries concerning the life cycle of scab and its relation to temperature and humidity. Apparently a scab infection can be predicted with 95 percent reliability by measuring rain, length of leaf wetness, and temperature. Using this information, a grower can eliminate weekly spraying and treat only when conditions make infection likely.

Warren also learns about treatments of leaf litter, including low-heat burning and fertilizer or fungicide applications, which kill fungus spores in the winter and help prevent reinfection during the following growing season. These treatments are still new, and some involve risks. But Warren resolves to find out more about them and consider how they might affect the alternatives he has been considering.

Tradition and the status quo influence the alternatives we consider and the choices we make. But when traditional practices don't meet our criteria, we have to broaden the search to find alternatives that do. If we limit ourselves to familiar solutions, we will be stuck with their familiar shortcomings. Degradation, pollution, and depletion of air, land, water, forests, and minerals are byproducts of our day-to-day activities. If we want to change these consequences, we must search for unfamiliar alternatives that not only use these resources productively but equitably and

---

Warren's Alternatives So Far

present regimen
organics
integrated pest management
leaf-litter treatments
Nova
resistant varieties

sustainably as well.

Warren is not fully satisfied with the alternatives he has identified so far. He makes a list to keep track of them.

Refine alternatives.

The quality of the decision is limited by the quality of the alternatives considered. At this point we critically evaluate our alternatives. Is each one truly distinct from the others? Are there several variations on a theme? Can the variations be combined or considered as a set? Conversely, are there multiple alternatives masquerading as one? If so, we pull them apart. We want to make the alternatives as straightforward as possible.

Untried and unfamiliar alternatives may seem riskier than familiar alternatives, but we don't automatically eliminate potentially useful alternatives just because we don't know enough about them. Conversely, we avoid clinging to an alternative simply because it's familiar. If a familiar alternative clearly is inferior or doesn't meet our minimum criteria, we cross it off the list.

Reluctantly, Warren crosses out the alternative of staying with a traditional fungicide program. As far as he can see, that alternative will mean a continuing cycle of switching sprays as resistant fungi develop and worrying every time a new Environmental Protection Agency or Food and Drug Administration report comes out. The recent concern over Alar, a growth hormone, slowed sales of Warren's apples for a month and gave him a taste of what it might be like to have his fruit declared unsafe.

While Warren doesn't feel that he knows enough about Nova to evaluate it, he has read that it is widely used in France. He leaves it on the list. Although he can't replace all his trees with resistant varieties, he will consider trying a few acres of the new resistant strains. Warren decides to treat IPM, leaf treatments, and organics as one alternative. IPM combined with leaf treatments should reduce the need for spraying. He settles on three alternatives: organics combined with IPM, Nova, and resistant varieties.

Review the criteria and alternatives.

Does each criterion serve a purpose? Does it set minimum requirements or highlight differences among alternatives? Are all important criteria included? Cross out criteria that don't highlight differences; they won't affect the decision. Time spent gathering information on criteria that highlight differences is most productive. If we have any doubt, leave them in. Warren examines his criteria again. When he is finished, Warren organizes his criteria and alternatives in a decision matrix (table 4.4).

Table 4.4. Warren's decision matrix

	Alternatives		
Ranked criteria	Organics/IPM	Nova	Resistant strains
Maintain present level of production			
Consumer acceptance/marketability			
Cost effectiveness			
Demand on time			
Minimize risk of cancer and other health-related consequences			
Reliability to control scab			
Minimize soil compaction and chemical runoff			
Protection of beneficial predators			
Time-tested method			

4. What is the expected effect of each alternative on each criterion?

Decision-making Framework

1. What is the decision to be made?

2. On what criteria will I base my decision?

3. What alternative courses of action exist?

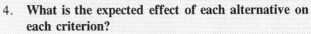

4. **What is the expected effect of each alternative on each criterion?**
   - Use available information.
   - Look for information that applies to the context of the decision.
   - Remember that some information is qualitative.
   - Gather information from a variety of sources.
   - Decide how much information is enough.

5. Which alternative is best?

6. How can the alternative be put into action?

The rows and columns of the decision matrix—criteria and alternatives—are *subjective*. The matrix's inner cells are filled with *objective* analysis based on factual information describing the expected consequences of each alternative on each criterion (table 4.5).

Table 4.5. Warren's filled-in decision matrix

	Alternatives		
Ranked criteria	Organics/IPM	Nova/IPM	Resistant strains
Maintain present level of production	Good, same now	Good, maybe better	Good when trees reach production; short-term loss
Consumer acceptance/marketability	Possible damage to appearance	No apparent problem	Possible problem but getting better
Cost effectiveness	Organics more expensive per dose than Benomyl but IPM reduces frequency of spraying; "natural" apples sell at premium price	Same as with organics	Cost effective only where trees are now past prime period of production
Demand on time	Higher than present; increased demands on a regular basis	Higher than present; increased demands on a regular basis	High initially; lower than present on a regular basis
Minimize risk of cancer and other health-related consequences	OK	Good	Excellent
Reliability to control scab	Good	Potentially good, but not proven in U.S.	Good
Minimize soil compaction and chemical runoff	A problem, but IPM will reduce need to spray when wet	Excellent because of kickback effect	Excellent
Protection of beneficial predators	A problem, but IPM helps	Good	Excellent
Time-tested method	Fairly widely used	Widely used in France, untested in U.S.	Method is proven; some individual varieties need more testing; questions on consumer acceptance

■   To evaluate the IPM organic spray alternative, Warren asks, "What will be the probable effect on productivity, marketability, cost effectiveness, and so forth?" He asks the same question about Nova and about planting resistant varieties until he has evaluated each alternative's effect on each criterion.

As he considers each alternative, Warren uses the information he gathered when he was developing his decision matrix (table 4.5). He is mindful, for instance, that by using IPM techniques to monitor the conditions that contribute to scab infection and by treating leaf litter in the winter, he can greatly reduce the frequency of spraying with Nova, just as he could reduce the need for organics. He revises the Nova alternative accordingly.

Gathering cause-and-effect information is an objective step. We need to be careful that our emotions don't influence our information gathering. We may find ourselves selecting information that supports one alternative or re-ranking criteria to fit the information we gather. If this happens, we need to stop and figure out why. Perhaps our criteria are not complete or we haven't been honest with ourselves in ranking the criteria.

Let's go back to Dorothy Richards' search for a job. Suppose she had settled on two criteria: flexible work week and staying in her hometown. One of her alternatives is a position in an exciting environmental advocacy firm located in Philadelphia. She finds herself thinking, "Philadelphia isn't such a large town, really; it's almost like staying where I am." This statement is not objectively true. What may be true is that a small town quality of life is not as important as she thought it was. Moreover, her need to specialize in environmental law is a criteria. She won't improve her decision by misrepresenting the effect the job will have on the criteria she has specified. Her decision will be improved by including the forgotten criterion and reassessing how she ranked her criteria, looking at the effects her alternatives have on the full set of criteria.

Use available information.

Complete the matrix, using the highest quality information available. The purpose of decision making is to make the best decision possible given available time and information. There is always more information we could gather, but there is rarely more time. Often there is a window of opportunity when the time is ripe for action or change. If you let the opportunity pass, you may not be able to act on the problem for some time. Sid, the inspector in the Powder River illustration, is in that position. He has to act right away while the threat of fines and lawsuits is fresh in people's minds and before conflict embitters them. Two months from now, the parties involved might not be willing to cooperate with each other. Warren is in a similar position.

His fungicide isn't working effectively, and scab season is approaching. He can't wait for more information. Moreover, he has several acres of trees that have passed the age of peak production. He needs to decide with what to replace them now.

Look for information that applies to the context of the decision.

Predicting the probable effect of an alternative on a criterion—let's say of Nova/IPM on soil compaction—depends on cause and effect *and* on the unique context in which the decision will be implemented. Warren has read that French orchardists like Nova because it can be applied up to 90 hours after the fungus infection begins, so they rarely have to spray when the soil is wet. He needs to think about Wisconsin rains and Wisconsin soils. Will 90 hours be long enough for *his* soil to dry out?

Remember that some information is qualitative.

Some criteria call for quantitative measurements; others for qualitative assessments. Our technical training leads us to discount the value of qualitative assessments because they make us feel uncomfortable. This is particularly true for those of us trained in the biophysical sciences and economics. We want numbers; we don't trust words.

It is obvious that if Warren discounts qualitative information, he will make his decision solely on the basis of productivity and cost. He will clearly be dissatisfied with his decision if he decides to use a method that produces the greatest numbers of apples at the lowest cost but sacrifices the quality of the apples, endangers his workers, or compacts the soil. We can see the importance of quality in this case, but we are often unwilling to accept qualitative information in making other decisions about which quality is just as important. Our criteria are chosen because they reflect our values, not because they make it easier to measure the outcome.

Discomfort with qualitative information has led to the development of pseudomeasures for qualitative data—"numbers" that we substitute for qualitative descriptions. We might decide to rank alternatives first, second, third, and so on with respect to a criterion, as though they were scaled. We might assign a numeric value to opinions on a scale of 1 to 10. Ranking alternatives is probably better than no information; the danger is that we are tempted to use the ranking or the scale as if it represented an objective measure. These numbers are still subjective opinions ordering subjective alternatives on subjective criteria. Assigning a number to qualitative information doesn't make it quantitative and ignores the nuances embedded in the original words.

For example, Warren has limited information on Nova. His friend George Morgan tells him that his cousin used Nova last year in Washington County, and it wasn't very effective. Warren could use this information to give Nova a lower ranking on the "reliability" criterion, or he could note "Morgan's cousin." If he chooses the qualitative approach and later on it seems that Nova's reliability could affect his decision, he could call Morgan's cousin. He may find that the cousin hadn't used Nova at all but a more traditional pesticide. If he simply enters a "3" for Nova under reliability, the true breadth of the qualitative information is lost.

The preference for quantitative measurements of cause and effect has important implications for equity and sustainability. We can measure performance and profit, but we do not have widely accepted measures for equity and sustainability. Our discomfort with qualitative assessments has led us to discount these important criteria, so that equity and sustainability are rarely fully represented in our resource decisions.

Gather information from a variety of sources.

Choose the most reliable source for the kind of information needed. Information may be obtained from applied research, theory, systematic observation, informed experience, or reliable impression. Different kinds of information call for different sources. One source isn't inherently better than another. Choose the most reliable and valid information. If you question the reliability or validity of a critical piece of information and it makes sense to put more effort into your search, check another source and verify its accuracy and applicability to your unique context.

Applied research and theory: Much of our understanding of cause and effect comes from applied research. We tend to trust the reliability and validity of research results. Our trust is well founded. However, we need to be vigilant when we apply research results in a context that is different from the context in which the research was conducted.

Most research is discipline specific and typically disregards influences of factors outside that discipline's domain. Most decisions, on the other hand, transcend disciplines, encompassing biophysical, social, and economic aspects. As a result, research results often ignore factors that may have important influences on the outcome. Research results must be interpreted carefully for use in real-world decision making.

The developers of DDT, for example, were right when they said that the pesticide would kill harmful insects, but they failed to anticipate the consequences of introducing the chemical into the complex, real-world ecosystem. Laboratory experiments didn't lead them to expect the rapid development of resistance or the harm to other species. In contrast, Warren is attracted to the IPM approach and leaf-litter treatments because they focus on specific conditions in his orchard.

Scientific theory helps us organize our expectations, but expectations based on theory should also be applied with careful consideration of context. When the assumptions on which theory is based differ from the real-world context, theoretical cause and effect is not a reliable predictor. For example, microeconomic theory assumes perfectly competitive markets, but many markets are only imperfectly competitive. Yet we often use microeconomic theory as though it were a reliable predictor of economic behavior.

Research and theory are good sources of information, but they are not the only reliable sources. If we use only information that has been proven in a scientific environment, we may become paralyzed, unable to make any but the most conservative choices. As professionals working in the midst of resource management problems that call for action, we often cannot wait for hypotheses to be tested true or false. We act when the time is ripe, drawing information from the best sources available at the time.

Systematic observation and informed opinion: We may draw either quantitative or qualitative information from systematic observation. Quantitative association drawn from a data set is one kind of systematic observation. Causal analysis using the framework described in chapter 9 is another kind. Systematic observation intentionally analyzes the full range of data available, looking for patterns of association from which to generate plausible explanations of cause and effect.

Informed opinion resulting from thoughtful observation of a situation over time can be a valid and reliable predictor. Some people are better than others at seeing the chain of causal relationships. These are the people we want to seek out for informed opinions—people who ask "why" and learn from experience. However, informed opinion inevitably carries with it the baggage of individual perspective. Observers may want to subtly encourage or discourage one course of action or another. Use informed opinions that hold up to critical scrutiny, but bear in mind the perspective of their source. For example, Warren's definition of protecting the environment is likely to differ from that of an environmental worker or that of a chemical salesperson. For this hard-to-define criterion, Warren may gain a more thorough understanding by talking to several people and reading from several sources with different perspectives. He can improve the reliability of his information by selecting people and sources he knows and respects.

In the process of gathering information, Warren talks to growers he knows who have tried various methods of pest control. He asks questions based on his criteria and makes sure he records his information. He gets conflicting responses. One grower says that he tried to grow a couple of acres of apples using organic sprays but found it too expensive. Another says that with IPM and organic sprays he has to keep up with what is happening in his orchard but doesn't spray as often as before and gets better prices. Warren decides that the second grower is probably more reliable since he seems to have taken a more serious approach to the issue and, unlike the first grower, is aware of the IPM techniques. The only person he can find who knows about Nova is a friend whose distant cousin tried it, and Warren can't find him to talk to him. He decides that a lack of information is a serious mark against this alternative. He visits an orchard in the next county that has several acres of 'Liberty' and 'Prima' apples, varieties resistant to scab. The grower speaks highly of their taste and appearance.

Decide how much information is enough.

The decision matrix has a dual role in guiding the search for information. It defines what is relevant and what is not. Any information that describes how one of the alternatives will affect a criterion is relevant. All other information is not. When a decision is complex, it is extremely helpful to know what one does not need to consider.

For example, when Dorothy Richards' husband died, she was the beneficiary of an excellent paid-up health plan that will cover her and her children until she remarries. Dorothy doesn't care what health benefits the jobs she considers have; she's completely satisfied with her family's current health plan. All the complex information about alternative health programs is irrelevant to her because health benefits are not among her criteria.

Relevant information may or may not be available. Whether or not it is worthwhile to expend the time and effort necessary to find it depends on a number of factors. First, is it known and available? Relevant information may be

- known and in hand
- known and readily available
- known and potentially available
- known but unavailable
- unknown but knowable in a reasonable time frame
- unknown and unavailable

Beginning with what we know and have in hand, we enter this information in the appropriate cells of the matrix (table 4.4). The spaces highlight where we need more information. Selecting topics where we need to know more to rank alternatives, we collect pertinent information that is known and readily available. The next step is to determine what information is missing. We ask, "How important is this information to the quality of the decision?" Information describing the consequences of our eighth or ninth ranked criteria may not be very important to the decision if other criteria discriminate among alternatives sufficiently. However, we must have information on our most important criteria and criteria that set minimum requirements for all alternatives, regardless of ranking. Missing information will be readily apparent. Unfortunately, Murphy's law says that for every decision there will be at least one piece of critical information missing—and a pile of interesting but useless information that doesn't fit into the matrix.

How much time and effort we will put into searching for that critical piece of missing information will depend on the importance of the decision, whether it is reversible and at what cost, and the time available. It makes sense to put more time and effort into collecting information for important decisions. The accuracy of prior information is less important if decisions can be made in small, reversible increments—we can learn as we go. Conversely, accuracy of information is critically important for decisions that have large and irreversible consequences. For every decision, the amount of information we collect will be constrained by the time available.

If a critical piece of information is not readily available, we must decide how to proceed. If the decision is important and the consequences are irreversible, we eliminate the alternative with missing information. If we feel the alternative with missing information promises to be the most attractive, we may take the time to search for additional information. If more information would be helpful and the decision is ongoing or repetitive (e.g., species selection in reforestation), a pragmatic action approach suggests a two-step response: Choose the best alternative now, using existing information, and continue to seek out additional information for the next time around.

5. Which alternative is best?

Decision-making Framework

1. What is the decision to be made?

2. On what criteria will I base my decision?

3. What alternative courses of action exist?

4. What is the expected effect of each alternative on each criterion?

5. **Which alternative is best?**
    *   Evaluate the probable effects.
    *   Choose among the alternatives.

6. How can the alternative be put into action?

Evaluate the probable effects.

Beginning with the first criterion, we ask, "Objectively, which alternative yields the most desirable outcome for *this* criterion?" We rank each alternative based on *this* criterion. Then we move to the second criterion and rank each alternative. We continue until we have ranked each alternative for each criterion. Where two or more alternatives are equally acceptable for a criterion, we rank those as *equally* acceptable. We eliminate alternatives that do not meet minimum requirements, and we eliminate criteria that don't highlight differences among alternatives.

This step requires critical evaluation. The consequences described in the matrix provide an objective basis for comparison. The comparison, however, has a subjective quality; there are no right answers. Given the same criteria, alternatives, and predictions, two people may choose different alternatives. One may have more confidence than the other; one may be willing to take greater risk than the other. One may have a deeper understanding of the context than the other, leading him or her to assess the risk differently.

Even if two people agreed, however, their subjective agreement does not necessarily lead to the "right" decision. The consequences are facts that can theoretically be tested and improved. Current information may be later proven wrong, and insufficient information can erroneously make one alternative seem better than another.

We base our evaluation not only on what is written down but also on the detail and nuance that numbers and words cannot capture. The matrix is a kind of short-hand notation to remind us of the breadth and depth of the information we have collected, and to organize it so it effectively informs our decision making. We consider the probable consequences of each alternative as we record them in the matrix. But we also take into account the reliability of the information's source, our confidence that an alternative will achieve the desired results in the specific context, and our willingness to take risks given the importance and reversibility of the outcome.

Warren ranks the most desirable outcomes, working across one row at a time (table 4.6). He critically compares the predicted outcomes for each alternative, criterion by criterion. Recalling the conversations he has had with other growers and all of his reading, he tries to evaluate each alternative as accurately as possible. Warren compares what he has read to what he has heard, trying to find instances in which one source might challenge or support another. He sorts out the emphatic "yes's" from the "yes, but's." Finally, he tests his confidence in the matrix, asking himself if he has left anything out and if he really is ready to risk a change in pest-control method or in the varieties of apples he grows.

Choose among the alternatives.

To choose, we compare alternatives overall. We choose the alternative that best meets our criteria and enables us to achieve our objectives effectively. Again, there is no right answer. In choosing, we express an informed preference, not a dispassionate mathematic solution. Our choice depends on our objectives, our criteria, and the richness of the alternatives we consider. Time and information constraints affect our choice. What we know about the underlying causal relationship affects the decision. The biophysical, social, economic, and political realities of the decision in context will affect not only the choice but also the action that follows. While there is no right answer, alternatives that let us achieve our objectives effectively are better than alternatives that do not.

Few choices can be reduced meaningfully to a weighted average— whether the weights are subjective probabilities or prior probabilities from

Table 4.6. Warren's revised decision matrix

Ranked criteria	Alternatives		
	Organics/IPM	Nova/IPM	Resistant strains
Maintain present level of production	Good, same now ②	Good, maybe better ①	Good when trees reach production; short-term loss ③
Consumer acceptance/marketability	Possible damage to appearance ③	No apparent problem ②	Possible problem but getting better ①
Cost effectiveness	Organics more expensive per dose than Benomyl but IPM reduces frequency of spraying; "natural" apples sell at premium price ①	Same as with organics ①	Cost effective only where trees are now past prime period of production ②
Demand on time	Higher than present; increased demands on a regular basis ①	Higher than present; increased demands on a regular basis ①	High initially; lower than present on a regular basis ①
Minimize risk of cancer and other health-related consequences	OK ③	Good ②	Excellent ①
Reliability to control scab	Good ①	Potentially good, but not proven in U.S. ②	Good ①
Minimize soil compaction and chemical runoff	A problem, but IPM will reduce need to spray when wet ②	Excellent because of kickback effect ①	Excellent ①
Protection of beneficial predators	A problem, but IPM helps ③	Good ②	Excellent ①
Time-tested method	Fairly widely used ①	Widely used in France, untested in U.S. ③	Method is proven; some individual varieties need more testing; questions on consumer acceptance ②

other sources. Ultimately, the decision maker must weigh the written and unwritten, the quantifiable and unquantifiable, the tangible and intangible, and the probability of success and the risk of failure to make a decision. No decision rule can substitute for critical thinking.

The framework does not eliminate the need for choice. Choice is ultimately subjective. As a result, two people may make different choices even with a completed matrix in front of them. The framework makes our criteria explicit, encourages us to consider multiple alternatives, and structures information to help us compare alternatives. The process steps free us to be creative when creativity is called for and critical when evaluation is called for without confusing the two. Similarly, the process steps highlight differences between subjective and objective thinking so that we can explore freely the values on which our criteria are based *and* bring greater rigor to our analysis of alternatives.

Had he limited himself to two alternatives, Warren would have faced many tradeoffs. Traditional sprays are effective and cheap but dangerous and subject to increasing resistance. Organic sprays are safe but expensive and potentially damaging to fruit quality. Warren's search for a wider range of alternatives has given much more flexibility to reduce tradeoffs among his criteria.

As he considers the alternatives, Warren realizes that spraying and planting resistant varieties aren't mutually exclusive. Since productivity is falling off in some of his trees, he will have to replace them anyway. He will be taking a minor risk since consumer acceptance of the new varieties hasn't been proven in the marketplace. But these varieties have the potential to be more cost effective and safer to workers and consumers in the future. His other two alternatives present more tradeoffs. Nova/IPM clearly seems to be better in many areas, but it hasn't been used by anyone he knows. Thus, it carries a greater risk. Does the potential, but untested, benefit outweigh the risk? How does the potential benefit compare to that of the less risky alternative with known drawbacks? What level of production risk is acceptable?

As the number of criteria and alternatives expands, there is a tendency to let the data decide, reducing the choice to a comparison of weighted averages based on rankings. We must avoid this trap. We believe values should be looked at independently first; then the tradeoffs among them must be made explicit in the final choice. Weighted averages are easy to calculate, but they avoid the necessarily difficult, subjective work of deciding what we really want. All the effort of gathering and structuring our information is trivialized when we resort to an easy mathematic calculation at this point in the decision process.

Like most of us, Warren prefers alternatives that have assured outcomes.

He knows that growers have been successful with organic sprays combined with IPM and resistant varieties. On the other hand, he thinks that Nova combined with IPM may turn out to be the best alternative in the long run. He finally decides that the window of opportunity for Nova hasn't yet arrived. Committing to a particular spray is a decision that he can reverse when more information becomes available. He decides to try the best organic spray he can find along with integrated pest management strategies. Warren really likes the idea of taking a more active part in deciding what his trees need and spraying when his knowledge and instruments indicate it is necessary, rather than following someone else's instructions. At the same time, he will try replacing some of his least productive trees with resistant varieties since that seems to him to be the most sustainable approach to pest control. This involves some degree of risk. But his research makes him confident that the risk is acceptable and the possibility for improved sustainability and lower cost is great.

Not making a decision in the face of a problem is a decision in itself. In Warren's case, not deciding or accepting someone else's decision would have meant choosing damage to his crop from resistant fungi or simply accepting a potentially dangerous chemical as a substitute for Benomyl. More often than not, no choice is the same as choosing the status quo. To move in the direction of sustainability, we must make choices; we must find alternatives that reconcile tradeoffs between productivity, equity, and sustainability; and we must be willing to risk change.

Warren's case clearly illustrates this. Had he limited himself to two alternatives, he would have had to choose among productivity, equity, and sustainability—between a pest-control program that maintains productivity by potentially endangering others and isn't sustainable and one that is safe and more sustainable but limits his ability to make a profit. By phrasing the question in terms that call for the reconciliation of productivity, equity, and sustainability, Warren leads himself to search for more acceptable alternatives. By finding out about IPM, leaf-litter treatments, organic sprays, and resistant varieties, he is able to broaden his choices and resolve the tradeoffs.

6. How can the alternative be put into action?

Decision-making Framework

1. What is the decision to be made?

2. On what criteria will I base my decision?

3. What alternative courses of action exist?

4. What is the expected effect of each alternative on each criterion?

5. What alternative is best?

6. **How can the alternative be put into action?**

Once an alternative has been chosen, the decision maker can begin planning. What are the steps necessary to get this idea into action? Who needs to do what and when? Chapters 7 and 8 deal with these issues.

Designing New Alternatives

Warren's choice is limited by the alternatives he considers. If IPM and resistant varieties had proven to be undesirable alternatives, Warren could have tried to design a new alternative. Identifying a new alternative requires Warren to view the problem differently and his alternatives creatively.

Look at the problem from new angles.

It is easy to get stuck when we try to see the problem and our solutions from different angles. We resist moving too far from the familiar; we set up mental blocks. The process doesn't have to be this difficult, however. Most new alternatives are developed by improving an existing alternative or by juxtaposing ideas in a new way. For example, Warren could have looked at his present biocide spray program and asked, "Isn't there a better way to control scab that reduces the amount of chemical applied, minimizes build-up of resistance, reduces damage to beneficial predators, reduces soil compaction, and still keeps protection costs in line?" The structure of the question is based on his criteria.

Warren answers this question tentatively, exploring additional possibilities. He thinks, "Any program that reduces the amount of chemicals sprayed is likely to put off build-up of resistance and reduce damage to beneficial predators. I can reduce the amount of spray by reducing the concentration of spray per treatment or by reducing the number of treatments. However, soil damage is related to the number of treatments, not the amount of spray. Reducing the concentration of treatments or number of treatments will reduce pesticide cost. Labor costs will decline only if the number of treatments is reduced."

Thinking about his criteria singly and as a whole, he asks himself a series of questions about his present spraying program: "Can I adapt what I am doing presently? Can I reduce the concentration of spray used with each treatment? The number of treatments? Can I substitute a different spray? A more effective spraying schedule? Can I alternate sprays? Can I use different equipment to spray? Can I combine several small improvements?"

Perhaps he could spray alternate rows with each treatment to reduce the amount of pesticides sprayed. Alternatively, he could combine IPM surveillance methods with a biocide spray as needed to reduce both the amount of spray and number of treatments. He may be able to alternate biocide sprays to forestall resistance problems. He could combine IPM surveillance with an as-needed spray schedule and alternate sprays.

Let the group improve creativity.

When we can't get past our mental blocks by ourselves, other people may be able to show us another way of seeing the problems and our alternatives. Warren could consult an extension agent or farm supply dealer to expand his search. If this doesn't help, he could pull together a group of people with different perspectives. Perhaps together the group can generate ideas that no single individual would have. Sometimes putting a group in a new situation helps them look at a problem with new eyes. Several techniques have been developed and tested that encourage groups to think creatively and generate new alternatives. While these are beyond the scope of this book, many of you may find it useful to pursue processes like brainstorming, team idea competition, and nominal group techniques in further reading at your local libraries.

At each moment, the future exists only as a set of possibilities in our minds. It never arrives, and we can know it only insofar as we are willing to consider those possibilities in the present and work to give them reality. If we wait for someone else to develop sustainable alternatives and present them to us in a way that doesn't involve risk, we will always choose the status quo. If we assume that productivity is always in opposition to equity and sustainability, we guarantee that the problems of the present will continue to shape the future. Only by challenging apparent tradeoffs among productivity, equity, and sustainability and asking our questions in ways that reconcile those factors can we begin to shape a future that is more productive, just, and sustainable than the present.

5

■ Making Decisions When You Are in Charge

Making decisions in groups is a large part of everyday work. One person often is accountable for the group, but working together as a group, even deciding who is in the group, also affects the way decisions are made. Thus, in organizations, the decision question is not simply which alternative is best.

This chapter discusses decision making in structured groups—groups that share a history of working together. Group members have expectations of their own and each other's roles, responsibility, and authority. Structured groups most often are thought of in connection with the workplace, within departments and operating units of businesses, government agencies, and nonprofit organizations; but they also may be found in committees, boards of directors, and other voluntary groups.

Manager's Perspective

This chapter considers the Powder River situation from Paul Hartner's perspective. As you recall, a washed-out logging road on Northwest Forest

Products' land caused Sid Riedel and the state Department of Environmental Quality to take notice of the Powder River's sedimentation problem. Now, Northwest has to decide what to do about the logging road. Paul Hartner, Northwest's forest-operations manager, is in charge.

Sid Riedel, the state inspector, is sitting in Paul's office. He explains why he has come and fines Northwest $5,000. At the same time, he explains to Paul that the state will bring legal action if the company doesn't take care of the road within the next few days. He warns Paul that if another section of the road slides in the interim, the next fine will be $10,000.

The conversation takes an unexpected turn. Sid apologizes in a backhanded way. "Just doing my job, Paul. I'd rather work with you to find a long-term solution to this sedimentation problem than come out here and fine you after the damage is done." Paul nods his head, waiting for Sid to continue. "There's a group of farmers and foresters who will be meeting next week to discuss the basin-planning option in the Forest Practices Act. We'd like you to join us." Paul hesitates. He hadn't expected this turn of events. Paul asks some questions, which Sid answers. Sid finishes, "I don't need an answer now. Think about it, and I'll get back to you in a couple of days."

Paul relays the conversation to Charlie Reynolds, the forest engineer. "We'll deal with the basin-planning option later. Right now, we have to figure out what to do about the immediate problem. That branch creek road has been nothing but a headache from the day we built it." Charlie answers, "You have two alternatives. You can band-aid over the problem, or you can fix it. Those new logging road standards go into effect five years from now. We might as well do it now."

Paul answers, "I want you to get a crew working on the immediate problem this afternoon. Rain is forecast tonight, and we don't want to pay a second fine if another section washes out." Charlie goes to the phone and arranges for a crew to begin work after lunch. He asks, "What about bringing the road up to specifications?"

Paul responds with a question, "What's involved?" Charlie explains, "First, we'll have to regrade the entire road. Then, we'll have to haul in rock to shore up the slide area. To prevent new slides, we'll have to reinforce the rock with a heavy wire mesh. The state won't let us bring one section of the road up to standards and leave the rest of the road unattended. We'll have to haul in rock and reinforce a couple of other problem areas too. When the entire roadbed meets the state's load-bearing requirements, we'll grade it, haul in crushed stone, and grade it again. When we're done, we'll submit a maintenance plan to the state. They will come out and inspect the road and approve it—if we do it right." Paul says, "What's it going to cost? Can you work up some cost numbers for me?"

Paul decides to talk to Ron Hastings about the branch creek road. Ron is an experienced forester with a common sense approach, and Paul often goes to him for advice. After listening to Paul's description of the problem, Ron responds, "Charlie's on target, if you're sure you need the road. But have you thought about abandoning it? It might be cheaper to abandon the road now and build a new one when you need access to those areas later." Paul answers, "What do you mean abandon it? That was supposed to be a permanent road. I know the construction was lousy, and it's been a problem ever since we built it. At least with Charlie on board, we shouldn't have any more like it. We need that road." Ron responds to Paul's outburst, quietly asking, "Are you sure?"

Paul isn't sure. Experience tells him if you ask an engineer to solve a problem, you get an engineering solution. Maybe Ron's right. Paul talks to Betsy Tomlin, the forester who reported the washed-out logging road. Paul values her advice. She has a big-picture understanding of Northwest's operations.

Thinking out loud, Paul questions, "Abandon the road, and do what? How will we get up to those ridge sites later?" Betsy interrupts, "How long until you need access to the ridge sites? You might be able to abandon the road now and build a permanent road that meets state standards or even a temporary road later—and save money. You have at least three alternatives, Paul, and maybe others. You just need to work out the numbers, figure out what's best given what we need to accomplish right now, and when we're going to need to harvest the branch creek area."

Paul needs to make a decision soon. He doesn't want to pay another fine. While the work crew will take care of the immediate threat this afternoon, heavy rains will quickly undo their work. If a hard rain hits, other sections of road will surely slide. This is a decision that requires careful thought and analysis. Paul decides to bring his team into the process. They have more information than he does, and they will carry out the decision.

The Decision-making Framework

The framework presented in chapter 4 can improve the outcome in group as well as individual decision making. The decision-making framework is identical however many individuals are involved. As you will recall, the framework asks a series of questions: What decision? What criteria? What alternatives? What consequences? Which alternative is best? The criteria and alternatives form the vertical and horizontal axes of a matrix. The interior cells describe the consequences of each alternative on each criterion.

The process steps guide groups through a logical sequence of steps to answer the framework's questions. They follow the same logic for the individual described in chapter 4, separating discussion of subjective and objective information, and creative brainstorming from critical evaluation. These process steps are even more important when groups make decisions. This separation encourages group members to share their deepest held values without fear of judgment. It also encourages groups to consider wider-ranging, more innovative alternatives; group members know even their wildest ideas will not be rejected as out of hand. This separation also helps groups avoid confusing facts with value statements, inviting more rigorous examination of the facts.

Decision-making Matrix

Alternatives

Criteria	A	B	C
1	A1	B1	C1
2	A2	B2	C2
3	A3	B3	C3

Group Process Steps

Several steps are added to those steps presented in chapter 4 to accommodate a group. They are added to help assure all group members the opportunity to participate without fear of rejection, which is needed to build trust among group members. Steps also are added to strengthen group members' commitment to the decision and to assign responsibility for follow-up action.

Decision-making Group Process Steps

1. What is the decision?

2. Whose decision is it?

3. Who should be involved?

4. How will the meeting be carried out?

5. What is the best alternative given the context?

6. Is the group committed to the alternative selected?

7. What is the next step?

1. What is the decision?

Decision-making Group Process Steps

1. **What is the decision?**

2. Whose decision is it?

3. Who should be involved?

4. How will the meeting be carried out?

5. What is the best alternative given the context?

6. Is the group committed to the alternative selected?

7. What is the next step?

How you phrase the decision question is just as important as how you define the problem. You cannot phrase a good decision question if you don't first have a problem statement and question that calls for action. Often you discover your question that calls for action is not as good as you think it is when you find it difficult to phrase a decision question.

Paul Hartner defines the problem like this: "A logging road has washed out, dumping sediment into a branch stream that flows into the Powder River, a state-designated salmon stream. Another section of road may slide with the next heavy rain. Other sections also are weakened. The state has fined Northwest $5,000 and threatens legal action and additional fines if Northwest does not take action to prevent the erosion. What should I do?"

Paul is unsure of what the decision question should be, which suggests that he has not defined the problem clearly. If he listens to Charlie, the question will be

How should Northwest repair the logging road to reduce sedimentation in the branch creek?

In its simplest form, this *how* question calls for planning. The question contains within it a solution—repair the logging road. The question asks how to repair the road. Questions that start with *how* rarely are good decision questions. They are almost always questions that call for planning—how to accomplish an already decided upon objective. Thinking about his talk with Ron, Paul considers another decision question:

> Should Northwest abandon the logging road now and build a permanent road later?

Paul quickly realizes this is not a good decision question either. It sets the decision up as a "yes/no" question and excludes the possibility of other alternatives. Questions that can be answered with yes or no rarely are good decision questions. Paul knows Ron intended to broaden his perspective when he offered the alternative. So Paul phrases a broader question.

He describes the problem and asks, "What should I do?" This question doesn't narrow the call for action. It is too broad; it doesn't state what he wants to accomplish. What should I do to avoid fines? To comply with state regulations for logging roads? To reduce erosion? To protect salmon? Paul isn't sure what needs to be accomplished yet.

After thinking about it, Paul realizes that Ron is right. Choosing how to repair the logging road excludes too many viable alternatives. First he must decide whether the road is needed or not. The company's goal is not to maintain a road but to minimize production costs and maintain profitability. He words the decision this way:

Problem statement: The branch creek road washed out, blocking a salmon stream regulated by the state. As a result, turbidity in the Powder River is higher than acceptable levels. The state Department of Environmental Quality has fined Northwest Forest Products and threatened legal action and additional fines if action is not taken to shore up the road and prevent future washouts. New state regulations for logging roads will take effect five years from now.

Decision question: What is the best alternative to deal with the branch creek road situation?

Immediate objective: To reduce erosion from the branch creek road to levels that comply with state regulations and minimize cost

Long-term goal: To maintain Northwest Forest Products' profitability, preserve its management options, and maintain goodwill in the community

At this point, Paul is about where Warren Olson was when he began thinking creatively about his alternatives. Paul, however, has to decide who should help make the decision and what their role should be before he proceeds.

2. Whose decision is it?

Decision-making Group Process Steps

1. What is the decision?

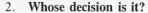 2. **Whose decision is it?**
- Who has the authority?
- Who will be held accountable?

3. Who should be involved?

4. How will the meeting be carried out?

5. What is the best alternative given the context?

6. Is the group committed to the alternative selected?

7. What is the next step?

Warren Olson, the orchard owner from chapter 4, is solely responsible for his production decisions. He confidently addresses problems knowing he owns and operates the orchard, and decisions about how it is managed are his alone. In organizations, responsibility for decision making is not always as clear as in Warren's situation. Responsibility defines the problems staff are expected to address. Authority defines the kinds of decisions they can make, including their power to command people, money, and equipment to get a job done. Accountability is the organization's way of ensuring that short-run objectives are met and progress is made toward long-run goals. When these are clearly defined, staff can make decisions with confidence.

Authority and responsibility are not always clearly defined. When this is the case, staff may not know who should make a decision, and problems go unaddressed. Even when they are clearly defined, new problems inevitably arise. Unless an organization is quick to assign authority and responsibility, these problems may fall through the organizational cracks until a crisis arises. Or unrelated individuals in different parts of the organization may independently assume responsibility for making decisions leading to chaos.

At any given point in time, these structural issues must be taken as part of the context—a given. However, problem solving is made easier where authority, responsibility, and accountability are linked. At Northwest, Paul is responsible for managing the forest. While he delegates authority and responsibility, he is ultimately accountable. Paul's raises and promotions are affected by the decisions he and his subordinates make; so is his professional credibility. Paul must decide how to handle the branch creek situation—a nonroutine management decision. While he will delegate responsibility for carrying out the decision to a staff member, he will be held accountable for the outcome by his boss, the vice-president for operations at company headquarters.

3. Who should be involved?

Decision-making Group Process Steps

1. What is the decision?

2. Whose decision is it?

3. **Who should be involved?**
   - How will you involve others?
   - Who will be involved?
   - Why?

4. How will the meeting be carried out?

5. What is the best alternative given the context?

6. Is the group committed to the alternative selected?

7. What is the next step?

Who is involved in making a decision will influence what is chosen. Think, for example, what the likely choice would be if just Paul and Charlie made the decision. Charlie has already decided what choice should be made: Northwest should bring the branch creek road up to state specifications now. If just Paul and Ron made the decision, they might decide to abandon the road and rebuild it later.

Who is involved in decision making strongly influences the criteria considered, the range of alternatives considered, and the alternative selected. Politicians and ministers understand this better than most. If they want a consensus, they make sure that their supporters attend while their detractors sit at home watching TV unaware a meeting has been called. Of course, the minister or politician in question knew what he wanted decided before calling the meeting.

The quality of a decision hinges on the values and capabilities of the people who make it. While having good information is essential, capable people know where to find and how to use information. The information does not determine what decision is made, people do.

Involve staff in decision making.

As operations manager, Paul has wide-ranging options. He can

- Make the decision himself and direct his staff to carry it out

- Ask his staff to provide information and analysis so that he can make a more informed decision

- Make the decision in consultation with one or more key staff members, asking for recommendations but reserving the decision for himself

- Make the decision with his staff, seeking a consensus of the group

- Delegate authority and responsibility for the decision to a staff member, providing broad guidelines that structure the choice, holding him or her accountable for the outcome

- Delegate the decision to a group of staff, providing broad guidelines that structure their choice, and holding them jointly accountable for the outcome

Paul wants the best decision possible. To do so, he must first decide who, if anyone, among his staff to include in making the decision and how they can contribute most effectively.

Paul decides to make the decision with several of his staff who can improve the quality of the decision. He includes a new staff person to develop her professional skills and identification with the group. He thinks about what each person can contribute to the decision's quality as he makes a list.

Paul includes Charlie and Ron. They approach the problem from different technical backgrounds and perspectives. Charlie is an engineer and Ron is a forester. Charlie is convinced by detailed technical arguments; he is impatient with qualitative data. Ron is more reflective. He trusts experience. When they discuss a problem, their combined perspectives often bring out critical detail and nuances that would not have been apparent from a single perspective, thus improving the quality of the decision. Moreover, both men will be involved in implementation, so their commitment to the group's choice is important.

Betsy Tomlin has been working on a special project for Ron, analyzing the efficiency of Northwest's operations and developing operational plans. Her analysis will enable her to contribute to the decision at hand. In addition, Paul values her ability to quickly identify the critical points in Charlie and Ron's sometimes wide-ranging discussions, separating important issues from interesting detail. This ability to find the common ground provides a basis for Ron and Charlie to trust each other more than they might otherwise. It also strengthens both the group and the decision.

Paul also includes Cindy Avesta, a recent forestry graduate in her first professional position. Participating in this decision will be a good chance for her to learn to appreciate Ron's experience and help her feel more a part of the team. Her recent academic work may make her aware of alternatives and technical information others in the group may not be.

Dick Jordan, a cost accountant in the finance department, is also on Paul's list. Paul invites Dick to department meetings whenever there's the slightest chance accounting may object to a decision. It's better to include them at the outset than deal with their objections after the fact, he reasons. Paul likes to work with Dick. He's an accounting whiz, so his peers listen to his recommendations. Just as importantly, he understands forestry. Dick is more empathetic to production issues than many of his peers. He has worked with Paul's team enough that they trust and rely on his judgment.

Include people for a reason. Ideally, people participate in making a decision because of what they can contribute or gain. When people are invited out of habit or tradition rather than real need, blind commitment or uncritical participation may result. In either case, the group may be an automatic rubber stamp for one person's decisions.

Decisions can be improved simply by reevaluating who participates on a decision-by-decision basis, and inviting people based on what they have to contribute to the decision and the group. Different decisions call for different requirements. Group composition is as varied as the decisions you make. Who you involve depends on the unique combination of creative energy, skills, experience, information, and insight needed, and the mix of these each potential group member possesses.

Include people who will improve decision quality. A clearly defined decision question highlights what is needed to make a wise decision, making it easier to determine who should be involved in the decision. Who is included influences the decision that results. Technically-focused people tend to identify technical solutions. Discipline-bound people prefer discipline-specific alternatives. People-oriented people choose people-centered solutions. Analytic people may find it difficult to make subjective choices, and creative people may disdain analysis.

While these stereotypes do not always apply, individuals come to decision making with their own biases and familiar approaches. Most solutions require both technical and human components. Real solutions generally cross superficial disciplinary and professional boundaries. Few people are equally comfortable generating new, exciting ideas one moment and carefully analyzing their consequences the next—or discussing subjective beliefs and then dealing in hard facts.

The best decisions result when group composition is tailored to the decision at hand and the strengths of the people available. You may include individuals in the group because of their similarity or diversity. A group with similar characteristics increases the precision and accuracy of information considered, enabling greater discrimination among similar alternatives. A diverse group expands the breadth of criteria, alternatives, and information considered, and has the potential to be more creative.

Choose the mix of skills, knowledge, and attributes that will result in the best decision possible. As you consider whom to include, consider the following kinds of contributions:

- Practical or theoretical knowledge of the underlying problem's causes
- Information about the context or alternative solutions
- Understanding of what factors are important to make a wise decision
- In-depth understanding of one or more possible alternatives
- Knowledge of the range of possible alternatives
- Needed skills (analytic, facilitation, human relations, financial)
- Practical experience with the problem or its alternative solutions
- Representation of differences in values

Include people who will implement decisions. Decisions are only effective when they are followed up with timely, purposeful action. Who is included in making a decision influences its implementation in several ways. By including those who will follow through, it is easier to determine whether or not the decision is feasible with the time, technology, equipment, people, and skills available and within budget. These factors are particularly critical when careful coordination is required among several departments or many individuals.

People don't like having decisions dictated to them from above, especially when they think the decision makers don't understand or care about the nuances of implementation. Including those who will coordinate the decision's implementation also generates commitment to the decision and trust in the decision makers' judgment. This commitment and trust can make the difference between half-hearted and enthusiastic implementation. While detractors look for excuses to explain why a decision can't work, a decision's enthusiastic supporters will do what is necessary to make a decision work. *Include individuals to develop their skills or professionalism.* Paul includes Cindy Avesta to develop her professional skills and personal identification with the group. As a new employee and a recent graduate, Cindy needs time to mature in her job and to learn about Northwest. By including Cindy in decision making, Paul can speed up the maturation process and increase her value to the company. Both the company and Cindy benefit.

Several years ago, Paul noticed that Betsy Tomlin intuitively considered small decisions within the broader institutional context. To develop her innate skill, he has included Betsy in many meetings and decisions she wouldn't have been involved in otherwise. Now his investment is paying off. Betsy is handling the department's long-range planning as well as or better than Paul himself could have.

Include people to strengthen the group. In the workplace, employees have a mental picture of the organization's purpose and where they fit in relative to other people. Paul, Betsy, Charlie, Ron, and Cindy more or less know which decisions they can make and which decisions must be handed up to a higher authority.

While Northwest has written statements of goals and purpose, job descriptions, and an organization chart, these documents do not reflect the who and how of decision making. They present the organization as senior management wants others to see it, not necessarily as it is. The company's goals and purpose are apparent in its accumulated accomplishments. Consequently, the company's criteria are constantly unfolding in the choices its employees make.

To the extent that Paul and his staff are confident about what is important to Northwest and in their relationships to each other, shared purpose, trust, and team spirit result. These qualities provide a foundation on which they can make decisions that meet Northwest's immediate objectives and move the organization toward its long-term goals. When group members make decisions together, these qualities are strengthened. The process generates mutual trust, reinforcing the group's commitment to the decision and to each other.

When group members are not confident in their relationships to each other, trust is often lacking. They are surprised and offended when group members do not act or react as expected. Petty professional jealousy and defensive turf protecting can result. They withhold information from each other, impairing their collective ability to make the best decisions. Individual members seek conflicting outcomes, or the group chooses alternatives at cross-purposes to their long-run objectives. While this situation can produce a self-reinforcing downward spiral, it can be turned around by using the framework and process steps to promote understanding.

In part, Paul draws his staff into departmental decisions so that important group qualities are strengthened and renewed. But Paul knows that whether or not the decision-making process results in these positive benefits depends on how the process is handled. A mishandled decision-making process can destroy trust and demoralize team members. He uses the decision-making framework and process to guide group decision making because experience has shown him that these tools make the difference between a process that strengthens the group and one that demoralizes it.

Include people to affirm organizational values. Decision-making groups affirm values in two ways. Organizational values are clarified and affirmed as work groups make choices. These values are demonstrated and made public in the group's shared commitment to the chosen action. An organization's stated values rarely influence individual values as much as constructive interaction in small groups.

A work group's values must be examined and reexamined. As new situations arise, the group examines and adjusts what it thinks is important. When a group does not discuss what is important and why, group members become unwilling to suggest innovative ideas or think critically. Even constructive criticism seems capricious when group members do not share a sense of what is important. Fearing ridicule or rejection, discussion is inhibited. Group members become blinded to innovative ideas and take few risks within the group. Over time, the group becomes a rubber stamp for decisions that have already been made.

While consensus is more readily achieved in groups that share basic values, there is the possibility of discovering new common values or refining old ones when group members hold wider ranging values and perspectives. In organizations like Northwest, staff with close working relationships generally hold similar values. Shared values enable co-workers to agree on core criteria related to work problems much of the time. This agreement provides the basis for commitment to the group and enables its members to commit readily to group decisions.

Groups can, perhaps, have the greatest impact in helping organizations achieve their long-term goals. Groups help organizations discover, clarify, and affirm the values that underlie organizational behavior. Whether formally or informally, groups help instill organizational values in new staff members. This socialization process ensures that organizational behavior reflects an organization's goals and vice versa.

Weigh the benefits and costs of expanding group size. Group decision making provides an opportunity to improve the decision and strengthen team spirit. There are also costs, however, including the real cost of an employee's time. Use of time and energy in decision making precludes other uses. Deciding whether the benefits exceed the costs requires good judgment and common sense. The benefits are likely to exceed the costs when

- The decision is important and the risk is high.
- The problem is poorly understood.
- The consequences are irreversible.
- The status quo is not an option.
- Implementation will require substantial reallocation of resources (e.g., money, people, equipment, processes, information).
- There is shared responsibility among unrelated units, departments, or organizations.
- There is organizational conflict over who is responsible for the problem, decision, and action.

4. How will the meeting be carried out?

Decision-making Group Process Steps

1. What is the decision?

2. Whose decision is it?

3. Who should be involved?

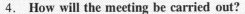

4. **How will the meeting be carried out?**
   - What agenda?
   - When will the meeting be held?
   - Who will facilitate?

5. What is the best alternative given the context?

6. Is the group committed to the alternative selected?

7. What is the next step?

Group decision making is typically coordinated in meetings. Asking how the meeting will be carried out ensures that the costs of including group members is minimized by using their time productively. Most professionals spend a substantial portion of their workday in meetings. Many decision-making meetings fall short of expectations because decisions aren't reached, decisions made aren't acted on, or staff time isn't used wisely.

A group's time and energy are frequently its most valuable resources. Using group members' time effectively is essential to maintain trust and a commitment to work together. While the decision-making framework and process steps help, careful preparation before the meeting and sensitive facilitation of group interaction during the meeting also are essential. In addition to using the frameworks and process steps, an effective decision-making meeting will include four steps.

Announce the meeting in writing.

The meeting announcement answers six basic questions.

What decision? The announcement clearly states the decision question and identifies what the decision needs to accomplish, enabling group members to come to the meeting prepared.

Why is the meeting necessary? The announcement explains the underlying problem that makes the decision necessary. Group members need this information to gather their thoughts about the decision. Explaining why a decision is necessary implicitly communicates that you are willing to share ownership in the problem and its solution. Promoting a sense of ownership now sets the stage to gain commitment for the decision later.

What is known? Make group members aware of relevant background information—what has taken place so far, what issues have been raised, what information is available, and so on. This reduces meeting and preparation time.

When will the meeting begin and end? Clearly stated times for beginning and ending the meeting enable group members to schedule their time efficiently and create a sense of urgency that encourages efficient time use. Organizations that start meetings on time and end meetings as scheduled show respect for their staff members' time. Respect, like trust, encourages commitment.

Who will attend? Knowing who will participate in the decision enables group members to prepare for the meeting together. Group members know each other's strengths and weaknesses. They will prepare differently depending on who is invited. If Charlie isn't invited, Ron will have to bone up on technical relationships between alternatives and outcomes. If Betsy isn't there, Ron will have to come to the meeting prepared to use Betsy's planning data. Listing those who will attend also demonstrates the group leader's willingness to share ownership and trust. Decision-making meetings are most efficient when a small number of people are involved. A larger group makes decision making cumbersome and can make agreement difficult.

Where will the meeting be held? The meeting room cannot ensure effective decision making, but it can preclude a productive meeting. Schedule meetings at a location convenient for the majority of group members. Choose a meeting room that encourages participation—large enough so the group can work around a table. The room should be comfortable, with adequate ventilation, temperature controls, and a clean, neat appearance. Visual aids should be available in the room—chalk board and chalk, flip chart and pens, overhead projector and transparencies, screen, or whatever aids might promote efficient and effective decision making.

Tell all group members what is expected of them.

Meetings are more efficient and the decisions reached show greater wisdom when group members come prepared, knowing what they are expected to contribute. Depending on the nature of the decision, preparation may require more or less effort—gathering data, analyzing it, or identifying alternatives.

The person calling the meeting reasonably can expect that group members will gather their thoughts about the problem and decision before the meeting. In return, group members can reasonably expect that their participation will contribute positively to the decision. In organizations where people are routinely invited to decision-making meetings without being asked to contribute, groups typically automatically approve decisions that have already been made and perceive preparation as a waste of time. In organizations where group members routinely come to meetings unprepared, staff time is wasted in unproductive meetings and decisions are often less effective.

Provide all group members with an agenda.

The agenda clearly states what is to be accomplished and lists all items to be discussed in the order they will be considered. The agenda is a plan that lays out how the meeting's purpose will be met. If a meeting has more than one purpose, each purpose is listed and priorities noted. An agenda sets boundaries for the discussion. An agenda gives group members a standard to judge the relevance of their ideas, opinions, and information to the task at hand. An agenda also gives the facilitator a rallying point to encourage constructive contributions and discourage unproductive digression from the meeting's purpose.

Facilitate the meeting.

Facilitation guides group interaction, moving the group from one process step to the next, making sure that the group completes each task before addressing the next, and encouraging discussion relevant to the decision before the group. The facilitator encourages all group members to participate and discourages those who attempt to dominate the decision-making process. The facilitator allocates meeting time, continually moving the group forward until the decision is made and productive tasks are assigned.

A facilitator asks questions that direct group attention to the steps required to complete the task—in this case, decision making. The facilitator clarifies, rephrases, and reflects on member response. The facilitator tracks progress and summarizes what has taken place at key points. He or she can invite participation from reluctant members, support fledgling ideas, probe promising lines of thought, and identify relationships between ideas as they come up.

The role of facilitator often falls to the individual responsible for the decision. However, this is not always the case nor is it always best. Someone else may be formally assigned to the task. In the absence of a designated facilitator, a group member often facilitates, unconscious of the role he or she plays.

5. What is the best alternative given the context?

Decision-making Group Process Steps

1. What is the decision?

2. Whose decision is it?

3. Who should be involved?

4. How will the meeting be carried out?

5. **What is the best alternative given the context?**
   - List criteria without discussion.
   - Discuss and refine criteria.
   - Rank criteria in order of importance.
   - List alternatives without discussion.
   - Refine alternatives.
   - Review criteria and alternatives.
   - Predict probable effects.
   - Choose the best alternative for each criterion.
   - Choose the best alternative.

6. Is the group committed to the alternative selected?

7. What is the next step?

Paul has very thoughtfully decided whom to invite and what the meeting's agenda will be. He circulates the meeting announcement (figure 5.1).

MEMORANDUM

DATE: September 19, 1993

TO: Cindy Avesta   Dick Jordan   Betsy Tomlin
              Ron Hastings   Charles Reynolds

FROM: Paul Hartner, Forest Operations Manager

SUBJECT: Washed-out logging road

The Problem: A logging road has washed out, dumping sediment into a branch stream that flows into the Powder River, a state-designated salmon stream. Another section of road may slide with the next heavy rain. The state has fined Northwest $5000 and threatens legal action and additional fines if Northwest does not take action to prevent the erosion.

Background Information: I have spoken with Charlie, Ron, and Betsy about the problem. Charlie recommends bringing the road up to state standards. Ron recommends that we rethink whether or not we need the road at this time. Betsy indicates we will not need the road to haul out logs for 15–20 years. There is an alternate access route maintenance crews could use in the interim. To make a decision, we will consider present and future needs, costs, and state regulations.

You may recall that the state Forest Practices Act sets standards for logging roads. While all new road construction must meet standards, there is a grandfather clause for existing roads. We have five years to bring existing roads up to standard. "Major repairs" cannot be undertaken unless all the road is brought up to standards. However, the definition of "major repairs" is fuzzy.

Northwest has 60 days to address the problem. However, the state inspector has threatened a second fine if there is another slide in the interim.

Meeting Purpose: We will focus on the broader question raised by Ron. What is the best means to reduce erosion from the branch creek road to levels that comply with state regulations and minimize costs? This decision will be our only agenda item.

Time and Location: Please plan on meeting Tuesday at 9 A.M. in the map room. The meeting will last no later than 10:30.

Preparation: Please come to the meeting prepared with ideas and information. I will contact each of you before Thursday to discuss in more detail what you can contribute to the decision and how you can prepare for the meeting.

Thank you for your cooperation. I look forward to a productive meeting.

Figure 5.1. The memorandum that was circulated before the meeting.

Paul starts the meeting. "Thank you for coming. I appreciate your willingness to help us make this very important decision. I know you are busy this time of the year, so we will conclude the meeting promptly at 10:30." He restates the meeting's purpose and asks whether everyone understands and agrees with the meeting's primary objective—to choose a strategy to deal with the branch creek situation. He reviews the immediate objectives—reducing erosion to comply with state regulations and minimizing cost—and the long-term goals—maintaining profitability, corporate flexibility, and goodwill in the community.

Charlie responds, "Does this mean that we're back where we started—deciding whether or not we need a road?" Paul says, "We're not back where we started. We have a road in place—a road with serious problems. At the same time, we won't start with the assumption that the road must be repaired whatever the cost. We will consider a full range of alternatives. However, I would like to wait to discuss their advantages and disadvantages until we have a complete list of alternatives. Do you mind, Charlie?" Charlie is familiar with the decision-making framework and process so he knows that there will be ample time to discuss alternatives later. He defers.

Paul restates the meeting purpose. "We will focus on the broader question: What is the best means to reduce erosion from the branch creek road to levels that comply with state regulations and minimize cost?"

Paul reviews the decision-making framework and process. He reminds the group that while there will be plenty of opportunity for discussion and input, they are going to go through a logical sequence of steps. Paul reserves the right to structure and guide the discussion so that the group stays on task and progresses to a decision in the time allotted.

List criteria without discussion.

Paul asks for criteria. Criteria are subjective. If everyone participates, the list will include what each person thinks is important. If only a few participate, the list will reflect what those individuals think is important.

To encourage everyone to contribute, Paul instructs the group. "List criteria, but do not discuss them. When the list is complete—when no one has anything to add—we will discuss and refine our criteria." Paul adds, "At this point, don't worry if the list is too long or criteria conflict. Also, don't worry about clarifying what you mean. We'll sort out meaning later."

Paul continues, "By listing all criteria before discussion begins, each of you has the opportunity to contribute to the list with confidence that your creativity will be respected and your ideas accepted. If you choose not to contribute to the list, I will take that to mean that you have nothing to add."

Paul concludes his remarks, reminding the group that he will not accept any discussion of criteria before the list is complete. "We all have a tendency to explain ourselves. Please don't take it personally if I cut you off when you explain too much. There is a fine line between explaining and justifying. If we get into a discussion before the list is complete, some people won't get a chance to add their criteria to the list."

Group members tend to list a criterion and discuss it, list a criterion and discuss it, discussing each criterion as it is placed on the list. The facilitator's job is to separate the creative listing of criteria from the critical discussion. Nothing stifles creativity faster than criticism, no matter how constructive.

When group members discuss each criterion as it is listed, one or two individuals come to dominate the discussion. Domination by a vocal few inhibits participation by others. Those who dominate may want to make sure the group chooses their alternative. They may dominate through the strength of their conviction, consciously or unconsciously railroading the group by making sure their criteria top the list. Other times, those who dominate are articulate and knowledgeable people who don't realize that their confident domination inhibits others from participating. Those who dominate may simply be rude, interrupting, rambling, and digressing from the point at hand. Whatever its causes, domination has the same effect. Would-be participants fail to share and do not contribute to the decision at hand. At the least, their time has not been used wisely. At the worst, the quality of the decision suffers because silence is mistakenly interpreted as agreement and creative ideas are missed.

Paul asks for criteria. As criteria are listed, Paul writes them on a flip chart. He asks Ron to start the list. Ron begins, "I think the decision should hinge on two factors. When will we need the road to haul logs out and what is the cost to repair the road now compared to building a new road when we need it?" Charlie interrupts. "It's not that simple, Ron. You can't just abandon a logging road and assume that the problem is solved."

Before Ron can respond, Paul intercedes. "We're listing criteria right now. We'll get to the analysis soon enough." He turns to Cindy. "Can you restate the criteria Ron just listed?" Cindy answers, "Timing of harvest and cost of repairing the road now compared to later." Paul turns to Ron. "Do you agree with Cindy's interpretation?" Ron nods.

Paul turns to Charlie. "Is there a criterion implied in your last statement?" Charlie starts to explain his statement in detail, saying the costs of abandoning the road will surely exceed any savings, especially if you consider fire access. Paul starts, "Charlie, I understand your impatience, but let's try to stay on task here. Can we hold the analysis until we've constructed the matrix? Do you want me to add fire access to the criteria list?" Charlie nods.

Paul turns to Cindy, who is sitting beside Ron. "What criteria would you include?" She adds meeting state regulations to the list. She asks about interim access. "How will maintenance crews get access to the areas served by the branch creek road for brush removal and pest control if we abandon it?" Paul thanks Cindy and turns to Dick.

Dick starts, "We have to consider two kinds of costs, the initial investment and recurring maintenance costs. We need to make the comparison using net present value rather than today's dollars." Paul interrupts, "Can we hold the discussion of analytic method for later? Do you have any additional criteria, Dick?" He shakes his head, so Paul turns to Charlie.

Charlie adds criteria that constrain the timing of implementation—heavy equipment and crew availability. Paul thanks Charlie and nods to Betsy.

She replies, "It seems to me that we should be concerned about Northwest's image in the community. This is an opportunity to demonstrate that Northwest is concerned about the environmental impact of its operations."

Paul reads the list of criteria from the flip chart:

- access to haul mature logs out of the sites that the road serves
- cost—initial and recurring
- fire access
- meeting state regulations
- access to controlling and thinning weeds
- equipment/crew availability
- goodwill
- access for brush removal and pest control

"Before we begin the discussion, do you want to add any criteria?" Betsy laughs, "Haven't we forgotten an important one? What about reducing erosion!?!" Paul chuckles, "You're right. That's why we called the meeting, isn't it?"

Discuss and refine criteria.

When the group stops offering criteria, Paul asks a series of questions to help the group evaluate and refine their criteria.

- Are there important criteria that are not on the list?
- Do the criteria listed describe what you think is important? What is important to the company? Are any of the criteria trivial? If so, cross them out.
- Do criteria overlap? Can you combine overlapping criteria?
- Are there criteria that are too broad and need to be stated more narrowly or too narrow and need to be stated more broadly?
- Are multiple criteria masquerading as one? Can you split them in two?
- Can you restate any criteria to make them more easily understood?

Dick Jordan remarks, "I agree that the timing of our need to get into the areas served by the branch creek road is critical. However, the issue is really timing of costs rather than timing of needs. If we analyze both the costs and timing of costs using net present values, we can eliminate timing of need as a criterion." Paul starts to cross off need.

Betsy interrupts, "Wait a minute, Paul. When you start rolling up qualitative factors like need into quantitative benefit-cost calculations, you run the risk of forgetting how important need is. Frankly, I don't trust numbers to highlight the importance of needs. I'd feel a whole lot more comfortable leaving it in."

Turning to Betsy, Dick queries, "It's my understanding that the earliest we will need that road for harvest access is 30 years from now. Is that right?" Betsy indicates the branch creek road serves naturally regenerated and replanted stands ranging from 20 to 35 years in age. "Assuming it takes 50 to 55 years to reach harvest age, we'll begin harvesting in 15 to 20 years. We won't need interim access for brush removal and pest control. But fire access is a major issue." Paul crosses out access for brush removal.

Dick questions, "Is the issue meeting state standards or avoiding fines? There can be a big difference." Paul adds, "The standards issue is further complicated when you compare the state standards that apply to us today with the standards that will apply to us when the regulations are fully in effect five years from now. And we can expect even tighter standards as time goes on."

Answering Dick's question, Ron asserts, "First, I think we should be concerned with the standards rather than avoiding fines. Second, I think we need to treat standards as two distinct criteria: meeting today's standards and meeting the standards five years from now when the regulations will be applied to existing roads. The state's timetable for enforcing standards should influence our choice."

Charlie says, "I'd like to get back to reducing erosion. Doesn't that overlap with meeting state standards? The state sets standards for roads. If we meet those standards, the effect should be reduced erosion."

Paul explains, "As usual, it's not that simple. There are two sets of standards: turbidity standards for the Powder River and construction standards for logging roads. Even if we meet the construction standards, we may not meet the turbidity requirements. If we can successfully claim that our repairs are not major, the road standards won't apply to the branch creek road for five years. However, I don't think Sid Riedel will let us get away with a band-aid approach. With the Powder River designated as a salmon stream, he's going to hold our feet to the fire on erosion—even if we meet the road standards now. I think we had better keep reducing soil erosion on the list."

"I don't know about anyone else," Charlie continues, "but I have a problem with reducing erosion as a criterion. How much do we have to reduce erosion? Do we have to eliminate it entirely? How much reduction is enough?"

This time Ron responds, "That's a good question, Charlie. Unfortunately, we don't know how much reduction is enough. Sid is going to enforce the state's turbidity standard on the Powder River. The standard indicates the maximum acceptable level. However, we're not the only ones who contribute sediment to the river. It's unclear how much of the river's sedimentation problem we cause, so it's not obvious how much reduction is enough." At this point, Dick joins the discussion. "Let's reword the criterion—reducing erosion to a level sufficient to avoid fines."

Clenching his jaw, Ron argues, "Let me restate what I think you mean. What's important is avoiding fines, not soil erosion." Dick nods his head hesitantly, thinking about what Ron is saying. Ron continues, "I have to confess that if that's the case, I'm disappointed. I thought Northwest was concerned about erosion. I'm not so naive as to believe that Northwest can prevent erosion entirely, but I find it hard to believe that we have no concern at all. If you carry that logic to an extreme, we could consider the fines a cost of doing business and simply include them in our cost analysis."

Seeing emotions rise, Paul starts to interrupt. But before he can say anything, Betsy speaks: "I've been with this firm for ten years. Northwest is concerned about erosion and not just to avoid fines. The firm was concerned about erosion when there were no standards. On the practical side, we've always had to weigh our concern against the financial returns. Generally, we've kept erosion at acceptable levels. We're dealing with an exception here. We all know that the design work on the branch creek road was faulty. The road should never have been built so close to the stream bed. I have to concur with Ron. I think the criteria should reflect Northwest's long-standing corporate values. I don't think we should change our values simply because our values are difficult to apply to the situation at hand. Reducing erosion is important for its own sake."

Paul surveys the group. Confronted with the truth of Betsy's assessment, each one nods agreement. Reducing soil erosion is kept on the list.

Rank criteria in order of importance.

Moving on, Paul says, "Before we continue our discussion, please take a moment to rank the criteria in order of their importance."

He gives the group a couple of minutes to quickly jot down their rankings. Then Paul begins, "Tell me what order you would rank these criteria?" Going around the table, he asks each person to share their rankings. He records the rankings on a flip chart.

Paul asks for discussion, saying, "Based on what you see, is this relatively important or unimportant?" The group discusses the relative importance of each criterion separately, ignoring for a moment the differences in their rankings. As group members talk, Paul takes notes. When they have discussed each one, Paul asks, "Does anyone want to change their rankings?" Paul takes a breath, and continues, "Now comes the hard part—reconciling our rankings. Which criterion do we as a group think is most important? Second most important? Third? And so on."

Dick starts, "It seems to me that the critical issue is timing of costs. When do we need that road to harvest logs? Second, is it cheaper to repair and maintain the road now or abandon the road now and build a new one later?"

Disagreeing, Ron contends, "I think reducing soil erosion should be at the top of the list. If it's not, how can we ensure that the alternative we choose will reduce soil erosion enough?" Charlie jumps into the discussion, "That's the million dollar question. How much reduction is enough? What kind of criterion is reducing soil erosion if we don't know how much is enough?" Ron responds, "That's precisely why I want reducing soil erosion at the top of the list. If we don't give it highest priority, we'll make the decision solely based on financial analysis of the timing of costs and financial returns. We'll meet state standards because we have to, not out of any real commitment."

Dick responds, "Ron, I'll accept reducing erosion at the top of the list, if you'll accept timing and cost next." Ron agrees. Paul turns to Charlie, "Is that order acceptable to you?" Charlie nods. Paul goes around the table. "Cindy?" "Betsy?"

When the discussion seems to be complete, Paul reads the ranked list.

Ranked Criteria

1. reducing soil erosion
2. initial and recurring cost
3. fire access
4. meeting state regulations
5. need for access at harvest
6. crew and equipment availability to do road work
7. improving image in the community

Then he goes around the table asking each one, "Does this reflect your understanding of Northwest's priorities?" The group agrees.

It is tempting to put criteria and rankings to a vote. If a majority agrees, include a criterion. If a majority lists a criterion first, it is most important. Voting is a technique that ensures that the majority's will prevails. However, majority rule does not assure good decisions. When the majority rules, an experienced person's contribution is weighted no differently than someone who is hearing about the issue for the first time.

Decisions made by majority vote can also lead to difficulties during implementation. A reluctant minority can derail the majority's decision to act even if the majority is right. This understanding of owning solutions underlies the more participatory styles of management, policy making, and action implementation.

Agreeing on how to rank criteria in the face of strong disagreement requires gentle leadership. Paul keeps the erosion problem before the group, constantly reminding them that they must take action. He provides leadership through his questions, subtly helping the group refine and rank criteria. While his questions shape criteria, he does not manipulate the list. To manipulate would negate the benefit of group decision making. Where individuals differ, he encourages them to explain why they think a criterion is more or less important. While they may never fully agree, they are more likely to accept an alternative other than the one they prefer if they understand the basis for the choice.

Sometimes group members need time away from the group to think through what is important before they can come to an agreement. If that had been useful, Paul could have concluded the meeting at this point and scheduled a second meeting to decide how to rank criteria and proceed. Many times differences are resolved relatively easily after group members have time alone to think.

List alternatives without discussion.

The next step is generating alternatives. This is a creative step. While old and favorite alternatives are sure to be listed, this step gives group members an opportunity to come up with new, unusual, or untried ideas. Now is the time to brainstorm. List ideas without discussing their merit. Be creative. Other members of the group can add to an idea, offer variations, or come up with new ones.

Accept and affirm all ideas regardless of their worth. Even the most innocently offered, critical statements will inhibit the group's creativity. Anything perceived as judgmental will lead group members to protect their egos, defending rather than generating ideas.

Sometimes ideas erupt like popcorn. Other times, the group is slow to visualize how other alternatives could meet their objectives. When a group can't generate alternatives, the facilitator may need to go around the group, asking each person for ideas. It is important to keep the flow of ideas going. Record each idea in a brief phrase on a flip chart or chalkboard. This public record often spurs the group to new ideas and helps structure discussion later. Now let's go back to Northwest Forest Products and the decision at hand.

Paul asks for alternatives. He reminds the group, "Right now, we are listing alternatives. So please, no discussion." The group lists three alternatives.

- Bring the road up to state standards now.
- Do temporary repairs now and bring the road up to state standards in five years as required by the state.
- Abandon the road now and build a new road when access is needed to harvest sites served by the road.

Before moving to discussion, Paul asks, "Have we got them all up? Let's take a minute and review the list for additions."

A group sometimes gets stuck and cannot generate alternatives. As individuals and groups, we have mental blocks that make it difficult to think any differently than we already do. There are several techniques that help individuals get past these mental blocks. Questions can help the group think differently about the possible alternatives.

- Have you seen the same problem in a slightly different form? In the same context? In a different context? Do you know of related problems in the same context? In a different context?

- How were those problems solved? Could you use those solutions? Could you use elements of those solutions? Could you learn from their results or their methods?

For example, a group in the Mississippi River Delta was trying to decide what they could do to improve the quality of education in their area. While they knew improving education was the key to unlocking the region's potential, they were at a loss about what they could do. They determined to look for ideas in the education reform programs that had been carried out in other low-income areas of the country. After several phone calls, they discovered an organization in the Appalachian region of Kentucky that had developed innovative education reform programs that were making a tangible difference. The Delta group realized, however, that the Delta differs from Appalachia in one very important aspect: In the Delta, the differences between the educated and uneducated are a partial result of racism. They adapted the program ideas they had seen in Kentucky to conditions in the Delta and ended up with a wide range of alternatives to choose from.

Sometimes these questions will not bring out additional alternatives. The group may have to redefine the problem itself.

- Can you identify alternatives to a closely related problem? Can you redefine the problem so that alternatives are more apparent? A more general problem? A more narrowly defined problem? Can you identify alternatives to solve part of the problem? Can you restate the objectives so that alternatives become apparent?

- If you still cannot identify alternatives, consider what caused the problem. Do you understand cause and effect? Is there a chain of events that caused the problem? At what point are you intervening in the chain? Can you define the problem so that you intervene at a different point in the causal chain?

When the group just can't think of any alternatives, it may help to redefine the problem from a different angle. An example illustrates how redefining a problem can make it easier to identify alternatives. A community organization wanted to help low-income women get jobs. They determined that lack of child care was the reason low-income women weren't working. Asked to generate a list of alternative ways they could meet these low-income women's child-care needs, they could identify only one alternative—open a day-care center.

They opened a day-care center. It quickly went broke and closed. The women they had hoped to assist still weren't working. Instead of giving up, the group decided to try once again to figure out what they could do. This time they looked at the problem from a different angle, listing alternatives that would reduce the cost of child care. They came up with the following list of alternatives:

- Create a sponsorship program, inviting community businesses to provide scholarships for children of working, low-income mothers at existing day-care centers. The group could act as a clearinghouse to evaluate mothers' needs and award scholarships.

- Help a local church to organize a day-care center for children of low-income mothers. The church already has the facilities and does not have to pay rent. This cost savings can be passed on to mothers.

- Create a directory and referral service to help low-income mothers find inexpensive, quality in-home child care. Child care in babysitters' homes often is less expensive than at a day-care center.

- Help a local factory, which is the largest employer of low-income women, open an on-site, subsidized day care.

- Organize a cooperative of local day cares so that they can purchase their food and supplies, purchase liability and health insurance, and process payroll jointly. By pooling these functions, they will reduce their operating costs, which they can pass on as a special credit to qualified, low-income working mothers. The cooperative could process and evaluate applications for the special credit.

- Encourage the local school district to develop school-based day-care centers for preschool children, offering subsidized rates to qualified, low-income mothers.

As long as they looked at the problem from the angle of day-care availability, they could see no other alternatives. When they looked at another facet of availability—reducing its cost—they had no problem generating alternatives.

Examining familiar alternatives can help group members identify additional alternatives or expand existing ideas to find alternatives with a new twist. Ask yourself, "Can I put something to a new use? Can I increase, decrease, or substitute? Can I rearrange, combine, or adapt?"

Refine alternatives.

Paul reads the list of alternatives and calls for discussion. There are three alternatives on the list.

- Bring the road up to state standards now.
- Do temporary repairs now and bring the road up to state standards in five years as required by the state.
- Abandon the road now and build a new road when access is needed to harvest sites served by the road.

To focus the discussion, Paul asks the following questions.

Is the list complete?
Are there multiple alternatives masquerading as one? Pull them apart.
Are there alternatives that can be combined? Put them together.
Are the alternatives straightforward? Clarify them.

Paul looks over the list. Betsy points out two different ways to abandon the road. "We can abandon the road and do the minimum amount of grading necessary to prevent further slides. Or we can restore the roadbed to its former condition—planting grass and trees and other streamside restoration." Paul adds another alternative to the list on the flip chart.

Abandon and restore the streamside roadbed to its former condition now, and build a new road 15 to 20 years from now when the area is ready to harvest.

"Can we clarify what 'temporary' means?" asks Charlie. "There are temporary repairs that last a couple of years, and there are temporary repairs that last until the next heavy rain. What kind of temporary are we talking about? Cost figures are meaningless without specifications."

"Charlie's right. 'Temporary repairs' is too vague," Ron answers. "I don't think it makes much sense to consider temporary repairs if we have to grade every time it rains. Erosion will certainly be a continuing problem." Charlie says, "Let's at the least consider a culvert and minimal roadbed work."

When the discussion slows, Paul asks, "Are you satisfied with the four alternatives listed here? If so, can we proceed?" Since no one speaks, Paul continues.

Review criteria and alternatives.

Paul asks the group to look over the alternatives and the criteria.

Are there any obvious revisions?
Do we need additional criteria given the alternatives?
Are the criteria and alternatives specific enough to predict consequences?

Charlie reminds the group, "If we do 'major' repairs, we're obligated to bring the road up to standard right away—whatever the state means by 'major.'" Cindy asks, "If we do extensive temporary repairs, what happens if the state considers our temporary repairs major?"

"Yeh," Charlie answers, "that's a good question. The statutes don't give us an answer, and there is no precedent yet. I'm not sure we want to be a test case."

Ron raises another issue. "I'm not sure what difference it makes. But I feel uncomfortable trying to anticipate what the costs of rebuilding a road will be 15 to 20 years from now. I feel just as uncomfortable assuming that particular road will be needed. I've heard headquarters is trying to negotiate a land swap right now that would give us easier access to the branch creek area. If the rumors are accurate, we may never rebuild the branch creek road."

Paul responds cautiously. "I am aware that the company is trying to initiate negotiations, but we are a long way from any agreement. I don't want to make any assumptions that we might regret later, so I'm not prepared to ignore the costs of rebuilding. On the other hand, it seems reasonable to keep this in the back of our minds and discuss it again after we've completed our initial analysis."

Looking at his watch, Paul says, "If there is no more discussion, let's move on. Does this table (5.1) reflect the structure of our decision so far?"

Table 5.1. The group's decision matrix

Ranked criteria	Temporary culvert now: meet standards in 5 years	Meet road standards now	Grade now and abandon; rebuild road in 20 years	Grade, grass, and abandon now; rebuild road in 20 years
Reduce erosion				
Minimize cost				
Provide access at harvest				
Comply with standards • road • turbidity				
Maintain fire access				
Make crew/ equipment available				
Enhance or maintain image				

Predict probable effects.

Paul asks, "What is the expected effect of each alternative on each criterion?" This is an objective question that calls for a critical response. The group uses the best information available. The quality of their analysis depends on the group's understanding of cause and effect, their access to information, and the time available. In many cases, a decision must be made before a meeting's close. Then, the quality of information group members carry in their heads and how well they prepared for the meeting determine the quality of the decision.

Paul's group has prepared because Paul expects everyone invited to participate in a decision to come prepared. His impatience with staff who don't prepare is widely known. Nearly everyone who works with Paul appreciates him for it.

In preparing for the meeting, Dick put together cost analyses for three of the four alternatives. He hadn't anticipated the fourth. In the process, he gathered engineering specifications from Charlie and operational plans from Betsy and Ron.

Handing out the completed analysis, he describes his analytic method. "Costs include initial investment and maintenance over a 20-year period. I compared the net present value of total costs. Net present value is a measure of how much Northwest would have to invest today to ensure that there is enough to cover expenses as needed over the 20-year period. Net present value lets us take into account the timing of costs and simplifies comparison. We only have to compare one net present value of total cost for each alternative."

With help from the group, Dick estimates the total cost and net present value for the fourth alternative—restoring the abandoned road to its natural state and rebuilding the road later. The group ranks net present value of costs from least expensive (1) to most expensive (4) for ease of comparison, knowing that the actual analysis is available if needed.

Betsy brings draft operational plans for the sites currently served by the branch creek road and detailed topographical maps of the area. In preparation for the meeting, Ron studied the state regulations for salmon streams and Charlie studied state standards for logging roads.

The group fills in the matrix with information at hand. Some effects are easy to predict; others are more difficult because of conflicting information, uncertainty about the information's quality, or lack of information. Paul puts question marks beside information that is questionable. Table 5.2 shows the decision matrix filled in.

Their filled-in matrix might have been different if Dick, Betsy, Charlie, and Ron had not prepared for the meeting. If they had ranked the alternatives based on quick estimates calculated at the meeting, the cost analysis might have pointed to a different alternative. If they had less knowledge of state standards, another approach might have looked more attractive.

Choose the best alternative for each criterion.

Paul asks which alternative is preferred to reduce erosion. The group quickly agrees that abandoning the road and restoring the road bed is the preferred choice. Bringing the existing road up to state standards is the second best choice in the short run. In the longer run, abandoning the road and allowing natural regeneration is the second best choice.

Paul asks which alternative is preferred to minimize cost. In this case, the preferred alternative is obvious: Abandoning the road and allowing natural regeneration is the cheapest alternative. Abandoning the road and restoring it to its natural state is the second cheapest alternative.

Table 5.2. The decision matrix with effects filled in

Ranked criteria	Temporary culvert now: meet standards in 5 years	Meet road standards now	Grade now and abandon; rebuild road in 20 years	Grade, grass, and abandon now; rebuild road in 20 years
Reduce erosion	Erosion may still contribute too much sediment to Powder	Erosion should be reduced to minimum acceptable	Erosion may be a problem for 1–2 years until natural regeneration controls	Erosion may be a problem until grass well established; good erosion control stabilizes area; then after 6–9 months erosion control good
Minimize cost	3	4—most expensive	1—cheapest	2—??
Provide access at harvest	flexibility good	greatest flexibility	flexibility limited	flexibility limited
Comply with standards road	???—state could consider repairs "major"	yes	yes	yes
turbidity	almost certainly won't meet standards	??—probably will meet standards	probably will meet standards	almost certainly will meet standards
Maintain fire access	yes	yes	no—but could get access through adjacent property land swap—???	no—but could get access through adjacent property land swap—???
Make crew/ equipment available	10 days w/ interim grading immediately	In 90 days w/interim grading immediately	10 days w/interim grading immediately	10 days for grading; 60 days for restoration
Enhance or maintain image	Community may think NW being uncooperative	Will maintain image	Will maintain image	Could improve image

As Paul circles the ranked alternatives for each criterion, it becomes obvious that some criteria differentiate among alternatives more than others. If the effect on a criterion is the same regardless of which alternative is chosen, that criterion will not affect the outcome. For example, three of the four alternatives will meet the state's new road standards. Crew and equipment availability is not an issue because in each case interim work can be done immediately. In contrast, effects on erosion, turbidity standards, cost, fire access, and the company's image do differentiate among alternatives. These are the criterion that ultimately will determine which alternative is chosen (table 5.3).

Choose the best alternatives. Is there sufficient information to choose? When the group has decided which alternative is best for each criterion, the group must determine if there is sufficient information to proceed with a choice. They can make this determination one of two ways. They can determine how much additional information would improve the quality of the decision, asking

- Will additional information change the result?
- Is additional information available?
- How accessible is it? Who has it? What will it cost? How long will it take?
- Is it worth postponing the choice and incurring the cost to get more information?

Alternatively, Paul can test the adequacy of the information by asking the group to choose. If they appear to be comfortable with the information available and reach consensus readily, additional information is probably unnecessary. Preferring not to postpone a decision, Paul chooses this strategy. He asks, "Is there an alternative we can all agree on?"

What additional information is needed to make a choice? The discussion that follows indicates there is no obvious choice. Each alternative has problems. The first alternative may not meet state regulations, and its cost is third highest. Meeting state road standards now is the most expensive alternative. With the third alternative, there may be continuing erosion problems for a year or two. Access to fight fires is limited; however, it is the lowest cost alternative. The fourth alternative reduces erosion most quickly and effectively; however, it costs more than may be necessary and eliminates fire access.

Table 5.3. The decision matrix showing best alternative by criterion

Ranked criteria	Temporary culvert now: meet standards in 5 years	Meet road standards now	Grade now and abandon; rebuild road in 20 years	Grade, grass, and abandon now; rebuild road in 20 years
Reduce erosion	Erosion may still contribute too much sediment to Powder (4)	Erosion should be reduced to minimum acceptable (1)	Erosion may be a problem for 1–2 years until natural regeneration controls (3)	Erosion may be a problem until grass well established; good erosion control stabilizes area; then after 6–9 months erosion control good (2)
Minimize cost	(3)	(4)—most expensive	(1)—cheapest	(2)—??
Provide access at harvest	flexibility good (2)	greatest flexibility (1)	flexibility limited (3)	flexibility limited (3)
Comply with standards	(2)	(1)	(1)	(1)
road	???—state could consider repairs "major"	yes	yes	yes
turbidity	almost certainly won't meet standards (3)	??—probably will meet standards (2)	probably will meet standards (2)	almost certainly will meet standards (1)
Maintain fire access	yes (1)	yes (1)	no—but could get access (2) through adjacent property land swap—???	no—but could get access (2) through adjacent property land swap—???
Make crew/ equipment available	10 days w/ interim grading immediately (1)	In 90 days w/interim grading immediately (1)	10 days w/interim grading immediately (1)	10 days for grading; 60 days for restoration (1)
Enhance or maintain image	Community may think NW being uncooperative (3)	Will maintain image (2)	Will maintain image (2)	Could improve image (1)

Paul asks, "What additional information do we need to make a decision?" Charlie begins, "If we make the decision based on the matrix before us, we'll likely abandon the road. Yet maintaining access to control fires is a key issue. I think maybe we need to give it higher priority."

"What's the probability of a fire in this area in any given year?" Cindy asks. Betsy answers, "About once every five years we have a fire in that area, but only about a third of those are likely to become major losses." Cindy continues, "I haven't been with Northwest long enough to know. What's our policy on fire? How much risk are we willing to take?"

Ron answers sarcastically, "We don't have one. We fight them all." Cindy apologizes, "I'm probably asking too many questions. All of you know the answers. Sorry." Paul responds, "No, they're good questions. Continue." Cindy asks, "Is there alternate access to those timber stands other than the branch creek road?" Betsy responds, "There is another fire road, but it's hard to get to and it hasn't been well maintained. Then there's the possibility of the land swap—which would give us good fire access."

Ron joins the conversation. "The issue before us is a tricky one. For years, we've treated fire access as a constraint. We haven't abandoned roads because we assume that maintaining fire access outweighs all other considerations. As a result, we've ignored some of our more serious erosion problems. The state has brought the erosion issue to our attention, and they're telling us we have to deal with it. Yet I've just listened to a conversation that is leading us down a worn and familiar path. We're about to decide that maintaining fire access outweighs everything else once again." Ron pauses. Paul asks, "What do you suggest, Ron?"

"I think we have enough information to make a decision. We said reducing soil erosion is the most important decision criterion this time. Let's act on that basis. Besides, I think there's a good chance that the land swap is going to happen. I propose that we experiment. Let's abandon the branch creek road. It's our most serious erosion problem. At the same time, let's appoint a study group to look at the fire policy. The committee can make recommendations about how much fire risk is reasonable for the firm to take. If the land swap falls through, we can consider improvements to the alternate access road."

Decoupling related decisions. Leadership is needed at this point. While the fire policy issue is closely related to the decision before the group, it is off track. Paul is aware that Northwest foresters have been talking informally for years about the need for a carefully thought-out fire policy. He quickly acknowledges and deals with the digression. Then he gently brings the group back to the task at hand. Other times, he might ignore the digression entirely.

He starts, "The study committee is a good idea, Ron. I will set an agenda and appoint a committee later this week. I need to remind you, however, that while I have some influence over the firm's fire policy, I don't have the authority to establish policy. I will bring the committee's recommendations to the chief executive officer. And while I agree that a land swap could solve the fire access problem, that too is out of my control. But I do not think it is practical to put off a decision at this point."

Paul continues, "If possible, we need to make a decision before we close. We have 15 minutes remaining." He goes around the table, seeking the consensus of the group. "What do you think about Ron's proposal? Should we abandon or repair the road?" There is strong support for using the branch creek road as a trial.

Again Paul provides leadership, pushing the group to make a decision that can be implemented. "We can abandon the road in two ways. Which is better?"

- Do the minimum grading necessary and leave the road to natural regeneration. With this option, we expect to get erosion under control in one to two years.
- Do more extensive grading and restore the area to its natural state. With this option, we expect to get erosion more or less under control by fall this year.

Ron asks Dick the difference in cost between the two alternatives. Dick answers, "I didn't anticipate this alternative so I am just guessing. The additional cost of grass and seedlings will probably be $200 or so an acre. There will be some additional site preparation but not that much. Most of the cost of abandoning the road is rebuilding a new one in 20 years."

Betsy speaks, "If we're using this as a test case, let's go all the way and do it right. I recommend that we do whatever grade work is necessary and grass the abandoned road so that we get maximum reduction in soil erosion as quickly as possible."

6. Is the group committed to this course of action?

Decision-making Group Process Steps

1. What is the decision?

2. Whose decision is it?

3. Who should be involved?

4. How will the meeting be carried out?

5. What is the best alternative given the context?

6. **Is the group committed to this course of action?**
   • Adjust to disagreements.

7. What is the next step?

Paul states Betsy's recommendation as a trial choice. "Grading the branch creek road and restoring it to its natural state is the best choice." He quickly adds, "This isn't a precedent for similar decisions that may arise, but a trial to see how Northwest might balance the need to control erosion against the need to protect against fire damage."

Paul asks for a commitment from the group. Ron says, "I can buy that." Charlie adds, "I hope we don't forget about protecting those timber stands from fire. I'd like to amend the decision so that we explicitly recommend forming the fire policy study committee and providing alternate fire access to those stands." Paul restates the agreement. Cindy nods. Betsy and Dick agree.

Implementation depends on commitment to the decisions made. Acceptance of a particular course of action is the first step to commitment. When silence is mistakenly taken for acceptance, half-hearted commitment and resentment can lead to implementation problems, including sloppy work, scheduling problems, and generally uncooperative behavior. All too often sound decisions are made, but because commitment is lacking, the decision fails on follow through. Nothing changes. The problem goes unsolved.

Adjust to disagreements.

It would be naive to think that group members always will agree. They don't. Honest differences of opinion lead reasonable people to disagree. Paul seeks commitment to a course of action, as opposed to agreement. He understands that individual group members may still harbor reservations when the decision is made. However, Paul's group is willing to put aside their reservations because the process steps provided them an opportunity to raise concerns and discuss options. They are willing to trust the collective wisdom because experience has shown that the group makes good decisions. When a decision proves to be inadequate, the group is quick to reassess and adjust course.

When group members are unable to put aside their reservations and commit to a course of action, the person with authority and responsibility for the decision, Paul in this situation, has several options.

- Paul can adjourn the meeting to give group members time to reflect. Frequently, conflicts disappear when people have time alone to think about what they really believe to be the issues. There is rarely anything lost by temporarily postponing a decision when people disagree.

- Paul can continue to seek an acceptable alternative with which group members can agree by amending the existing alternatives or searching for new alternatives that reconcile tradeoffs. (Finding an acceptable alternative is different from negotiating a compromise, which assumes there is a "fixed pie" and you cut the pie so everyone gets a fair-sized piece. Compromise decisions are rarely effective, and groups can easily lose sight of the objectives that brought them together.)

- Paul can elect to make the decision himself based on the available information, announce the decision, and expect subordinates to carry it out. If he does this sensitively, group members may commit to whatever he decides without resentment.

Once a decision maker has delegated a decision to a group, however, it is sometimes difficult for the group to give up its sense of ownership. Those who disagree with the decision maker's choice may harbor resentment that can get in the way of implementation. Paul can avoid this situation if he makes clear at the outset that he is ultimately responsible for the decision and is seeking guidance versus a decision. Paul knows, however, communicating this distinction isn't as easy as it sounds. While he asks for guidance, his actions imply decision making. He encourages the group to take emotional ownership in the decision because he wants their commitment. Of course, he can simply tell subordinates what he has decided, and ignore their feelings.

- Paul can postpone making a decision until something changes to make agreement possible. It makes sense to postpone making a decision only if something is likely to change in a time that makes sense, and only if the expected change is likely to make it easier for group members to agree. If announcement of a land swap is imminent, waiting to make a decision probably makes sense. Waiting doesn't make sense if negotiations could take years. Many decisions are deferred without any reasonable expectation that something will change. When this happens, the problem goes unsolved.

Which of these responses is best depends on the problem, the context, the urgency and importance of the decision, and the likelihood that something could change in a time frame that makes sense. Each response to disagreement has strengths and weaknesses.

7. What is the next step?

Decisions don't solve problems, actions do. Many decision-making meetings end when the decision is made. It is taken for granted that somebody will act on the decision. More often than not, nobody acts on the decision until specific responsibilities are assigned.

Paul knows this. At a minimum, he will assign responsibility for the next step—action planning—to Charlie. An action plan lays out who will do what and when. Charlie can schedule another meeting to develop the plan, or he can develop the plan himself. When the plan is completed, Charlie will delegate each of the plan's steps to a person, establishing the link between planning and action. Only when the desired results are achieved will Paul and his group have completed what they set out to do.

6

■ Making Decisions When No One Is in Charge

External events can create problems in which unrelated people are thrown together in ad hoc groups. Members of these groups share nothing more than a stake in the same problem. None can solve the problem alone. They can only solve their individual problems through voluntary joint action. This chapter deals with the special challenges that arise as a result.

Several of this chapter's central characters will be familiar to you. In chapter 2, Sid Riedel, the inspector from the state Department of Environmental Quality, and Glenn Hoffmann, the mayor of Red Ridge, defined the Powder River situation as a question that calls for action. You will recognize Paul Hartner, operations manager, and Betsy Tomlin, who discovered the washed-out branch creek road, of Northwest Forest Products. In chapter 1, you were briefly introduced to Ray Green, a farmer who owns land on the banks of the Powder River, and in chapter 2 to Ron Banks, a Native American leader from the reservation downstream, which depends on salmon fishing for their livelihood. As chapter 2 ended, Sid and Glenn were listing who should be invited to a meeting to talk about using the basin-management option to solve the soil erosion problems on the Powder River. These individuals and others were on Sid's and Glenn's list. Most of the people know or know of each other. Sid and Glenn will bring together this new ad hoc group to confront the problem. To succeed, this diverse group of people must become an effective working group.

Three Simultaneous Processes

Without organizational structure, the individuals who share a stake in the Powder River problem will come together voluntarily bringing with them their diverse needs and perspectives. In the process of answering the decision-making framework's questions, the group organizers, Sid and Glenn, will facilitate the decision-making process in a way that encourages individual commitment to the group and its decisions. Throughout this group process, each individual will go through an internal process of self-questioning that causes them to make a commitment to the group and its decisions or to abandon the group. All of this will occur simultaneously, each process reinforcing movement toward a common decision.

Establishing purpose

As organizers and facilitators of the ad hoc group, Sid and Glenn have thought through who they are and what the problem is enough to conclude sedimentation is a problem that can be resolved if people who live and work along the Powder River are willing to develop a basin-management plan together. With their definition of the problem and their ideas about what can be done in mind, they take it upon themselves to bring others who are related to the problem together in an ad hoc group. As facilitators, Sid and Glenn will lead the group through the decision-making framework.

Group formation

Members of the ad hoc group collectively begin by asking, "What, if anything, is there for us to do together to solve the problem that brought us here?" Before they can move to other frameworks like decision making, ad hoc groups invariably struggle with problem definition and ownership.

In chapter 4, Warren Olson knows he is an individual making a decision about a problem that is his to solve. Paul Hartner's group in chapter 5 is well structured, and each person knows the roles they fill and the relationship among their roles. They work for Northwest Forest Products under the supervision of Paul Hartner. The problem is Paul's to solve and, at Paul's invitation, the problem becomes the group's to solve.

In contrast to Warren Olson's or Paul Hartner's groups, the ad hoc Powder River group must discover who *we* are as they decide what is the best alternative. They must answer two questions simultaneously: *What is the best alternative?* and *Who are we?*—the group asking the question.

Individual commitment

As individuals, each person comes to the problem from his or her own unique perspectives, conflicting expectations, and a confused jumble of impressions. Paul Hartner has accepted that Northwest Forest Products is partially responsible for the river's turbidity and has already decided to address the immediate problem—the branch creek road. Betsy Tomlin helped shape their decision to abandon the branch creek road and restore it to its natural state to reduce sedimentation of the Powder River in chapter 5.

Like Ray Green and Ron Banks, others are only aware of the problem as it affects them. They must decide for themselves whether or not to join the group effort to solve the soil erosion problem.

At each meeting and between meetings, individual group members go through an internal set of questions, asking themselves, "Is this my problem? Can I trust the group to help me solve my problem? Can they trust me? Is this our problem? Is there something we can do together to solve our problem? Should I continue?"

Each individual will determine whether the Powder River problem is his or her problem—as an individual and as a group. They don't ask these questions just once, but over and over until they feel comfortable with the answers or quit the group. Each evaluates their individual problem and its context against the group's emerging purpose, which is reflected in what it chooses to do. Most of the group's members will defer phrasing their own question that calls for action until they feel comfortable with what the group can (or cannot) do together.

At the outset, individual members may answer all of the questions "no" except the last one—"Should I continue?" As they come to understand that it is at least partially their problem, their willingness to trust and be trusted may grow. Eventually, individual members may come to accept this problem as *our* problem. Until there is something to do together to solve our problem, the realization that they share a problem has little meaning, however. So the questioning continues. Any individual group member can get stalled at any point. Whether or not that makes a difference to the group as a whole depends on who, when in the process, and how many falter.

When individual group members answer these questions "yes," trust evolves and group members begin to identify with the emerging group. Trust and identification with the group do not happen all at once, but little by little. And both occur in the process of deciding what the group can do together—in this case, answering the decision-making framework's questions.

Trust does not develop and group members do not identify with a group when it serves no purpose. Hence, answers to the question, "Who is asking the question?" are contingent on believing there is a way for the group to solve its problem together. Establishing purpose, group formation, and each individual's assessment of how they relate to the problem and the group are three inseparable, simultaneous processes. In this chapter these processes are shown side by side. The remainder of this chapter illustrates the special challenges that arise when ad hoc groups, in this case, the Powder River group, set out to solve a shared problem.

The Group Together

If unrelated individuals are to voluntarily meet to talk about whether they share a problem, those with a stake must move from recognizing a problem to accepting some responsibility, at least tentatively. This is no small task. Each one needs a good reason—a reason that makes sense to them. Few will participate simply because they should.

Three Simultaneous Processes

ESTABLISHING PURPOSE	GROUP FORMATION	INDIVIDUAL COMMITMENT
What is the problem?	How can I draw the group together?	How do I relate to the problem?
What is the decision to be made?	How can I help members participate productively?	How do I relate to the group?
What are the criteria?		
What are the alternatives?	How can I affirm membership in the group?	Is this our problem?
What is the effect of each alternative on each criterion?	How can I encourage group members to persist?	Should I continue meeting with the group?
Which is the best alternative for each criterion?	Who will lead the group forward?	
Which is the best alternative overall?		

Starting joint effort when people feel the pain of inaction

Ad hoc groups are most likely to form during periods of crisis or when external events cause individuals to feel the pain of inaction. Responding to a common threat, people put aside their differences to solve an urgent, common problem. Americans have a long history of coming together in times of environmental, natural, or agricultural crisis—whether it is cleaning up shore birds after an oil spill, fighting forest fires, rebuilding a barn after a tornado, or coming to the aid of neighbors in times of economic hardship.

More chronic problems, such as groundwater contamination or soil erosion, cannot lay claim to the same urgency. To form groups around intractable chronic problems with long-term consequences, there must almost always be a golden opportunity that will be lost and a threat of dire consequences if action is not taken now, that is, a carrot and a stick. A change in the context may provide an immediate opportunity or threat—a changed regulation, a court ruling, or new information. Sometimes a small event can take on symbolic importance, enabling people to see an opportunity where none appeared before. By itself, a threat is not sufficient. Without an opportunity, there is nothing for the group to do. An opportunity without a corresponding threat often fails to motivate group formation and change.

One environmental mediator says voluntary, joint action to solve an intractable resource problem depends on "feeling the pain" of inaction. The status quo must be unacceptable to all involved. While each person may feel the pain differently, each must believe change is necessary before all will work together.

Drawing the Powder River group together

In chapter 2, a washed-out logging road was the catalyst that caused Sid Riedel and Glenn Hoffmann to begin talking. In that problem situation, they discovered a long-term opportunity—the possibility of getting agreement on a basin-management plan to reduce soil erosion in the long run. They identified the people and groups with a stake in the problem and analyzed their roles, responsibility, and authority. Both Sid and Glenn defined the problem from their own perspectives. In this chapter, Sid and Glenn will expand ownership in the problem to include these individuals and groups.

Sid and Glenn call key people and invite them to a meeting at the Red Ridge elementary school. They invite people who will have to change their management practices to reduce sedimentation. At this point, they don't try to reach everyone; rather, they focus on opinion leaders who will influence others as the group expands.

In their telephone conversations, Sid and Glenn use a carrot-and-stick approach to entice these people to attend the meeting. They point to the state's threat of fines and legal action, which make the status quo unacceptable. Then they offer a positive way to avoid fines and legal action. The group can use the basin-planning option in the Forest Practices Act to develop a land-management plan that reduces sedimentation through voluntary action. After getting a tentative agreement to attend the meeting, Glenn sends a follow-up letter, confirming the meeting's purpose, agenda, time, and place.

Both Sid and Glenn realize that they will have only one chance to get the group's attention. If key people do not attend this first crucial meeting, the basin-planning option may not be an acceptable approach to solve the problem. Sid and Glenn carefully set the tone of the meeting in their phone calls and letters.

While Glenn and Sid tailor their words for each person, the basic message remains the same. They want to set the stage for informal, meaningful give-and-take, and they don't want group members to expect easy answers. They assure each one that the basin-planning option offers the group a chance to find an alternative that meets individuals' most essential objectives while reducing sedimentation to levels that protect salmon runs on the river. They affirm the legitimacy of each person's perspective. Yet they try to make each person aware that solutions will require the cooperation of all involved. Every person takes a risk in coming to the meeting, even Glenn and Sid. While Sid and Glenn make sure each person knows that the alternative to exploring this opportunity is fines and legal action, they focus on the benefits of voluntary action (figure 6.1).

TOWN OF RED RIDGE
Red Ridge, West Coast State 90000

Mr. Ray Green
Box 125
South End Road
Red Ridge, WC 90000

Dear Mr. Green:

Thank you for agreeing to come to the basin-planning meeting next Wednesday night. We will meet at 7:30 P.M. in the Red Ridge elementary school lunchroom. We will conclude the meeting no later than 9:00 P.M.

We will meet to see if there is interest in developing a plan to reduce sedimentation in the Powder River. As you know, turbidity is above the level set by the state Fish and Wildlife Service for salmon-bearing streams. Farm- and forest-management practices along the river contribute sediment to the river. The state indicates that runoff from your land contributes to the problem.

The Department of Environmental Quality offered us the option of developing a basin-management plan. If those who contribute excess sediment to the river can agree on a plan, we will avoid additional fines and legal action. We hope that all landowners along the river will join together to solve this troublesome problem so that the stream is cleaned up and individuals meet their own needs too. Everyone, including the state, knows that fines and legal action don't solve the problem. Working out an agreement is to everyone's advantage.

A group of seven to nine landowners and interested people will meet Wednesday night to lay the groundwork for the planning process. I have invited you; Paul Hartner and Betsy Tomlin from Northwest Forest Products; Bill and Laurie Kriesle, who own Cascade Farms and Nursery; Ron Banks from the Powder River Reservation; and Kathy Shield, who represents the state Forest Service. In addition, Joe Warren with the state Fish and Wildlife Service, and Sid Riedel and Jill Baker-Schofield from the state Department of Environmental Quality will join us. Joe knows the salmon regulations inside and out. Jill is familiar with the new Forest Practices Act and the basin-planning option. You probably know Sid, the environmental quality inspector for our area.

At this first meeting, we hope to get a variety of views on the table for discussion, so come to the meeting prepared to share your ideas and opinions. The discussion should be lively. If you have questions in the meantime or just want to find out more about basin planning, give me a call or stop in.

Ray, I appreciate your support for this community initiative and look forward to seeing you Wednesday night.

Sincerely,

Glenn Hoffmann
Mayor, Town of Red Ridge

Figure 6.1. A follow-up letter confirming the meeting.

Ad hoc groups forming under special circumstances

Ad hoc groups form because no person or organization singly holds the power to solve the problem and the effect of any individual action to solve the problem is so small that it hardly seems worth the effort. Ad hoc groups only are effective to solve problems with localized causes and effects. For example, most Americans know that their driving habits contribute carbon dioxide to the atmosphere. They also know that theirs is one of several million cars on the road. If they choose to drive less the effect will not have a discernible impact. Americans will change their driving habits when the government regulates our driving, when gasoline prices become so high we decide to drive less, when mass transportation becomes so attractive we prefer it, or when social customs change and "unnecessary" driving becomes socially unacceptable—as littering has become in many parts of the country. While the problem transcends individuals, it is unlikely that people will band together in ad hoc groups to voluntarily solve it. The causes and effects are too dispersed, both geographically and over time.

Unlike driving and carbon dioxide, soil erosion has more localized causes and effects. Sid can identify who contributes to soil erosion and how their soil erosion affects salmon. While no single landowner can change his or her management practices enough to solve the sedimentation problem, it is reasonable to think that 10 to 15 landowners jointly can decide to shift management practices enough to jointly reduce soil erosion to acceptable levels on the Upper Powder River. The boundaries of the problem and potential solutions are clear enough that Sid can act as a catalyst.

Who to invite to the group

The question of who to involve is the most important choice the organizers of an ad hoc group make. When people are invited to participate in ad hoc problem-solving groups based on who can agree versus who owns the problem and its solution, misunderstanding is the almost certain result.

Both the owners of the problem and the owners of the solution must be represented to exploit all the opportunities to solve a problem fully. This is because ownership conflicts are at the root of most of today's natural resource management problems. Those who own the solution hold the power to solve it. Those who own the problem are affected by it. Problems are relatively easy to solve when these two groups are the same. However, these groups may only partially overlap or include wholly different groups. Determining who owns the problem and who owns the solution depends on the context in which the problem will be solved and how the problem is defined.

In chapter 2, Sid and Glenn assessed the Powder River situation's context and defined the problem. They identified the people who own the problem as those affected by soil erosion and its impacts on salmon: commercial fishers, including members of the Tribal Association who rely on the salmon catch for their income; recreational fishers; those who value biodiversity; landowners; resort owners who rely on salmon runs to draw tourists and recreational fishers; those who believe that wild salmon contribute to the region's aesthetic appeal; and perhaps others who get value from the salmon. When Sid and Glenn defined the problem as soil erosion, they implicitly defined the landowners whose management practices create soil erosion as the owners of the solution.

As you will recall, Sid debated over whether to invite both those who own the problem and those who own the solution to the first meeting. He decided to invite mainly landowners to the first meeting, but he added Joe Warren, a fish biologist, because he understands the linkage between soil erosion and salmon fishery. He also invited Ron Banks because he is the most vocal representative of the Native Americans who depend on salmon for income. Any solutions the landowners consider will have to win the support of the Native Americans. The basin-planning approach was enacted to provide owners of the solution to soil erosion with a legally recognized means of joint, voluntary action. However, their solution must be acceptable to other owners of the problem—the fishing, tourism and recreation, and environmental interests. By having Ron Banks and Joe Warren present, Sid is trying to reduce the risk of a solution, unacceptable to other interests, being selected by the landowners.

A different problem, a different group

In a different context with a different opportunity, the mix of group members would certainly differ. For example, Joe Warren of the Fish and Wildlife Service could have observed the same symptoms—increased turbidity—and defined the problem as a fisheries-management problem. Without the opportunity that the basin-management problem provides, Joe might invite a different mix of people, including a different set of problem owners and solution owners. Some, like landowners, fall into both groups. In Joe's group, commercial fishers surely would be invited. As a representative of Native Americans dependent on salmon, Ron Banks would be a critical member. Representatives of environmental groups concerned with biodiversity, tourism, and recreational fishing might be included. Framed this way, with a different mix of people, the group almost certainly would address the problem in a different way than Glenn's group. Perhaps this group would negotiate reduced fishing as well as erosion controls and offer landowners assistance in streamside management.

Voluntary groups and the choice to change

In the Powder River situation, landowners have clearly defined property rights that give them legal authority to decide how to manage their land. While Sid can fine them if their management practices generate too much soil erosion, he cannot tell them how to manage their land. Sediment will be reduced when these landowners voluntarily choose to change their management practices. A landowner could choose not to change management practices and treat the fines as a cost of doing business.

Without the landowners' participation, Joe Warren's fisheries-management group would lack the power to reduce soil erosion because it would not own the solution. To voluntarily change their management practices, landowners have to decide that the proposed changes meet both their own individual and the group's requirements. While Joe's group might be eager to reduce soil erosion, it would have no clear opportunity for voluntary change without the landowners' participation. It is the meaningful participation of the landowners that grants authority to the broader group to recommend that farmers and foresters change their management practices. Without landowners' meaningful participation, Joe's fisheries group would have to turn to solutions that do not depend on voluntary cooperation, such as education, the courts, legislative action, or public opinion, to influence the landowners' management practices.

Group membership and ownership

Problems are best solved when people accept responsibility for their own problems. "Outsiders" may come in and tell people what to do without consulting those who created the problem or are affected by it. However, their recommended solutions often fail. Because outsiders generally fail to appreciate the complexity of the context, their recommendations are less effective than they could be, whether the outsiders are government officials telling communities how to serve the needs of their citizens; VISTA volunteers telling poor people how to improve their lot in life; or highly paid consultants telling management how to improve profits. Just as often, however, people abdicate responsibility for their problems and look to outsiders for solutions. As citizens, we often look to government to solve all of our problems, ranging from resource degradation to poverty and drug abuse. As managers, we tend to call in consultants to provide quick-fix solutions to problems we have created and probably only we can solve.

Community leaders talk about the importance of self-determination; managers call for freedom to conduct business unfettered; landowners insist on maintaining their property rights. However we talk about it, whatever we call it, the issue is fundamental: When we try to solve someone else's problems, we cannot be certain they will embrace the solutions we offer. If the individuals who own the problem and the solution don't help determine how to solve it, the outcome is likely to fall short. That is not to say advisors should not play an important role. Their role must be appropriate— suggesting, supporting, informing, initiating, and assisting rather than deciding and demanding.

Membership and values

People bring their own values to group interactions. Including people who value productivity, sustainability, and equity ensures that these values are considered. While Sid and Glenn invited mostly landowners to the first meeting, they selected people who represent each of the aforementioned values. Sid, Jill, and Joe represent the state. The state has charged them with sustaining fish runs. Paul Hartner, Ray Green, and the Kriesles have a stake in maintaining the short- and long-run productivity of their land. Ron Banks' participation will ensure that the decision is equitable and takes into account Native Americans' rights to receive an income from salmon. All are both owners of the problem and owners of the solution. With a different problem or in a different context, Sid and Glenn might have had to search more consciously for group members to represent other values.

Numerous groups exist to protect the environment, representing a wide range of sustainability values. Historically, these groups were not included in ad hoc groups seeking voluntary solutions because they did not own the solution. Excluded and ignored, they turned to the courts and public pressure. Their successes have helped environmental groups become recognized as partial owners of the solution. Only when the Sierra Club started to challenge timber sales from the national forests were they recognized in the courts as having a legitimate interest in how national forests are managed.

The interests of the impoverished and disenfranchised are often poorly represented in ad hoc groups. Individually, these people are directly affected by legislation to protect the environment. A farmer who barely makes enough income to feed the family cannot afford to implement expensive nonpoint source pollution controls. Increased tipping fees for landfills place a heavier burden on the poor than on others.

When environmental groups and timber interests negotiate a settlement that protects ancient timber stands and reduces the timber supply, jobs are lost. Those who suffer most are the working poor who have limited employment alternatives. Unless intentional steps are taken to ensure that equity values are represented in an ad hoc group's deliberations, their decisions may place an inequitable burden on the poor. As yet, the poor have not had the same success in making themselves owners of the solution as environmental groups have.

The First Meeting—A Common Understanding

As people arrive at the meeting, Glenn welcomes them. While most people know each other, Glenn makes a point of introducing those who don't. He wants to encourage as much informal interaction as he can.

Three Simultaneous Processes

ESTABLISHING PURPOSE	GROUP FORMATION	INDIVIDUAL COMMITMENT
What is the problem?	How can I draw the group together?	How do I relate to the problem?
What is the decision to be made?	How can I help members participate productively?	How do I relate to the group?
What are the criteria?	How can I affirm membership in the group?	Is this our problem?
What are the alternatives?	How can I encourage group members to persist?	Should I continue meeting with the group?
What is the effect of each alternative on each criterion?	Who will lead the group forward?	
Which is the best alternative for each criterion?		
Which is the best alternative overall?		

Encouraging everyone to talk about why they are present

Glenn asks everyone to sit around a table. When there aren't enough chairs at the table, he finds more so that no one will feel excluded from the discussion. He thanks everyone for coming and asks each person to explain why they have come.

Glenn starts with himself. "You all know who I am. As mayor, I'm here because sedimentation affects the town's water treatment plant. But more importantly, I'm here because land-use planning affects us all. And I'm concerned about the welfare of the people of Red Ridge and surrounding areas."

On his left, Sid introduces himself and explains that he doesn't want to have to police the river. He's here to see if there is some other way to reduce sedimentation. Next, Joe Warren from the Fish and Wildlife Service says he's here because Sid told him to be. When the laughter subsides, Joe says, "Really, I'm here to find a long-lasting means to reduce sedimentation on the Powder River so that my children and your children can enjoy the salmon runs too."

Paul Hartner from Northwest Forest Products skeptically tells why he's at the meeting. "I'm here to see if anything comes of this. While I don't expect much, Northwest Forest Products is committed to being a good corporate citizen. So as long as the group continues to meet, we'll be present." Betsy Tomlin introduces herself next. "Northwest has already decided how to make sure the branch creek road doesn't wash out again. We're going to abandon the road and restore it to its natural state. So I'm not sure what more we can do."

Ray Green, sitting to Betsy's left, explains, "I don't really know how any of this applies to me. I can't really see how you can expect farmers like me and the Kriesles to comply with those new regulations. If I have to do something, I guess I can fence my cows out of the bottomland, but what do you expect me to do about flooding? You'll put us out of business before it's all finished." His neighbors, Bill and Laurie Kriesle, nod in agreement as they introduce themselves.

Ron Banks sounds cautious as he speaks. "I was surprised to get an invitation to come to this meeting. I am here because this is the first time you folks have acknowledged a problem before my people called it to your attention. For those of you who are concerned about the cost of erosion controls, let me remind you that my people are concerned about their livelihoods. Salmon are an important part of our diet and our cash income. Now that our fishing rights are fully recognized, we don't intend to let upstream landowners destroy our resource."

Jill Baker-Schofield, Sid's boss, goes next: "I want to see the river meet the turbidity requirements established in the salmon-bearing stream regulations. As far as I'm concerned, we can enforce the standards with fines and legal action or you can avoid fines and legal action by developing a basin-management plan that meets both your and the public's needs." Kathy Shield, a fishery biologist for the state Forest Service, admits that "the Forest Service probably should have sent someone else. As a fishery biologist, I'm more concerned about the salmon than anything else. And I know from practical experience that unless we all reduce runoff, including the Forest Service, no single effort will be enough." Glenn thanks everyone and continues.

The group isn't a group until its members recognize that they share the same problem. At this point, each one perceives the problem differently. Some group members are concerned about salmon but don't see how the salmon are their problem. Some are concerned about soil erosion as it affects them personally but don't accept that it should be the group's concern. Some think the state regulations are the problem. To operate as a group, they will have to find some common understanding of what the problem is and agree on the specific choice to be made.

Staying on topic and developing a common base

Glenn asks the group to describe the problem. Instead, Paul asks why Clearview Lumber isn't represented at the meeting.

"Were they invited?" he demands. Bill Kriesle asks why the Krohls, who farm the opposite side of the river, aren't at the meeting. Others list names of people they think should be at the meeting. While Glenn fields the questions, Sid writes down people's names. Finally, Glenn holds up his hand. "I agree that anyone with a stake in the problem needs to be included. But can we come back to this after we talk about why we're here? When we're sure of our purpose, identifying people who need to be included will be easier."

Glenn asks Joe Warren to describe the problem from the Fish and Wildlife Service's perspective. Joe describes the declining population of wild salmon, explains why wild salmon are important, and tells how sedimentation affects salmon runs. He describes the turbidity standards that were established last year and the research that was done to determine at what level the standards should be set. Next, Sid explains how soil runoff contributes to sedimentation and the Department of Environmental Quality's role in enforcing the standards.

Those present ask questions. Joe and Sid answer the questions as simply as they can while keeping the relationships between wild salmon populations, salmon runs, turbidity, sedimentation, and soil erosion in front of the group. They focus on the relationship between soil erosion and sedimentation because this is what group members can do something about.

When the group has exhausted its questions, Glenn asks Sid to explain the basin-planning option and how it might work. "Basically," Sid says, "landowners develop a land-use management plan jointly. The state reviews the plan and accepts it or suggests amendments. Each landowner signs a contract saying that he or she will abide by the plan for ten years."

As Sid pauses, several hands shoot up. Glenn calls on Bill Kriesle. "Does anybody have any experience with this planning option, or are you asking us to be guinea pigs?" Sid responds, "Let me respond to the second part of your question first. We are not asking you necessarily to do anything. We want you to be aware that the basin-planning option is available and that you may want to consider whether it makes sense for those of you who own land along the Powder River. Whatever you do—either individually or as a group—you must choose."

Sid continues, "That doesn't mean the state doesn't have an interest in what you choose. We do. My job is to make sure that the Powder River can support wild salmon, and that means turbidity levels cannot exceed the standard. As some of you know, I take my job seriously. At the same time, I know you all have to make a living too. I don't mean to sound aggravated, but we all have to accept the responsibility that is thrust upon us. Your job is to do whatever you must to make a living. My job is to make sure you bring soil erosion under control. I can't tell you how, and I certainly can't ask you to develop a basin-management plan. Besides, that would defeat the purpose of the program. It is intended to give you a wider range of options so that you can voluntarily choose what's best for you."

Going on, Sid says, "I know I've said more than I should, but I want to answer the first part of your question, Bill. People up around Vine City used the basin-planning option last year. Glenn and I went up and talked to them, and almost everyone was pleased with the results—at least so far. Of course, their situation is a little different from yours. The land there is almost all forested. But I encourage any of you with questions to give the mayor a call. Better yet, arrange to talk to some of them like Glenn and I did."

Sid answers more questions about the basin-planning option as candidly as he can. He doesn't want to oversell nor undersell the basin-planning option. He wants to give those at the meeting the information they need to pursue it or not. On some questions, he admits he doesn't know the answers but promises to get an answer before the next meeting. Glenn writes down the questions that need to be answered.

Getting commitment to continue

Glenn glances at his watch; it's 15 minutes before nine o'clock.

"Before we conclude, we need to answer four questions," he says: "Is this a line of thinking we want to pursue? If so, what should we do at our next meeting? Who should be present at the next meeting? When and where should we meet next?" He finishes, remarking, "Let's take the questions in order, please."

"I can't speak for anyone else," starts Bill Kriesle, "but I don't feel like we have discussed the basin-planning option enough. I sure can't say 'yes' to basin planning right now. But I can't say 'no' either. I think we need to keep meeting." Paul Hartner nods in agreement. "I think that's what I said at the beginning of this meeting. I don't expect anything to come out of this, but if there's any chance that this basin-planning thing can help us avoid fines and legal action, we need to keep talking."

Ray shakes his head, "I'm not as sure as you guys. It's planting season, and I can't be spending my time attending a lot of meetings." Glenn asks, "Does that mean you won't come to the next meeting?" Ray answers, "I didn't say that, did I? If everyone else decides to meet again, I'll be there. Just don't think I'm going to be going to weekly meetings for the next two years or anything."

Glenn continues, "What I hear you saying is that we'll take one meeting at a time and go from there. Have I interpreted what you are saying accurately? If so, can we go on to the next question?" Observing nods of agreement, Glenn proceeds. "What should be on the agenda at the next meeting? Just give me your ideas now. We'll discuss them after we have all the possible agenda items on the table."

Paul begins, "I would like to talk to the people from Vine City. And I don't want to talk to the mayor. No offense, Glenn. It's just that we need to be talking to the people who have to live with the plan." Glenn writes down "Vine City" on a flip chart. "Anything else?"

Bill answers, "I agree with Paul. There's another thing we need to talk about too. I can't decide whether or not developing a management plan for the basin makes any sense until we decide what we're planning for." Ray asks, "Can you explain, Bill? I don't get what you mean."

Bill answers with a question: "What is the plan supposed to achieve? What are our objectives? Wasn't it Pogo who said, 'Any plan will get you there if you don't know where you're going?' I want to know where we're going. I think there are some important decisions we have to make before we begin planning."

On the flip chart, Glenn writes "decide what we're going to decide," and asks, "Is this a fair summary of what you mean, Bill?" He answers, "That's it." Glenn prods, "Anything else?"

Paul responds, "If no one minds, I would be happy to arrange a meeting at Vine City before the next meeting. If you don't mind, I think it would be helpful if only we landowners met with them." Bill laughs, "When did you buy Northwest Forest Products, Paul? I didn't know you were a landowner." Grinning, Paul answers, "I wish I owned more of the company. Seriously, Glenn, would you and Sid and Joe mind if we talked to the Vine City people by ourselves? I think all of us would feel more comfortable talking about this basin-management option if we had private assurances that it works from people like us."

Sid says, "Paul, I think that is a good idea. As I said earlier, the state is not telling you to do anything. You have to feel comfortable with whatever you decide. As you say, you will have to live with the plan." "Good," Paul answers,

"I'll take care of the arrangements and be in touch with everybody."

"Before we go on to the next topic," Kathy Shield asks, "I want to clarify a point with Paul. The State Forest Service will have to enter into a basin plan for it to work. However, if you private landowners would prefer to meet with the Vine City people without the Forest Service present, we can meet with our district ranger up there separately." Paul responds, "Thanks, Kathy. I think that would work best."

Taking care of details

Glancing at his watch, Glenn continues.

"We have two more questions to cover: Who should be invited to the next meeting? and When and where should we hold it? What do you think?"

Paul offers to contact Clearview Lumber, saying they own a tract of forest-land in the basin. Ray and Bill volunteer to talk to the Krohls and several other farmers who farm the river's bottomlands. Bill adds Pineview Resort to the list, explaining they own several hundred acres of recreational land in the basin. Kathy adds the name of the state's timber management person, Stan Nevin.

Paul asks Kathy, "Will you represent the Forest Service?" She shakes her head and says, "I'll let you know later." Other names are added to the list, and someone is assigned to contact each person on the list. The group talks about what information these people will need to be given. Paul volunteers to invite those they have added to the group to talk with the Vine City people.

When the discussion ends, Glenn asks, "When can we meet next?" The group chooses a date two weeks away. Glenn turns to Sid, "Since you took notes, can you write up minutes? We don't need anything elaborate, just who attended and what was decided." Without waiting for an answer, Glenn asks if there is anything else to be discussed before they close. Anxious to get home, no one speaks. Glenn adjourns the meeting at 9:20, saying, "Next time we'll adjourn on time."

Sharing a base of information

People in ad hoc groups must build a shared base of understanding. Structured groups come to decision making with a common base already in place; members of ad hoc groups rarely come to decision making with the same information or understanding. Not only are their perspectives different, but some members know more than others. Some have access to better information than others. The same words and concepts mean different things to different people.

Different understanding, like different perspectives, can lead to confusion, conflict, and anger. Differences can also contribute novel solutions, offer more thoughtful criteria, and cause a group to test its assumptions more thoroughly. Whatever the starting point, the common base that is shared grows as the group does. Keeping track of the shared information that is developed, recording information so that an individual's knowledge is accessible to other group members, and listing agreed-on meanings enhances the process.

At the first meeting of the Powder River group, Joe Warren talked about the cause-and-effect relationships between wild salmon populations and soil erosion. Sid talked about turbidity standards, his agency's powers to enforce the standards with fines and legal action, and the basin-planning option. This information provided a base of shared information. At each meeting, this base will be expanded. As new members are added to the group, effort will have to be made to share the same information with them as well.

Getting commitment to meet again

Glenn did not assume that the group would meet again; rather, he let them decide. Faced with the certainty of fines and legal action if they don't find another way to reduce soil erosion, they quickly decided to continue. Glenn could have simply scheduled another meeting. By asking the question, skeptics like Ray had to decide "Will I go to the next meeting or not?" Notice however, Glenn didn't ask for a commitment to basin planning. He asked for a commitment to attend the next meeting. Group members do not have enough information to commit to basin planning yet. Asking for that commitment would have been like asking your next door neighbor to dinner a year in advance. *It depends on what comes up between now and then!* In contrast, he asked a narrow question and got concrete commitments.

Looking at Sid's and Glenn's role

As the group's organizers, Sid and Glenn played a key role. Glenn and Sid were the catalysts who drew the Powder River group together. They decided who should attend the first meeting. Glenn facilitated. Sid provided information and took notes for a permanent record. Throughout the early stages of group formation, Sid and Glenn will continue to be critical resources to the group—inspiring, enabling, facilitating, and shaping the group's thoughts. This role is essential, yet carries within it the potential seeds of failure. At the outset, the group may see the problem through the eyes of its organizers, perhaps even phrasing the initial call for action as they would. This is neither surprising nor bad; it is a starting point. If the group takes the organizers' vision and shapes it into its own unique vision, then the group's decisions will be consistent with its members interests. If, however, the group fails to shape its own vision, the group may make decisions inconsistent with its members' interests, failing even as it succeeds just as an eager-to-please son may succeed at a career chosen by his parents only to find it unsatisfying at mid-life.

As the group's organizers, Glenn and Sid cannot avoid influencing the group. The information Sid provides and the kinds of questions Glenn asks as facilitator influence the group. Even if they say nothing, their presence will influence the group. Sid is a constant reminder of fines and legal action if the group does not act. At the same time, his continued interest holds out hope of finding an alternative.

Rather than trying to avoid influencing the group, it is important that Sid and Glenn do all they can to transfer responsibility for establishing its purpose and formation to the group. Sid and Glenn must provide support while taking every opportunity to shift ownership in small increments. Incremental shifts will be made by using the decision-making framework and group process steps and thoughtful facilitation to structure subsequent meetings. If the group feels abandoned by Sid and Glenn, particularly in its early stages, the group will almost surely fail.

When Glenn asked, *"Who should be present at the next meeting?"* he accomplished two important objectives: First, he invited members to take ownership in the group when he asked them to name who should be involved; second, he effectively opened the group to anyone with a stake in the outcome.

Humor is an important tool in a facilitator's kit. While group members differ on many issues, they usually are willing to laugh at the absurdity of their differences. To the extent Paul, Ron, and others can step back from their situation and laugh at themselves, they are more likely to view other people's perspectives with empathy. As facilitator, Glenn sets the tone. By encouraging people to laugh, he encourages them to see both the reality and absurdity of their differences.

Using the decision-making framework

With the first informational meeting completed, Sid and Glenn will structure succeeding meetings around the decision-making framework's questions. Glenn will use the group process steps to guide the group as it answers each question. The questions are the same as those presented in chapters 4 and 5: What will you decide? What are the criteria? What are the alternatives? and so on. However, instead of answering all the framework's questions in one or two meetings, this ad hoc group will answer the decision-making framework's questions over a period of weeks or even months.

You may wonder why Sid and Glenn are using the decision-making framework for basin planning. Planning is only possible when a group has mutually agreed-upon objectives and when it knows what it wants to do. Before the group can begin planning, it must set objectives that translate into criteria, identify alternative strategies to achieve those objectives, and choose the best strategy. There are too many landowners and too many factors to approach basin planning as a "how" question without a decision in principle about "what" will work.

Using the decision-making process, the group will agree to a broad strategic plan in principle. They will evaluate alternative strategic plans in their entirety. When the group has decided what strategic plan is best in principle, then they can answer the action-planning framework's detailed questions about how to implement the chosen strategy: What specific steps? Who specifically? Where specifically? When precisely? Each group member will have to negotiate what precise steps he or she will take one at a time. This detailed negotiation, which is how action planning is done in ad hoc groups, is virtually impossible unless the group has agreed in principle on a strategic plan.

The Second Meeting—What to Decide

Sid and Glenn must decide whether or not to explain the framework and process steps to the group. Either way, they run a risk. If Glenn explains the framework and process steps to the group, the methodology could detract from achieving the meeting's purpose. If they do not explain the framework and process steps, the group could rebel against what appears to be arbitrary structure. A group's organizer must decide on a case-by-case basis what to do.

In this case, the group trusts Glenn as a facilitator. Glenn can guide the group through the questions and use the process steps so that they strengthen the group's interaction without seeming to be arbitrary. The group already has a lot of information to sort out. Adding a description of the framework and process steps on top of soil erosion, sediment, salmon, and basin planning could be the proverbial "straw that breaks the camel's back."

At the second meeting, the group will start formulating a decision question. As facilitator, Glenn will encourage group members to reveal the objectives that a plan must meet. With new group members present, he realizes that he may have to allow some digression. Before group members can discuss their objectives, they have to make a tentative commitment to basin planning. However, they do not have to commit to developing a basin plan, only to pursuing it as far as it makes sense.

Three Simultaneous Processes

ESTABLISHING PURPOSE	GROUP FORMATION	INDIVIDUAL COMMITMENT
What is the problem?	How can I draw the group together?	How do I relate to the problem?
What is the decision to be made?	How can I help members participate productively?	How do I relate to the group?
What are the criteria?	How can I affirm membership in the group?	Is this our problem?
What are the alternatives?		Should I continue meeting with the group?
What is the effect of each alternative on each criterion?	How can I encourage group members to persist?	
Which is the best alternative for each criterion?	Who will lead the group forward?	
Which is the best alternative overall?		

Letting people know what to expect

Two weeks later, the expanded group meets again.

Glenn welcomes the group and again asks people to introduce themselves. When everyone has spoken, Glenn adds, "Ron Banks called to say he couldn't be present but that he will be at future meetings." Continuing, Glenn points to a flip chart that lists the meeting's agenda. It says

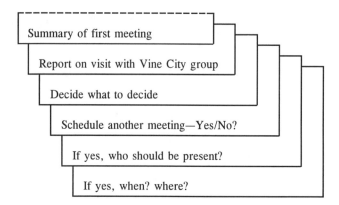

Glenn asks if there are any additions to the agenda. Seeing none, he asks Sid to summarize the information that was presented at the first meeting for the group's new members. Sid hands out the minutes and a three-page handout giving background information about how soil erosion leads to sedimentation, which reduces salmon populations. He talks for five minutes and offers to answer questions after the meeting.

Glenn asks Paul Hartner to describe the group's visit at Vine City. Paul starts, saying, "Glenn, I have to tell you I was pretty skeptical about this basin-planning option at our last meeting. But after talking to the people at Vine City, I see how it might help landowners here in the Upper Powder River basin get erosion under control." Continuing, Paul describes what he learned; Bill Kriesle elaborates. Looking at Ray, Bill adds, "I'm sorry you couldn't be with us. I think you would feel better about this idea if you had." Paul concludes the report, telling the group, "No one at Vine City said it would be easy to develop a plan. In fact, every single person we talked to said it was one of the hardest things they have ever done. But I guess what most amazed me was when I asked them whether they would do it over again, everyone said 'yes.'"

Deciding what to decide

Moving down the agenda, Glenn changes subjects.

"Our primary purpose here tonight is to decide what to decide. Is it fair to say that we want to find the best way to reduce sedimentation in the Upper Powder River basin to increase salmon runs?" Ray answers, "It depends on what you mean by 'best.' If 'best' means I can't use my bottomlands then that's not why I'm here." Glenn encourages Ray to explain further. "What would be best for you, Ray?"

"The least cost and trouble. As far as I'm concerned, this whole thing is a damned nuisance. Looks to me like you're in cahoots with the state, Glenn, coming in here telling us what we can and can't do with our land. Who do you think you are anyway? And, Paul, I'm not about to talk to those Vine City folks. People like Sid, here, brainwashed them as far as I'm concerned."

Glenn ignores the personal remarks. Carefully phrasing a question, he replies, "So you want to reduce sediment but at the least cost and the least amount of your time?" Ray nods. "The issues are time and trouble. I don't see any advantage in making changes that are going to add to my workload," Ray declares. Others around the table offer similar comments.

Dick Miller, the owner of Clearview Lumber, adds, "I wasn't at the first meeting so maybe I missed something, but I'm not here to reduce sedimentation. And I'm not going to go out of my way to protect salmon although you can't be from these parts and not care about the salmon. I am willing to talk about how I can reduce soil erosion on my land. But like Ray, here, it better not involve much time or trouble." "Or money," adds a farmer.

Betsy breaks in, "At the last meeting, I said I didn't hold out much hope for this basin-planning option. And as I listen to the discussion around the table, I'm even more skeptical. Listen to us. To protect salmon runs, we've got to reduce sedimentation. To do that, we all have to reduce soil erosion. Otherwise anything any one of us does won't have enough effect." Several people nod. Joe Warren agrees. "It's not any single change that makes a difference. It's the effect of everyone doing what needs to be done at the same time."

Focusing on the benefits, but not letting the group give up

The atmosphere is tense and questioning.

John Robertson, a landowner, slams his fist on the table. "No matter what we do, it won't be enough. Somewhere, sometime, a logging road is bound to wash out or a culvert will go. If we're going to fail regardless of what we do, why do anything?" Others quickly follow John's questions.

"That's a good question, John," says Glenn, turning to Sid for a response. Sid's boss, Jill, responds tersely, "I need to remind you there are consequences in doing nothing. The state is happy to play the game however you choose. You can take voluntary action or court-ordered action. If you want to pay fines and court costs, that's up to you." Joe jumps in to soften the impact of Jill's response. "I know it sounds like we're asking for a lot. But once we get the turbidity levels down, the river will be pretty resilient."

Ray asks, "What do you mean by 'pretty resilient'?" Bill Kriesle explains that the river is like soil. Once you get pH in bounds, it can handle a shock once in a while. Kathy adds, "Once the sediment load is down, the risk to the fish population from a single event is much lower. Within limits, the main stream can handle a slide or bank collapse in a side stream."

Allowing the discussion to digress

The group is now looking at the problem from many perspectives.

Trying another angle, Joe comments, "There's another reason to take a good look at this basin-planning option now. The courts have supported Native American claims to fish stocks. If fish runs don't come back up, the regulatory code likely will become stricter over time. And the Tribal Association could try to hold individual landowners liable for loss of income if salmon numbers continue to decline."

"What you're saying is if we don't take some responsibility now, we could be required to later—at a higher cost." Dick Miller of Clearview Lumber concludes. "We really don't have much choice, do we?"

Sid clarifies what he sees as an important distinction. "You have a choice but there are boundaries on your options. Doing nothing is not an option. I can tell you what I think will be enough. Nobody can tell you what is the minimum necessary." Sid continues, "Right now, you have a more fundamental choice to make: (1) You can take one step at a time and see if you can develop a plan; (2) you can each go home, implement whatever erosion controls you can, and see if it is enough; or (3) you can do nothing and wait for the state to take legal action. Whatever you do, you can be sure that the regulations will get more demanding every year until the fish runs improve."

A landowner asks Jill, "If we draw up a basin-management plan, how long are we protected from stiffer regulations?" Jill answers, "The plan is good for ten years, with a review at five years." The speaker insists, "A five-year review? That means we're only protected for five years." Jill answers, "The five-year review is for everyone's protection. Yes, the state can request more effort but it gives the landowner an out as well. If you have a buyer who doesn't want the plan, you can withdraw from the plan at five years."

Ray asks, "What if I want to sell my land before five years?" Jill answers, "The buyers will have to agree to abide by the terms of the plan. If they don't, both you and the buyers will be held jointly liable." Ray shakes his head, "That's pretty risky if you ask me."

"C'mon Ray, five years is nothing when the farm has been in the family as long as yours has," Bill teases. Others ask questions about the basin-planning option and how it works. Unlike the questions from a week earlier, people are asking questions about their specific concerns rather than general points of information.

Dealing with impatience

After listening awhile, Bill Kriesle speaks.

"I know I said this at the last meeting, and I can't speak for anyone else, but it seems to me that we have little choice but to continue. We are so far off the agenda right now, I'm not sure we'll get back. How about it, Glenn, can we get back to deciding what to decide?"

Glenn responds, "You're right, Bill. We have gotten off the topic and I promised you we would end on time tonight. Before we close, let's come back to the decision question."

Coming back to the decision question

Paul leads the group back to the main task of the meeting.

Paul replies, "I think what you said earlier is OK." Ray cautions, "As long as I can keep farming . . ." Betsy adds, "That applies to Northwest as well. We have to protect our bottom line, too." Seeing the direction the discussion is taking, Glenn summarizes the group's common ground. He wants the meeting to end positively. "Based on our discussion here tonight, let me restate what I think the decision question is," Glenn declares. "'What is the best plan to reduce soil erosion so that sedimentation does not threaten salmon runs and landowners have the least cost and fuss possible?' Is that it?"

Ray nods, "That's a lot better than the first question you asked. At least it says my needs are as important as those damned salmon." Dick Miller of Clearview Lumber replies, "C'mon, Ray, we all care about the salmon, and you know it. But I'm like you, I have to put food on the table before I can concern myself about dying salmon." Turning to Glenn, he says, "I'm satisfied."

Getting commitment to attend the next meeting

Changing the subject, Glenn turns to some housekeeping details.

"Am I correct that you want to schedule another meeting?" Seeing nods of approval, Glenn continues, "We have accomplished a lot tonight. Between now and our next meeting, I want you to think about your own objectives—your bottom line, so to speak. Next meeting, we'll revise the decision question if we need to. Then, we'll talk about what factors, or criteria, we should use to evaluate alternative plans. If you know of other landowners who should be present, please invite them. Is two weeks a good interval between meetings? Is Tuesday night a good night?" After a brief discussion, the group sets a meeting date and Glenn closes the meeting.

Focusing on opportunities—using threats sparingly

At the meeting, Glenn emphasizes the positive benefits of planning—controlling erosion, voluntary action, and community empowerment. He facilitates and motivates the group. Juxtaposed against Glenn's forward-looking approach, Sid makes the need for a choice real to group members through his presence, body language, and words. He carries the stick of increased state regulation, but he does not threaten. He downplays the negative threats when the group is moving forward, using them only when needed. He gently soothes Ray's anger, which is close to the surface. At one point when the group seemed close to giving up, Jill made the threat of regulation more urgent and explicit, sparing Sid the need to jeopardize his sympathetic relationship with the group.

Sid knows that threats can push people away. If he bludgeons group members with threats, they may decide that they cannot accomplish enough to avoid fines and legal action. The rational response to inevitable fines and legal action is to delay as long as possible, to organize, and to fight in the courts. Threats effectively draw people together to solve problems if

- They are coupled with a clear opportunity to avoid the negative consequences threatened.

- The consequences of inaction are so great and so immediate that no thinking person can stand by and do nothing (i.e., during crises). Even then, there must be a clear-cut approach available or people will not act together.

Too often, threats put people in a "damned-if-I-do, damned-if-I-don't" situation. When this happens, many choose to continue as they have in the past. The threatened person thinks, "If there's nothing I can do to avoid the negative consequences, then I might as well continue doing what I'm doing as long as possible, avoiding the disruption change brings and hoping something will change so I can avoid what now seems inevitable." We see people employ this logic every day: Cities and farmers across the Southwest know they must reduce their water usage. Rather than adjust their usage voluntarily, they have desperately fought any change that would reduce their allocations and distribute water more fairly.

Empty or exaggerated threats can make problems harder to solve. During the 1970s' energy crisis, we were told that oil reserves would be depleted in 20 years. Many of those who bought smaller, energy-efficient cars felt they had been misled when the immediate crisis was resolved and a glut of oil brought gasoline prices down. Buyers returned to larger cars mistakenly convinced that the threat was empty. Those who proclaimed the crisis lost credibility. And perhaps Americans became a little more jaded—harder to convince that resource problems call for action.

Encouraging individual commitment

Individual commitment is essential to move the group to choice. At the outset, group members make a conditional commitment to come to a meeting to see what develops. After each meeting, each individual asks, Is this *my* problem? How do *I* relate to this group? How is this *our* problem? Is there anything we can do to solve *our* problem together?

In most cases, the individual must affirm his or her membership in the group over and over. Ideally, each affirmation brings a deeper commitment so that at some point, there is no doubt in the individual's mind. However, an individual's commitment doesn't always deepen. Sometimes people make conditional commitments from one meeting to the next, always waiting to see what happens, always ready to give up at the least slight. Other times people's commitment may not deepen, but participation becomes habitual; they stick with the group out of habit.

The basis of individual commitment often shifts as the group matures. When a threat brings the group together, group maturation hinges on shifting the basis of individual commitment to something positive. Just as different things bring the group together, group members commit to different aspects of the group's purpose. Some individuals make a personal commitment to the group of people involved or to the group's leader. Others commit to solving the problem and taking action. Some make an ideological commitment to the ideals the group represents. Members' expectations of the group differ depending on the basis of their commitment.

Affirming diversity and encouraging realistic expectations

To mature, new groups have to affirm the diverse basis of members' commitments and, at the same time, create realistic expectations. Failure to create realistic expectations leads to inevitable defeat. Failure to affirm diversity leads to a homogeneous membership that almost certainly excludes people who need to be involved in solving complex problems.

On the surface, affirming diversity and creating realistic expectations seem to conflict. However, they need not if the group can agree on what the problem is and what needs to be decided—constructing a carefully worded decision question that identifies the group's multiple objectives. The question and process that creates it can result in realistic expectations while affirming diversity.

These objectives are achieved by creating an environment in which group members feel free to express their needs, opinions, and concerns about the decision to be made. Group members learn to know each other as they experiment with alternative decision questions—trying them on, experiencing how they feel, and thinking about where they might lead.

Articulating the choice to be made in concrete terms is risky for each party in the new group. Group members don't know each other well. They are naturally hesitant to reveal too much, fearing rejection, disinterest, or conflict. Group members must come to grips not only with the decision at hand but also with their position in the evolving group. Often individual group members represent a larger group of people. For example, Ron Banks represents his Tribal Association. Kathy Shield represents the Forest Service. Paul Hartner represents Northwest Forest Products. These individuals must present values, needs, and wants of their group or parent organization. Kathy is not sure she can represent the Forest Service's interests well while Paul Hartner feels confident of his ability to represent his employer.

Finding direction and leadership

In the process of group formation, groups grope for direction, potential leaders emerge, and roles evolve. Just as a shopper tries on new clothes, the group tries on directions, leaders, and roles in the early stages of group formation. It is hard for a group to evaluate direction without trying it on, experiencing how it feels, and seeing for a moment where it might lead. The group may seem fickle, following one path at one meeting and another at the next.

Potential leaders jockey for position and compete for followers—sometimes consciously, at other times unconsciously. In our illustration, Glenn is in a unique position. Sid asks him to lead the meeting—to be the "front man" on basin planning, drawing attention away from the threat of fines and legal action. At these first meetings, Glenn functions as both leader and facilitator. He wants to inspire a shared vision among group members, which is a leadership role; he also wants to facilitate group interaction, encouraging constructive and purposeful participation. Sid also has a unique status. Although Glenn leads the meeting, all present know that Sid, representing the state's regulatory apparatus, is the reason they are meeting.

When questions that require authoritative response arise, he answers.

Groups groping for direction and leadership are unstable. Group members' commitment may wax and wane from meeting to meeting. It is difficult to predict whether the group will come to agreement or disband.

Groups that succeed in coming to agreement and making a commitment to action choose a direction and leadership. Direction and leadership are inseparable. Whether the group chooses a leader who sets direction or a direction that determines who leads is unimportant. What is important is that, in choosing, the group sets down *a* path of discovery—one that differs from other paths they might have chosen.

Distinguishing leadership and facilitation

It is important to distinguish between leadership and facilitation. A group may formally choose someone to lead meetings—to facilitate group interaction. A facilitator encourages constructive and purposeful participation, monitors progress, and keeps the group moving forward. In contrast, leaders provide a vision that gives direction. Sometimes these roles conflict.

John Robertson, the landowner who pounded his fist on the table, challenged Glenn's vision when he asked, *"If we're going to fail regardless of what we do, why do anything?"* Taking their cue from John, others started asking similar questions. Glenn, the facilitator, thanks John for the question and asks Sid to respond, expecting that Sid will gently remind the group of both the opportunity and threat, providing the leadership needed to give the group direction. In this case, Glenn's role as facilitator and leader conflict. If Glenn asserts leadership at this point, the group's trust in him as facilitator will be diminished. At this point, the facilitator's role is critically important, and other group members can be counted on to provide leadership so Glenn responds to the challenge as a facilitator.

Leadership is a function of the group. Leaders emerge from a group as they voice a vision of the future shared by the group. Sometimes leadership is divided—or shared. But shared or not, leaders can improve their contributions to a group by becoming aware of leadership attributes and skills.

Leaders see problems as a challenge and a call to action. They own the problem. Leaders take action purposefully. First, they question: "What vision will guide us? What values inform the vision? Who will share it?" Leaders inspire a shared vision of what the future can be. At the same time, they are realists, searching for concrete ways to solve the problem at hand. They are not satisfied with easy solutions that temporarily resolve the problem but come no closer to their vision. Rather than asking, "What is the easiest way?" leaders ask, "What is the best way?" When presented with new and better ways of doing things, leaders ask, "Why not?" They encourage innovation, experimentation, and risk taking to move forward. Leaders ask, "Who are we? Who can we involve?" As enablers, they encourage collaboration, build teams, and empower others to act, sharing ownership with all who have the vision. When solutions seem beyond reach, leaders instill confidence that those working together have within themselves the tools to persevere and meet the challenges they face. In this situation, leaders do not ask "What are our deficiencies? How do we make up for them?" but "What are our strengths? How can we build on our accomplishments so that each step moves us closer to our vision?"

In contrast, facilitators play a different role. Typically, they do not own the problem or the solution. Consequently, they are more-or-less disinterested participants free to observe and expedite group interaction. Facilitators help a group of individuals function as a group by helping them communicate to find common ground instead of talking past each other. Instead of articulating a vision, a facilitator helps a group find its own vision.

Facilitators ask questions just as leaders do. However, a facilitator does not actively participate in answering them as leaders do. When the question calls for factual information, a facilitator helps group members sort out what they know and what they don't know. When a question calls for value-based answers, a facilitator helps the group affirm individual differences while searching for some common values.

Skilled facilitation is both an art and a craft. Facilitation requires thoughtful listening and the ability to discern meaning from not only words but body language, tone, and other nonverbal communication. At the same time, facilitators use several techniques to promote constructive communication. They include the following:

- *Encourage thoughtful participation by all.* Sensitive facilitation is needed to encourage thoughtful participation and constructive discussion. The facilitator strives to create an environment where people who may not know or understand each other well can reveal their values, wants, and needs without feeling threatened.

- *Affirm diversity.* Recognizing the need to affirm diversity yet encourage realistic expectations, Glenn encourages open discussion at the first meetings. He asks the group to suggest alternative decision questions. He keeps the discussion open ended, encouraging members to express a wide range of viewpoints. He restates and clarifies without judging. To keep the discussion going, he uses a roundtable approach, moving around the table, actively soliciting comment.

- *Encourage variations on a theme.* Glenn asks for additional comment. To avoid polarization, he encourages variations on a theme rather than dialectically opposed opinions. He wants to expand the discussion and reduce individuals' commitment to narrow viewpoints. Point-counterpoint discussion implicitly encourages people to choose sides.

- *Restate and clarify points.* Rather than cutting off repetition, Glenn encourages group members to restate and reinforce each other's opinions. Repetition and reinforcement clarify confusing points and highlight common ground.

- *Reduce personal risk.* As facilitator, Glenn reduces risk even further by asking people to "think off the wall." He assures the group no one has to commit to anything right now. Throughout the meeting he reminds the group, "Nobody will hold you to anything you say. Tonight, we're here to think this problem through."

- *Highlight common ground.* Glenn concludes each meeting by identifying the common ground revealed in the discussion. He will start the next meeting with this point of agreement. Recognition of common ground provides a sense of accomplishment and creates anticipation for what is to come. Beginning the next meeting with agreement on the decision question gives group members a sense of progress. While it does not always work out so nicely, it is important to give group members a sense of direction, which is measured by accomplishment, anticipation, and progress.

- *Give members who represent an organization time to touch base.* Putting off agreement is also practical. Deferring agreement to the next meeting gives those who represent an employer or organization a chance to report on the meeting and gain institutional support. These group members have to make sure they don't get too far out in front of those they represent. Influenced by participation in the ad hoc group, these representatives' understanding evolves. If those they represent do not evolve at the same time, their representative may agree to something that isn't supported by the parent group.

- *Keep the group moving forward.* The Powder River group agrees on who should be involved in decision making. The group realizes that the status quo is unacceptable and that change will be necessary. Glenn's ability to hold up a vision that others can accept establishes his position as leader, at least in the short run. As the second meeting ends, the group has established a sense of direction and has begun to define roles. They decide to meet again.

Without Glenn's skilled facilitation, the diverse Powder River group might never become a group. To become a group, its individual members must reconcile answers to their own questions with the group's answers to the decision framework's questions. Glenn's facilitation helps individuals accept differences without withdrawing from the group. As facilitator, Glenn asks himself, "How can I draw the group together? How can I help members participate productively? How can I affirm individuals' membership in the group? How can I encourage individual members to persist?"

The Third Meeting—
The Decision Question, Values, and Criteria

Glenn and Sid structure the meetings so they can use the decision-making framework and process steps without having to explain its structure and logic to the group members. They plan the next meeting according to the framework's structure.

Three Simultaneous Processes

ESTABLISHING PURPOSE	GROUP FORMATION	INDIVIDUAL COMMITMENT
What is the problem?	How can I draw the group together?	How do I relate to the problem?
What is the decision to be made?	How can I help members participate productively?	How do I relate to the group?
What are the criteria?	How can I affirm membership in the group?	Is this our problem?
What are the alternatives?	How can I encourage group members to persist?	Should I continue meeting with the group?
What is the effect of each alternative on each criterion?	Who will lead the group forward?	
Which is the best alternative for each criterion?		
Which is the best alternative overall?		

Planning for the next meeting

Sid and Glenn develop an agenda for the next meeting. The first agenda item is getting agreement on the decision question.

Sid suggests rephrasing the decision question in a way that makes it easier for group members to list their own objectives. "How does this sound? 'What is the best plan to reduce soil erosion in a way that meets landowners' needs and increases fish runs?'" Glenn agrees, "I think that's what we need."

Next, they add "discussing criteria" to the agenda. They talk about the point of this step. Sid says, "We want to find out what criteria are important to each individual. We don't want to push the group to agree to a set of shared criteria." Glenn agrees, "Everybody needs to understand what's important to the others. If we push them to agree, they'll only try to convince each other that their criteria are most important. We'll have a free-for-all."

Finally Glenn says he would like to see a leader emerge from the group. "Don't get me wrong. I can lead the group, and I'm willing if it's necessary. But I think the group would have a better chance of coming to agreement if someone with a direct stake in the outcome took the lead." Sid disagrees, "They feel comfortable with you, Glenn. The fact that you aren't a direct stakeholder makes it easier for them to trust you. What if Paul Hartner tried to lead the group? The group would never trust him. They would always be trying to figure out what his hidden agenda was. They would question his motives." Glenn concedes, "You have a point there, but I'm still not convinced. Let's wait and see what evolves."

Starting where the group left off

The meeting is well attended. Glenn opens the meeting.

He asks everyone to introduce themselves. He puts the revised decision question on a flip chart and asks for comments. Each person is given a chance to add their objectives to the decision question. The group lists the following needs:

- Maintain income
- Minimize cost of erosion controls
- Require minimum amount of labor to implement and manage
- Share burden among landowners

After several people speak, it becomes apparent that the question captures the general sense of the group's purpose. However, nearly everyone suggests word changes and superficial modifications. Rather than bog down in nuance of word meaning, Glenn suggests that they move on, deferring detailed revisions until later. After seeking consensus, Glenn moves to the next agenda item.

List but do not discuss criteria.

Glenn asks each person to list their criteria on a piece of paper. He explains that criteria are those things that are important to the decision—the basis on which individuals choose among alternatives. When everyone finishes writing, he goes around the table asking each person to read their list.

He cautions the group that no discussion will be allowed, explaining, "We each need to know what is important to our neighbors because any solution has to meet not only our own criteria but our neighbors' as well." Sid records each person's criteria on a flip chart.

Ray turns to Glenn and says, "You can't meet all of those conditions. You have a conflicting jumble up there." Glenn explains, "That's all right for the moment. We'll talk about the criteria when everyone has had a chance to get what's important to them on the list." Sid reminds Ray of the list but does not discuss rules.

Revising criteria

When everyone has had a chance to add their criteria to the list, Glenn asks for discussion. The discussion that ensues is heated.

Each person tries to convince the group that his or her criteria are the right or most important ones. While one person talks, the others think about how they can make their arguments more effectively. People talk more than they listen. Glenn remains silent as he realizes the discussion is directionless.

After an hour, Glenn calls a halt to the discussion and suggests a coffee break. During the coffee break, the most vocal group members corner anyone who will listen and continue their efforts to gain support for their criteria. Sid and Glenn go into a corner to talk about how they can get the discussion back on a more purposeful track.

The group comes back from the break more agitated than when they left. Before reopening the discussion, Glenn reminds the group of three points.

- Criteria are not right or wrong, they reflect an individual's values, needs, and wants.

- What's important to one person may not be important to anyone else.
- Each person's criteria are legitimate.

He concludes, "The purpose of this discussion is to learn to understand our neighbors' criteria and why they are important. We're not asking you to give up what is important to you. We just want to find whatever common ground we have. Surely we have something in common."

Bill Kriesle is as frustrated with the earlier discussion as Glenn. But now he worries that Glenn's sermonette might turn some people off. He decides to give Glenn a little ribbing to ease the tension. "Don't be so sure, Glenn. We're a pretty independent bunch of folks. Right, Paul? You and Ron ought to be able to answer that one. Do you have any common ground? Have you two ever agreed on anything?"

Ron Banks from the Tribal Association smiles slowly. "If we have, neither of us will admit it." Paul lights up. "We agree on one thing. We've never agreed on anything. Is that the common ground you're looking for, Glenn?" By this time, everyone is laughing. Always the politician, Glenn takes the ribbing good naturedly.

When the discussion resumes, the group listens more actively and Glenn facilitates. He affirms statements, asks for clarification, encourages new people to contribute, and protects people's ideas.

Generating an inclusive list of criteria

Criteria will almost always differ in ad hoc groups that come together to address complex resource problems. The group process step *list, but do not discuss* allows individuals to explore and clarify their own criteria before discussing and critically evaluating them. When structured groups use the framework, the purpose of this step is to develop a single list of criteria for the group. In ad hoc groups, a single list often is not possible and may not be necessary. Listing criteria makes each group member aware of what is important to other group members. At its best, discussion of criteria enables group members to see the basis of choice from each other's perspective, even if just for a moment. Through this process, group members can gain empathy for others' perspectives and learn to accept the legitimacy of criteria other than their own.

While possible, it is rare for individuals to make drastic changes in their own criteria. It is difficult to imagine Ray Green thinking about the problem as a fisheries-management rather than a land-management problem. He is a farmer, not a fisher. However, a better understanding leads people to accept a more inclusive list of criteria. People come to acknowledge that everyone's criteria are critical to making a decision because all of the people present are critical to solving the underlying problem.

Many people find it difficult to list their criteria. Unaccustomed to stating what is important to them in precise, clear language, they confuse criteria and alternatives. They cannot separate narrow criteria from broader objectives. Glenn is careful to describe criteria in several different ways to help people understand their role in decision making. He gives clear examples to illustrate how criteria influence a simple decision. People can list criteria without ever even hearing the word. It isn't the word but the concept that's important. Criteria answer two questions: On what basis will we decide? Ideally, what specific conditions should our alternatives meet?

Some people have thought about what is important to them more than others. Setting aside time for each person to think about their criteria and to write them down before stating them gives group members a chance to participate more equally. Next, the facilitator goes around the room asking each person to add criteria to the list. The facilitator continues to ask for additional criteria until all group members see their criteria included. The facilitator can clarify additions to the list in several ways. For example, Glenn can ask contributors to clarify their additions. He can ask another group member to paraphrase an addition to the list and then ask the contributor to confirm the restated criterion. Glenn writes all contributions on a flip chart. He thanks each person for their contribution without judgment, affirming the contributor's participation in the group.

Letting the group discover its common ground

The group members pause to think about how they relate to the group.

Midway through the discussion, Bill Kriesle says, "I think we have more common ground than we realize. At one level or another, we're all concerned with productivity. Only our specific interests vary. Take Ray Green, Andrew Krohl, and me. We're farmers. We have to keep our land producing or we won't have any income. Paul, you and the other timber producers have the same concern. If the land doesn't produce trees, you won't have a job." He turns to Ron Banks and Joe Warren. "You guys are interested in fish runs. But, Ron, you manage your forestland for timber too. You have to be concerned with productivity of both fisheries and forestry. Even the town's concern for water quality can be seen as a productivity issue." Glenn responds, "Right, it's a question of how much clean water costs."

Probing the group for a leader

Bill's observation stops the discussion for a moment. Before anyone raises a new point, Glenn points out the time.

"It's 8:45. If we're going to close at 9:00 as we agreed, we had better take care of some housekeeping details now." No one clamors to continue the discussion so he goes on. "I am still happy to make arrangements for these meetings and Sid has offered to continue taking minutes, but is there anyone who is willing to lead the group?"

When no one responds, Glenn resumes. "I think it's important that someone who has a more obvious stake in the outcome lead the group. I have to admit I feel a little bit hypocritical standing up here when I'm not the one who will have to make any real changes. I think one of you needs to lead these meetings. Any volunteers?"

Everyone praises Glenn's logic, but no one volunteers. Someone suggests Joe Warren. He shakes his head. "I'm not the right person for the same reason Glenn isn't the right person. I'm not going to have to make any changes. Besides, just two weeks ago you all were worried that the state was coming in here telling you what to do. And I am here representing a state agency."

After more discussion, Paul Hartner suggests Bill Kriesle. Bill was deeply involved in the evening's discussion. He had buttonholed Jill Baker-Schofield before the meeting and at break to find out more about the basin-planning option. He has a reputation for being direct and sure of himself. Everyone turns to Bill.

He asks some questions. Then he responds, "In all seriousness, folks, this is *our* meeting. What we need is a neutral chairperson to keep us from each other's throats and to help us figure out what we can agree on. Frankly, I want to feel free to say what I think needs to be said without having to worry about keeping the peace. I recommend we let Glenn continue doing what he's been doing." Looking at Glenn, Bill concludes, "I can only speak for myself but I want you to know I like what you've been doing. I think we need you."

After some discussion, Glenn agrees to lead the group. Laughing, Bill stands up. "Who said anything about leading us? We asked you to chair our meetings, keep the peace, facilitate, whatever you want to call it. Nobody said anything about leadership. I'm not sure we've got any followers but we have plenty of leaders in this room."

Glenn laughs, "OK, OK. I get the picture. Now, when do you want to meet next?" Everyone agrees to meet the following week, same time and place. As people walk to the parking lot, they joke about Bill and Glenn. Paul warns Glenn, "Watch out for Bill. He might just take this leadership business so seriously he runs for mayor next election."

Confirming individual leadership

At the third meeting, an essential step in group formation occurs. They confirm Glenn's critical role as facilitator and acknowledge Bill's leadership.

These events are a key step in group formation.

Taken literally, these events improve the likelihood that the group will continue to progress. Glenn has formally accepted responsibility to see the process through—to help the group laboriously move from one step to the next until a plan is agreed on. This is a critical role. Without a strong facilitator, ad hoc groups almost inevitably get mired in complexity and fail to reach a joint decision.

As symbolic gestures, these events represent a shift in ownership from the politicians and bureaucrats to the group. As Bill and other group members assert their leadership, the group is more likely to take ownership over the decision-making process. If they feel that they own the process, then they are more likely to commit themselves to implementing the decisions that result.

Since group members don't know what will be decided, their commitment to stay with the process is based on a growing trust that the group's efforts can result in an acceptable plan. As an articulate and thoughtful member of the group, Bill helps group members discover their common ground. Group members listen to him. By the end of the meeting, they are looking to him to help make sense of the jumble of ideas and perspectives in a way that is sensitive to everyone's needs. They are beginning to trust him to set a direction for the group.

Leadership, direction, and trust do not always evolve so easily. When group members see each other as adversaries, strong but sensitive facilitation is required to help group members discover their common ground. Any hint that the facilitator sympathizes with one faction or another impairs the facilitator's effectiveness. Ideally, a courageous leader will emerge to draw the group together even in the most polarized groups. In some groups, this leader never materializes, and group members never develop the trust necessary to move forward. Even those who want to find common ground can become impatient and quit.

Coping with the organizer's changing role

In the early meetings, the group's development depended on Sid and Glenn. Group members identified with Sid and Glenn rather than the group. If either had missed a meeting, the fragile group might have collapsed.

Now individuals are beginning to identify with the group. Rather than attending the mayor's meeting, they are working with the Powder River group. When they talk about the group to their friends, they are more likely to explain, "A group of us who live and work along the Powder River are trying to develop a basin-management plan" than "The mayor's asked me to attend a meeting."

As group members have begun to identify with the group, Glenn's role has as organizer becomes less important. This shift is an important step in group formation and one that increases the likelihood that a group will reach agreement.

Once group members begin to identify with the group, it is relatively easy for most groups to accept the organizer's role. It is not always easy for the organizer to accept a reduced role in the group. While Sid and Glenn accept their reduced role gracefully, many do not. Mixed feelings are natural, much as parents worry about letting go of their teenage children. Occasionally an organizer will actively resist the loss of control, manipulating the group consciously or unconsciously so that it remains dependent.

As professionals, we are more likely than most to advise ad hoc groups. Often we are the catalyst for their formation in the first place. We have to put aside our insecurities and personal desires for the good of the group. When the time comes, we may have to step aside to allow someone with a greater stake in the outcome to assume leadership. Then we have to ease the transition, willingly accepting a diminished but important advisory role. If we do not, we impair the group's ability to reach a decision and subtly discourage group members from committing themselves to implementing whatever decision might be reached.

he Fourth Meeting—
he Search for Alternatives

Glenn stands at the door, welcoming people as they arrive for the next meeting. Bill makes a point of greeting each person as they come in. When they sit down, Glenn sits at the center of the table where he can see everyone. Sid, taking notes, sits to his left. Bill sits with the group, but it is clear he is a leader.

Three Simultaneous Processes

ESTABLISHING PURPOSE	GROUP FORMATION	INDIVIDUAL COMMITMENT
What is the problem?	How can I draw the group together?	How do I relate to the problem?
What is the decision to be made?	How can I help members participate productively?	How do I relate to the group?
What are the criteria?	How can I affirm membership in the group?	Is this our problem?
What are the alternatives?	How can I encourage group members to persist?	Should I continue meeting with the group?
What is the effect of each alternative on each criterion?	Who will lead the group forward?	
Which is the best alternative for each criterion?		
Which is the best alternative overall?		

Glenn opens the discussion, summing up the conclusion of the last meeting. "All of us are concerned about improving, or at least maintaining, productivity. That means different things for each of us. What does that mean to you?"

Ray answers, "To protect the fishery folks' productivity, Bill, the Krohls, and I have to quit plowing our bottomlands and put them in long-term pasture. To maintain *our* productivity, we have to keep plowing those lands. It's not that we want to, we have to. We have to produce enough crops to pay our bills. Those are some of my most productive acres. Unlike Bill, I don't have much alluvial benchland."

Hinging joint decisions on a sense of fairness

The discussion that follows is intense. Bill questions, "Is it fair for Ray or anyone else to bear the cost of solving this problem alone?" Dick Miller of

Clearview Lumber says, "No one can take Ray's productive land without compensation." Glenn answers, "It's not a taking issue." Betsy adds, "If it's not a taking issue, it's an issue of being able to pay the bills, show a profit, and keep the land in commercial forest use." Glenn says, "We've agreed that everyone has an interest in maintaining productivity. Whose productivity is going to be affected?"

Bill replies, "Let's look at this from a different angle for a minute. It seems to me—and I might be wrong—that we each have an interest in protecting each other's productivity. If the forests and farms aren't commercially viable, then we'll see 'gentlemen' farmers and 'horse acre' developments. None of us sitting around this table wants that."

Jill responds, "I agree with what you've said, Bill and Glenn. We do have to protect each person's ability to produce, but we also have to do things differently. We have to reduce sedimentation from plowed lands and silting from logging operations and clear cuts. We must have fewer roads wash out and less runoff. I'm not sure what the alternatives are, but I am sure that each and every person in this room will have to do some things differently." No one responds. To break the silence, Glenn proposes a coffee break.

Knowing where the group is going

During the break, Glenn, Bill, and Sid plan the rest of the meeting.

Bill asserts, "We have to get agreement on the idea that every one needs to look out for his or her neighbors' productive interests. If we can get agreement on that notion, then we can break into small groups to generate ideas about how to reduce sedimentation."

"Sounds good to me," Glenn responds. "What do you think, Sid?" Sid answers, "I think we're on the right track, but don't push them too hard on looking out for their neighbors, Bill. Each one of us will have to come around to the notion of collective responsibility individually. That takes time."

Summarizing where the group has been

Bill asks, "What if we start by asking someone to summarize what we've agreed on so far, Glenn? Then you can divide us into small groups to brainstorm about alternatives." Glenn nods.

Glenn calls the group back together. He starts, saying, "I want to be sure that we're all on the same track. Can someone summarize what we just said?" Betsy responds, "We've agreed that we need to find the best way to reduce sediment to increase fish runs. And each of us has an interest in maintaining or increasing productivity. But our interests differ and at times conflict. We also agree that it is not fair for one person to shoulder the cost of solving the problem alone. And it's pretty clear that each of us will have to do things differently. Does that summarize where we are?" Glenn looks around the group for nods of agreement.

List but do not discuss alternatives.

Glenn moves forward.

"Next, we'll divide into two groups. Each group will generate a list of ways that we can reduce sediment in the Powder River. Your task is to generate a list. It's unlikely that any idea will be complete or satisfy everyone. So for now, put every suggestion on the list without talking about its good or bad points. Sid and I will facilitate, so don't get upset if he or I cut you off when you start discussing instead of listing. We'll write your ideas down as you speak so that we have a written list. When we come back together, we will discuss them all. And I trust that we will be considerate of each other. Are there any questions?" Seeing none, Glenn divides the group so that farm, forest, and fisheries perspectives are represented in both small groups.

Facilitating and keeping the group on task

Although the facilitators have clearly stated the rules, they allow for flexibility.

Both Sid and Glenn bend the "no discussion" rule, permitting clarification and limited discussion about the alternatives. However, both are careful to discourage discussion that might deteriorate into an "us" against "them" argument or comments that might prejudice the group for or against an alternative.

The groups are still listing alternatives at 9:00 p.m. when Glenn calls the meeting to a close. He suggests that they continue working in groups next week. Everyone agrees. Afterwards, people cluster in groups of two and three, continuing the discussion as they walk slowly to the parking lot.

Often, the search for solutions is bounded more by the perceptions and emotional energy of those involved than by technological, physical, or social constraints. The extent of the search is a subjective choice the group makes consciously or unconsciously. The search itself can be as creative or as narrow as the group chooses.

The search for solutions is also a concrete step in group formation. The kinds of alternatives listed, the way suggestions are received, the energy and enthusiasm behind suggestions—all send signals. Group members form opinions about what kinds of actions their neighbors might be willing to consider or take. They use these perceptions to evaluate how far they might be willing to go and what personal risk they might be willing to take later in pushing one alternative or another.

The search for solutions is a critical step in moving the group from problem definition to action. Action depends on identifying and considering a mutually acceptable alternative. If no alternative meets the minimum requirements of all group members, joint action is impossible even if the group has agreed on a decision question, clarified criteria, and made great strides in group formation.

The Fifth Meeting—Common Ground

No one waits for the meeting to start tonight. They go into their groups and commence where they left off the week before.

Celebrating the turning points

Glenn is beaming when he calls the meeting to order.

"I'm sorry to break up your discussions just now, but I would like Bill and Ray to share with you a conversation they had after last week's meeting. I think you will find it as interesting as I did. The floor is yours, Bill."

Smiling, Bill starts, "Ray and I were in different groups last week. We compared notes. For the most part, our lists were pretty predictable. Everybody listed 'keep the cows off the bottomland' and doing some kind of streamside planting to reduce runoff."

Only half-jokingly Paul teases, "Get to the point, Bill. We want to get back to our work." Unruffled, Bill replies, "Just give me a chance, Paul. I may be slow to get to the point, but I usually have something to say. I'm not a politician, you know.

"As I was saying, Ray and I were talking about how to deal with the sedimentation from our farms. After a fair amount of saying it couldn't be done, we talked about the possibility of trading some of his lower land for some of my benchland where our farms adjoin." Bill has everyone's attention now. Jill can't believe what she is hearing.

Bill explains further. "Then I could use the lower part of Ray's bottomland to grow hay and Ray could use my benchland for crops. That won't reduce the flooding, but it might reduce the runoff. Frankly, I don't know why we didn't think of it before. We've shared equipment and helped each other over the years. This isn't that different really." "It isn't?" Paul asks. "Sounds pretty incredible to me. Are you sure you two are thinking clearly?" Ignoring Paul, Bill resumes, "Anyway, I thought you might want to consider a broader range of alternatives as we continue our group work."

Trusting the group enough to take a risk

In both groups, the discussion turns to Ray's and Bill's proposal. They don't have a lot of details. Both admit that they haven't talked it out, and neither is fully convinced a land swap is possible. But both believe that their idea represents the kind of thinking that is necessary to find a mutually acceptable plan.

Now people begin to offer more interesting ideas. They offer narrow solutions to specific problems rather than broad, fuzzy solutions to broad, fuzzy problems. Ron asks, "Can the surface-road drainage ditch be run into a settlement pond if the river outlets are blocked?" Dick Miller of Clearview comments, "Streamside planting isn't a big deal if someone can get seedlings." Kathy Shield from the Forest Service offers to find out if her agency can donate seedlings. Paul says, "Northwest might be able to avoid planned extensions to the '200' logging road if the company can get permission to improve and use the farm road that runs through your property, Ray. We'd also need special permission to exceed load limits on that county road to haul logs out."

Art Porter from Pineview Resort offers to buy a small, old growth remnant at the mouth of the branch stream. Tourists come to the resort to relax on the lodge balcony overlooking this beautiful, old timber stand. Art has worried for years that Clearview Lumber might someday harvest it, and put the resort out of business.

Paul adds, "I understand the state and the Nature Conservancy have started buying conservation easements. We need to look into the details."

Encouraging well-reasoned decisions

When the flurry of ideas slows, Glenn calls the groups together.

Each group presents its list. While enthusiasm is still high, Glenn closes the meeting promptly at 9:00. He doesn't allow time for discussion. He is convinced that things are moving too quickly. He doesn't want people making commitments to things they might regret. When the time comes, he wants solid commitments based on a thoughtful evaluation of the advantages and disadvantages. Right now, the group is focused on possibilities; they can't see the implications. They need time to think about the possibilities and their consequences in the light of day-to-day reality.

Before closing the meeting, Glenn asks for volunteers to check into the implications of each alternative. With volunteers and gentle arm-twisting, each alternative is assigned. Ron asks for clarification: "What kind of implications?" Glenn answers, "We'll need different information for each alternative. For example, how much streamside planting is necessary to reduce sedimentation and where? Can we get any help from the state or county? If we do everything that's been suggested, will it be enough to reduce sedimentation? Do we have to do everything? How much is necessary? Is the burden of change spread equitably? Who bears an unfair share of the burden? I'm sorry I can't be more specific, Ron. Is this helping?" Ron nods.

Minimum-Acceptable versus Best-Possible Solutions

When a group negotiates a political solution, alternatives are offered incrementally. Each side presents a negotiating position. Through cautious give-and-take, one gives a little ground and then the other. When an alternative meets all sides' minimum-acceptable requirements, the deal is sealed. Solutions are by necessity shortsighted. Often it is only months or a few years before all sides must negotiate a new solution to deal with the problems that arise out of the previous solution.

In contrast, those who search for the best-possible solutions seek ones that meet the parties' highest values, wants, and needs as opposed to their minimum-acceptable requirements. But there are times when the only possible solution is the one that meets minimum-acceptable requirements. Frequently, ad hoc groups settle for shortsighted solutions because those involved don't seek anything better. Opportunities are lost for lack of trying.

Establishing trust

In attitude and approach, the Powder River group started its search looking for an alternative that met the minimum acceptable requirements of each member. In the second meeting, Ray Green said he wanted the solution that requires the least change. They talked in generalities. They stuck to familiar alternatives. Group members discussed who might do what in the abstract, using words like everybody, anybody, and somebody—words that often translate into nobody.

The turning point came when Bill Kriesle announced a willingness to consider trading his more valuable cropland for Ray Green's less valuable bottomland to convert it to pasture. Bill felt a responsibility to enable the group to consider alternatives that meet more than the bare minimum. His willingness to consider an alternative that flies in the face of tradition demonstrates a willingness to entrust his welfare to the group. His willingness to trust compels other members to entrust their welfare to the group as well.

Bill also demonstrated a willingness to take risks. While listing an alternative does not imply a commitment, it commits Bill at least to give his own idea serious consideration. Any alternative seriously considered has the potential to be the alternative chosen. Bill would break trust with the group if he rejected his own idea without good cause later. The group will resent him for raising false hopes and acting in bad faith.

Trust within ad hoc groups is fragile. If trust is given and then capriciously withdrawn, a group can quickly disband in frustration. Consequently, moving the group to seek the best-possible as opposed to the minimum-acceptable solutions carries with it a greater risk of failure. A carefully thought out plan and objectives for each meeting help minimize this risk. Plans and objectives should focus not only on the decision making but also on the broader processes of group formation and individual commitment.

Common criteria driving the emerging "us"

Bill's dramatic announcement set the tone for the remainder of the meeting. The discussion shifted from "What is best for me?" to "What is best for us?" As the group optimistically moved from "me" to "us," common understanding emerged to motivate the new "us."

- We will all have to do some things differently.

- Everyone has to share the burden of change equitably.

- No one person should have to bear all the cost.

- An alternative should enable individuals to make progress toward their other goals rather than just to get by.

- We are all better off if land stays in agricultural and forestry production. Recreational housing or industrial development will negatively affect each of us.

Avoiding a fast-moving bandwagon

Enthusiasm, like malaise, is infectious. When one member begins to see opportunities, others follow. The shift from guarded to enthusiastic participation was dramatic in the Powder River group. Where once the group saw only timeworn ideas, now they see possibilities. An ephemeral, creative energy emerges and takes hold of the group. There is a snowball effect as each member jumps on a bandwagon driven by enthusiasm for the joy of creating ideas.

While pleased with the shift from me to us, Glenn reacts cautiously to the meeting's overreaching enthusiasm. Deferring discussion gives group members a chance to collect information and gather their thoughts. Glenn hopes the deferred discussion will retain some of the enthusiasm while focusing on practicalities. There is a risk, however, that the enthusiasm of the moment will be lost altogether. He is willing to take that risk. He realizes that momentary enthusiasm cannot substitute for sustained commitment to action. While necessary for commitment, enthusiasm must be fueled by something more lasting than the momentary joy of creating ideas.

The Next Meeting—The Choice

Grounding the decision on solid information

Glenn, Bill, and Sid meet the next day, Bill admits some doubts about the previous night's meeting.

"I wasn't fully prepared for the response last night," Bill says. "While I hoped our announcement would have the effect it did, I guess I didn't realize everything would move so quickly. I hope I'm not leading them down the wrong path."

"You were great last night, Bill," Sid says. "Yes," Glenn adds, "I've seen groups do that same thing once or twice before. The ideas develop a momentum of their own, separate from reality. The group gets on a roll, and there's no stopping them. But don't worry about it. Next meeting, you'll have the opposite to deal with. Everyone will be wondering why they ever agreed to consider such risky alternatives.

"Right now, we have an opportunity," Glenn continues. "We have to come to the next meeting prepared with solid information. We have to help the group think through the implications of their ideas so that they don't get needlessly bogged down trying to figure out the technical details of biophysical relationships. And we have to provide enough information so that each individual can satisfy himself or herself that the real benefits outweigh the real costs; then they can come to agreement in principle. We can work out details of the plan in later meetings."

Sid says, "I'd feel more comfortable if we had more than one person collecting information on each of those options. I'll take the laundry list of options suggested at the last meeting and put together some background information. For each option, I will provide as concrete information as possible about what would be entailed to make the change, who would be involved, and how much it might reduce soil erosion. Then I can talk about the cumulative effects of several combinations of options on sedimentation. That should put the discussion on a firmer foundation, don't you think?" Glenn laughs, "Did you just volunteer?" Sid chuckles, "Well, better a volunteer than a draftee."

Planning for all possibilities

In spite of his enthusiasm, Glenn worries about the next meeting. "On a serious note, Sid, we have to let group members report first. You should be ready to supplement as needed." He knows from intuition and experience that the group may not come together with the same level of agreement and commitment that they had when they left the last meeting.

In his mind, he sorts out his options. The worst that can happen, he reasons, is that the group will fall back to where they were before Bill revealed his startling idea of a land swap with Ray. He decides to talk with Ray and Bill to see if they are still working on the idea.

Meeting at the diner the next morning, Bill opens the conversation. "Ray and I have talked a couple of times." Ray nods in agreement. "We think the idea has merit, but there are several potential problems. How do we take into account the parcels' different values? What if our operations change in the future? We're going to have a couple of appraisals done to see how much money will be involved in a swap. Then we'll each have to evaluate our own cash position. We're also exploring some lease and buy-back options with our attorney." Ray continues, "We're not sure we can pull this off, Glenn. But at least we're committed to trying, and we're exploring some ways of doing it. We're also open to suggestions."

Glenn offers both thanks and encouragement, then asks for a favor. "Fellows, I'm not sure how the next meeting will go. But it could be real tough. If everyone is as positive as you two, we'll make progress. But if all our ideas turn sour by the time we meet again, we're in trouble." Sipping his coffee, Glenn continues, "I'd like to open the next meeting with your efforts. I think a demonstration of your progress and continued commitment would get the discussion off on the right foot."

Sharing Glenn's concerns, Bill and Ray agree. Ray adds, "I hear Ron Banks has been getting a lot of pressure from the Tribal Association not to sell out to the state or the town, and I'm sure Northwest's vice presidents are putting pressure on Paul to be careful about what he agrees to change."

Bill has heard the same talk, but he adds optimistically, "Glenn, you got all of us thinking about our shared values and problems. It may take more than the next meeting to reach agreement, but I think we will if you continue to have patience and help us summarize as we make progress on each issue."

Glenn is pleased with the encouraging words. He continues preparations for the sixth meeting, talking to Pineview Resort and Clearview Lumber to see if they have had any further discussions. They haven't. He checks back with Sid to make sure he is going to be ready with concrete information.

Making choices in principle

Glenn recognizes that he cannot expect a final decision at the next meeting. While the group may be able to make a decision in principle, they will not be ready to make a commitment. At one level, Ray and Bill have already made a decision in principle. They are committed to look for mutually agreeable solutions, and they are looking far more widely than either would have imagined a few weeks ago.

Others in the group must still be convinced. The resort and Clearview Lumber are talking about a potential sale. Ron Banks and Paul Hartner are trying to get their respective parent groups, the Tribal Association and Northwest Forest Products, to accept the idea that the process makes any sense at all. They will have to sell the choice to their parent groups before a decision can be made in principle and then again before they can make any commitments.

Evolving an overall plan out of many small decisions

Making all of the small decisions that go into a basin-management plan may take months. Each of the parties involved will have to agree in principle to make changes in the way they manage their land. A few big changes will be required; most will not be as dramatic as Bill's and Ray's land swap. The overall plan will take shape as the small decisions are made.

The group has made dramatic progress in a few short meetings. However, progress will slow as they reach agreement in principle on the pieces of the plan and begin to work out the details. Glenn hopes that each meeting will show progress from the previous meeting; but he knows that is not realistic. Progress will be sporadic, breakneck at times, painfully slow at others. There will be times when the process will appear to stall altogether. Glenn fully expects a year or more to pass before a plan is finalized—unless some crisis happens to speed the process.

Glenn is worried that the euphoria of the last meeting will bring people into the next meeting expecting to agree on a plan right away. Unrealistic expectations could cause group members to give up the process in impatience. He doesn't want to dampen enthusiasm too much. On the other hand, he feels that it is important that group members know what to expect. He will spend some time talking about what they can expect from here on out.

Confirming commitment to the overall plan

The Powder River problem will not be solved simply by reaching agreements in principle. Action must be taken. Action depends on the personal commitment of all group members to follow through. As the plan takes shape, group members' emotional commitment to it will grow as well. However, Glenn must be careful not to ask for commitment until there is something tangible to commit and everyone has enough information to make an informed decision. Glenn knows never to ask for a commitment too soon. The growing emotional commitment is conditional and depends on finding adequate answers to the questions that remain.

Commitment is one of those intangible qualities that each person defines differently. For some people, commitment is a sacred trust, not to be broken. For other people, commitment is purely utilitarian and conditional on getting something in return. In either case, commitment is at least in part an emotional response to the decision-making process. It flows out of each person's individual

- Sense of ownership in the agreed-on solution
- The feeling that he or she has been heard
- Trust in the group and its purposes
- Sense that he or she has been dealt with fairly in the process and the solution

In the Powder River case, the state is asking for signed contracts binding each of the group's members to a ten-year commitment to the plan. In most cases, commitment is not so public or binding. Follow-through depends on the depth of commitment. And the depth of commitment depends on the strength of these intangible feelings. A decision-making process that does not encourage these feelings at each step of the way will likely fail because people do not follow through or follow through only halfheartedly. Generating these positive feelings after a decision has been made is not easy.

Beyond Agreement

Action also requires operational plans for each of the small decisions that make up the plan. This is true whether it is Warren's choice of the best pest-management alternative to control apple scab, Northwest Forest Products' decision on what to do about the washed-out logging road, or the ad hoc group's decision on how to reduce sedimentation of the Powder River. Decisions lead to action if the commitment is there to follow through. Actions can be made more effective if they are based on plans and follow-up monitoring to make sure the results achieve the intended objectives. The next two chapters present tools for moving from decisions to timely, purposeful action.

7

■ Taking Action

Action links day-to-day choices to the dynamic accumulation of results. Action is the critical link between problems and solutions. It enables us to achieve our immediate objectives while the accumulation of day-to-day actions moves us closer to achieving our long-term goals.

Without action, immediate problems are not solved; progress is not made. However, action alone does not guarantee that problems will be solved—misdirected action can result in not achieving our objectives, thus impeding progress toward our goals. Action must be purposeful, timely, and effective. The effectiveness of our actions depends on carefully laid action plans that help to achieve these goals. However, planning doesn't guarantee that action will follow or that the action that does follow will achieve the intended result. Action is most likely to achieve the intended result when plans are laid before action is taken, and the results are monitored closely so that corrective action can be taken as needed.

Inaction and Misdirected Action

We have made a decision. We know what we want to do. We know what result we want to achieve. Now, it is just a matter of getting it done. And that is as far as it sometimes goes.

At breakfast, discussion centers on the family vacation scheduled for next month. One says, "We need to make our campsite reservations 30 days in

217

advance to be guaranteed a site." Everybody nods in agreement. At dinner, somebody asks, "Did you get the campsite?" Another frowns, "I thought you were going to call." Another responds, "No, I thought you were going to do it." Everybody thought somebody would do it. As a result, nobody did it. When somebody calls the next day, the campground is full. Now everybody must decide whether to go somewhere else or delay their long-awaited vacation.

We've all been in meetings where decisions were made and no one followed through. We've set objectives, developed strategies, and planned, only to see the completed document gathering dust on a shelf. Decision making has no effect unless action follows.

Alternatively, we see a problem, and we act before we think. But instead of solving the problem, the action makes it worse. To move in the direction we want to go, action must be purposeful, timely, *and* effective—in other words, result oriented. Otherwise, it may be misdirected. Progress is hindered or, worse, reversed.

You're driving along the highway when the radiator light starts flashing, and steam is rolling out from under the hood. Instead of stopping, you drive to the next exit, hoping there will be a service station. At the station, the service station attendant identifies the steam's source and replaces a split radiator hose. He asks, "How far did you drive it like this?" You respond, "Eight, maybe ten miles." The attendant replies, "Yeah, I can tell. You've ruined the engine block. Looks like everything's frozen up. What would have been a $10 repair is going to cost you $1,500 to $2,000."

Misdirected action or inaction leaves the problem unsolved and often changed in character. In these two illustrations, inaction and misdirected action create more troublesome problems. Once we know what we want to accomplish, and we have decided the best way to approach the problem, then we must plan "*how*?" (figure 7.1).

No effective action and worsening resource problems

Resource degradation, pollution, and depletion problems change in character as a result of inaction and misdirected action; often they become more intractable. The chain of biophysical relationships may become more complex. For example, we have done little to reduce sulphur dioxide emissions even though much of the Northeast has experienced acid rain for 60 to 100 years. Having done little to reduce these acid-yielding emissions, we are now confronted with acidified lakes and soil and are beginning to see damage to trees as well.

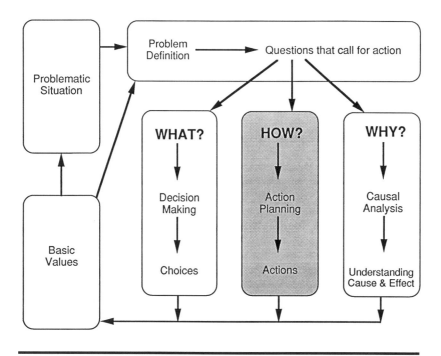

Figure 7.1. Problem-solving framework—actions.

Framework and Process for urposeful and Effective Action

Purposeful, effective action moves us closer to achieving our broadest goals. We can improve the effectiveness of our actions using a simple framework and process. The action framework is a simple six-question guide to organize our thoughts in three stages of timely, purposeful action: planning, taking action, and controlling results. It will help us move toward achieving immediate targets and long-run goals.

```
┌─────────────────────────────────────────────────────────────────────────┐
│                          Action Framework                                 │
│  What objective? _____      │
│                                                                           │
│  Planning              Action              Controlling Results            │
│  What steps?      Who?   When?     When done?   Effective?  Corrective action? │
│                                                                           │
│  1._____      ____   ____      _____    _____      _____   │
│                                                                           │
│  2._____      ____   ____      _____    _____      _____   │
│                                                                           │
│  3._____      ____   ____      _____    _____      _____   │
│                                                                           │
│  4._____      ____   ____      _____    _____      _____   │
│                                                                           │
│  What results?_____           _____       │
└─────────────────────────────────────────────────────────────────────────┘
```

Eight process steps structure our plans and actions and give us a measure of control over the results. They focus our attention on the relationships between task, immediate targets, and long-run goals. Ideally, completing a sequence of small tasks will enable us to achieve our targets while the accumulation of results moves us closer to achieving our broadest goals.

Process for Action Planning

PLAN: 1. Decide who to include in planning.
            2. Translate decision into a series of targets.
            3. Identify the steps necessary to achieve the targets.
            4. Gain commitment to the plan.
            5. Consider closely related targets.

ACT: 6. Implement the plan.

CONTROL
RESULTS: 7. Monitor progress, taking into account the influence
               of an everchanging context.
            8. Take corrective action.

Like all problem solving, planning is iterative rather than mechanistic. Uncertainty and a dynamic context make it necessary to plan and revise our plans continuously, taking a step and then evaluating whether it achieved its intended purpose. Through the process of planning, acting, and controlling results, the problem solver is constantly learning—collecting and reflecting on new information that will improve his or her ability to define problems and make decisions in the future.

Action plans that link planning, action, and results

An action plan is a set of steps to get from the situation as it is to some more desirable one. Like problem definition, an action plan takes into account time constraints, place, people involved, resources available, and other context-specific factors. Action planning

- Increases the probability that the desired results are achieved and reduces the risk of misdirected action or inaction

- Shows whether the physical and human resources available are adequate for the job

- Demonstrates how resources can be used more effectively, thereby reducing costs, conserving scarce resources, increasing output, or answering more equitable distribution of benefits

- Improves coordination so that the desired result can be achieved more readily

- Fosters personal commitment to the plan and improves the likelihood of getting people's best efforts by providing personal objectives. These objectives lead to an individual sense of accomplishment in contributing to a group's shared purposes.

Since planning alone does not ensure that we will achieve the desired result, purposeful action must follow. The process does not stop there, however. Even carefully planned and executed action can have unintended results. Result-oriented managers monitor progress at each step. If a step doesn't achieve the desired result, they adjust the plan midcourse. The plan is a temporal tool, useful only as long as it moves the problem solver toward the desired result.

Warren Olson's Implementation of His Decision—IPM

It is almost Thanksgiving. Warren Olson always looks forward with anticipation to the feeling of satisfaction he gets this time of year. The harvest is complete, the cider press stilled, and the equipment cleaned and put in its place for the winter. It is a long-awaited time of reflection—to look back and evaluate what went right, what went wrong, and why. This winter will be different.

Warren has decided to shift to integrated pest management (IPM), combining a variety of management techniques with a flexible organic spray regimen. He is determined to leave as little to chance as nature will allow. This winter, he will lay out a plan that will enable him to follow through on his decision. He will also rethink his marketing plans.

After a lot of reading and talking to growers, he has decided to abandon nearly 20 years of biweekly pesticide applications. His decision involves a five-part strategy.

- *Use a combination of integrated pest management techniques.* These techniques achieve two objectives: Scab predictors enable Warren to take preventive measures before an impending scab infestation damages the crop. Burning leaf mold and applying nitrogen fertilizers break the fungus' life cycle, reducing the likelihood of an outbreak.

- *Spray a sulphur-based organic fungicide when primary infestation of scab is imminent in early spring.* This will prevent or eradicate an initial outbreak that could cause a secondary infestation in the summer months, resulting in damage to the crop and trees. While it has drawbacks, the organic fungicide does not carry the health risks of Benomyl and other sprays and powders.

- *Shift marketing strategy and sell more apples at the orchard and fewer to wholesalers.* Spraying with copper sulphate can cause russeting and a higher proportion of blemished apples, especially in the first years as Warren learns how to use the more complex management strategy. Direct marketing gives Warren the opportunity to point out to consumers that the blemishes do not affect quality. In fact, blemishes signal the health benefits of IPM.

- *Plant several acres of scab-resistant 'Liberty' and 'Prima' trees.* In the long term, scab-resistant trees will reduce the cost and health risks of other alternatives. However, most scab-resistant varieties have not found market acceptance. Planting a few test acres will enable Warren to test marketability before he makes a large investment.

- *Watch the literature and other growers' experience with Nova.* This new product being used in France has shown promise for effective scab control without the negative consequences of traditional sprays.

Although Warren deliberated a long time, he is satisfied with his decision. This year he will implement it.

1. Decide who to include in planning.

Deciding who to include in an action-planning group is an important decision. Who is included influences whether or not the objective is achieved in three ways: knowledge, coordination, and commitment.

Process for Action Planning

PLAN:
1. **Decide who to include in planning.**
   People with necessary specialized knowledge
   People who must coordinate closely
   People whose commitment is needed

2. Translate decision into a series of targets.
3. Identify the steps necessary to achieve the targets.
4. Gain commitment to the plan.
5. Consider closely related targets.

ACT:
6. Implement the plan.

CONTROL
RESULTS:
7. Monitor progress.
8. Take corrective action.

Specialized knowledge

First, the participants in planning influence the quality of the plan. In all but the smallest organizations, tasks are assigned to specialists, who often know their jobs better than anyone else. They know how long it takes to complete a task, what skills are needed, and what resources are required. They know what they need from other people, when, and in what quantity. They have the kind of specialized knowledge that can only be acquired through experience. A thoughtful specialist can tell you how to improve quality or cut the time required to complete a task without research. In some cases, their specialized knowledge based on field experience will mean the difference between a well-conceived plan and a plan that is impossible to implement. It is particularly important to include these people when you are contemplating change (e.g., improving a time-tested procedure, shifting job responsibilities, introducing new equipment or technologies, or adjusting a time-sensitive schedule). However, including them in planning for familiar tasks may lead to new and better ways of doing these as well.

Coordination of a complex process

Second, including key people in planning can make coordination of action easier. This becomes particularly important when careful coordination is important to achieving the objective. Coordination's importance depends on the answers to four questions.

How squeezed are you for time? Do you have a pressing deadline, or can you afford to take a relaxed attitude toward time?

How are people organized to carry out the job? Are authority and responsibility clearly defined or does follow-through depend on each individual's commitment to the task? Are those involved in implementation separated by geography, time, or institutional boundaries?

What are the number and sequence of steps? Is each step highly dependent on completion of the previous step, or can steps be completed independently?

What are the consequences of misdirected action? What happens if you fail to achieve the objective on a timely basis? How much tolerance is there in meeting quality standards?

When many people repeat the same task supervised by one person, coordination is not difficult. Detasseling corn is a very intense activity. While timing is critical, little coordination is required once the crews are in place. One or two individuals can supervise large crews of high school and college students to get the job done with little coordination. In contrast, coordination is critical in designing and building a prototype for a new biomass energy system. Engineers in different departments, often at different locations, may work on highly specialized elements of a subsystem, bringing together all of the elements after long months of research, design, and redesign. Years of design work may be completed before all of the various systems are fully analyzed as a working whole.

Commitment to the plan

Third, who is included influences the depth of ownership a group feels in the plan and its objectives. When a plan is implemented, it is more likely to achieve the desired results if everyone involved feels a sense of ownership in the plan. It must be the group's plan. Those who don't make a personal commitment to the plan are less likely to follow through on the tasks assigned to them. Participation in planning enhances the sense of ownership and supports a commitment to carrying out the plan. However, there is a practical limit to the number of people who can be meaningfully involved. Planning groups with more than six or eight people tend to be either unproductive or dominated by one or two powerful individuals.

Warren, his son, and a trusted employee

Warren brings his son, Bill, and Jim, his crew foreman and right-hand man, into the planning process. Bill intends to buy into the orchard in a couple of years. Jim is Warren's only year-round employee. He has worked for Warren for 15 years. Warren has complete confidence in them; both counseled Warren as he made the initial decision; both will be deeply involved in making the changes work. Warren doesn't want any surprises.

2. Translate the decision into a series of targets.

Process for Action Planning

PLAN: 1. Decide who to include in planning.

> **2. Translate decision into a series of targets.**
>   Concrete results, not activities
>   Measurable
>   Time-specific
>   Realistic, yet challenging
>   Consistent with authority and responsibility
>   Compatible with goals and other targets

3. Identify the steps necessary to achieve the targets.
4. Gain commitment to the plan.
5. Consider closely related targets.

ACT: 6. Implement the plan.

CONTROL
RESULTS: 7. Monitor progress.
8. Take corrective action.

Warren's decision to shift to integrated pest management flows out of his goals, objectives, and criteria. Now he must translate these broad values, needs, and desires into performance targets. A target is a specific description of an end result to be achieved in a defined period of time. It describes what and how much must be accomplished by when. It does not describe how the results will be accomplished. The steps necessary to achieve your targets are identified later in the process.

Frequently targets are confused with objectives or goals. Warren's *goals* have not changed since he was a young man. He wants his work to give him and his family health and financial security in the long run. He has always felt a responsibility to protect the natural world that has given him both these things. His *objectives* express his goals in terms of the situation he faces today: He wants to maintain and improve the orchard's productivity and marketability of his produce, and he wants to do this in a way that doesn't threaten the health of his employees or his customers. Now he needs to translate these objectives into performance *targets* that state specifically what he plans to achieve in the foreseeable and controllable future. Targets are

* *Concrete results, not activities.* Using nouns and adjectives, targets describe achievements and accomplishments. If you find yourself writing targets using a lot of active verbs, you're probably describing "how to" activities rather than what is to be achieved.

* *Measurable.* Targets state how achievements will be measured, using yardsticks of quality, quantity, cost, and time. They answer this question: How do I know when I've achieved the desired result?

* *Time-specific.* Targets state a completion date. Without a date, targets differ little from objectives. A time frame gives immediacy to targets that objectives do not have.

* *Realistic yet challenging.* Targets are realistic given the time frame and context. If the target isn't attainable, it's just a pipe dream—useless except as a pleasant exercise. But unless the target represents a challenge to improve performance, it is unnecessary. It will be achieved whether or not it is stated. The best targets challenge the problem solver to improve productivity, sustainability, and fairness.

* *Consistent with authority and responsibility.* Targets should be consistent with the problem solver's authority and responsibility. The chief executive officer of a forestry firm is likely to set production targets for the company as a whole, rather than by individual sites. A site manager sets targets for the forest he or she manages, not the company or division.

* *Compatible with goals and other objectives.* Targets should be compatible with broad goals and short-run objectives. Ideally, a large, multilayered organization's targets would be consistent and complementary from the janitor to the chief executive officer. The sum of the target results at one level should add up to the targeted results at the next. Similarly, departmental targets would be consistent and complementary. This is not easy. When a complex organization achieves this, it stems from a clarity of purpose at all levels of the organization and a commitment to results. Planned targets are the means that links purpose to results.

Warren's targets

Warren knows what he wants: He wants to maintain and improve the orchard's productivity and profitability over the long haul. During his 20 years in the business, he has put just about every dollar he has earned back into the orchard, expanding acreage, planting improved varieties, and replacing unproductive trees. A few years ago, he expanded his cold storage.

In the early days, Warren strove to produce as many #1 grade apples and as few windfalls and lesser grades as possible. At that time, he didn't want to bother with marketing, preferring to pack and ship his apples through brokers who sold them to retailers. In the late 1970s, he diversified his marketing strategy. While he continued to pack and ship the majority of his crop, he advertised in local papers and sold apples directly to customers who would come out to the farm from July when the first apples are picked until November when the last apples are sold. He also bought a small cider press and sold cider to his local customers. His profits improved.

Now, he's decided to shift to integrated pest management and reduce production costs. Integrated pest management is riskier than the traditional biweekly pesticide application. Without careful and effective management, scab may blemish the fruit or, worse, denude and kill the trees. To market the cosmetically less-perfect apples he will harvest, Warren will need to exploit consumer preferences for apples produced without highly toxic pesticides. He may also need to press more cider than before. Warren starts planning with a single target:

- He will maintain apple production next season at more or less average levels, given the year's weather patterns, producing 60 percent #1 grade apples and 40 percent lesser grades the first year, increasing to 70 percent #1 grade apples and 30 percent lesser grades by year 5 while reducing the risk of scab infestation and the risk of deleterious health effects of toxic sprays to family, employees, and consumers.

Jim asks, "What do you mean 'average' production? I don't know that we've ever had an average year, and what does 'more or less' mean? Sounds to me like it's just words on the page."

Bill answers. "We're going to do our best to keep production where it's been, and that means learning how to use this integrated pest management system quickly. I think our first target needs to be getting a quick education in this new way of growing apples."

Jim adds, "We really didn't do any management when we sprayed every two weeks and after every rain. We sprayed whether it was needed or not. Now, we're going to have to learn how to predict and prevent infestations with integrated pest management and eradicate with organic sprays. Saying we won't resort to toxic sprays is like tying one hand behind our back. It's going to take some experience to get the right information at the right time and use it to make the best management decisions. The only way to get that is trial and error. It isn't like spraying on a schedule. It's the combination of many things done at just the right time that prevents scab. Timing is critical."

"You're right," Warren replies. "Let's make a *learning plan* first so by spring we have a better idea what to expect from IPM. We can accept these production targets for the time being and revise them later when we know a little more. While we're learning about IPM, we'll have to be getting ready to use it in the spring. We need to line up equipment so we'll have it in time. Some things we'll need to begin now—burning the leaf litter and applying nitrogen fertilizer—we can't wait till spring for that."

Jim raises another issue. "I don't see anything here about marketing. I hope we're not going to make all of these changes only to find out we have more second-grade apples than we can sell or press. That would be a helluva lot of work for nothing."

"It would be pretty shortsighted not to anticipate the effects of this change on our marketing strategy," Warren agrees. "Let's set targets for both marketing and processing. What do you think is realistic?" After a long discussion, they agree on two additional targets.

- We will create in the minds of local consumers the image of a health-conscious environmentally responsible Olson's Orchard by year 3. This will increase retail sales of premium-priced apples at the farm from the current 20 percent to 50 percent of the crop and thus reduce reliance on the wholesale market and improve income by year 5.

- We will expand cider press capacity to process 40 percent of the coming year's apple crop into cider. Currently, my press can process no more than 5–10 percent of a year's harvest.

While Jim isn't fully convinced the targets are attainable, he agrees to do whatever he can to reach them.

Returning to IPM, Warren continues, "After we've figured what we need to learn about IPM, we'll tackle the marketing issue. Let's spend an hour or so planning how we're going to implement the integrated pest management techniques and an hour on marketing. Getting these plans right is going to be a winter-long project, so we don't want to try to do too much in one sitting."

3. Identify the steps necessary to achieve the target.

Process for Action Planning

PLAN: 1. Decide who to include in planning.
2. Translate decision into a series of targets.

> **3. Identify the steps necessary to achieve the target.**
> List but do not discuss the steps.
> Check confidence in assumptions and predictions.
> Refine steps.
> Determine the sequence and timing of steps.
> Assign responsibility for each step.

4. Gain commitment to the plan.
5. Consider closely related targets.

ACT: 6. Implement the plan.

CONTROL
RESULTS: 7. Monitor progress.
8. Take corrective action.

Identifying the steps necessary to achieve the target is a listing process, and listing is creative. The level of detail will vary depending on the decision to be implemented and the people involved. Some individuals will fine-tune lists with several levels of steps. Others will list broadly defined steps that imply a sequence of smaller steps. People's experience and training may make them approach the targets from various angles, making different assumptions or identifying alternative paths to achieve the same targets.

List the steps without discussion.

Separating creative and critical thinking can improve the plan that results. As with creative steps in decision making, the rule is "list but do not discuss" during the creative phase. This encourages group members to suggest a wide range of ideas without fear of rejection. Discussion is deferred until the list is complete.

Warren begins, "Let's make a list of all the things we're going to have to do. Then we can talk about them and put completion dates on them. Bill, you keep track of the list."

Jim starts, "We need to do something soon about controlling leaf litter. The spores are spread by wind, and eliminating leaf litter will reduce spore counts in the spring. We also have to learn how to use the scab predictors to predict scab infestations."

Bill picks up from there. "Once we've learned how to predict infestations, we'll need to identify the best combination of management practices—with as little trial and error as possible. Sounds like we've got a lot of learning to do. There's an annual workshop on least-spray IPM in apple production at the state university. I think at least one of us should go, if not all of us."

Warren grins, "I'm one up on you. All three of us are signed up for the workshop that runs from December 5–9." Jim frowns, "That's OK for you, but I'd rather take advice from somebody who makes his living using this stuff. Those university people can tell you how it's supposed to work in theory, but they're not much help dealing with the everyday problems that inevitably come up."

Warren nods, "I agree with you, Jim. But it's a whole lot easier to get information from those growers when you know what questions to ask. If we spend a week at the university, we should learn enough to ask intelligent questions. Then we'll visit growers who have a few years' experience using least-spray IPM to predict and control orchard problems."

Bill adds, "One of us needs to spend a fair amount of time talking to salespeople. We need to learn as much as we can about their products and how to use them. Then we need to verify everything they tell us with people who've used the products in the field."

Confidence check

All plans are based on assumptions about the expected outcome of each task. In effect, a plan says, "If I do this, then I expect this outcome. If the expected outcome occurs and if I take the next step, then I expect another outcome." The planner makes a series of if-then statements that will result in the desired outcome if things go as predicted.

Warren's predictions are based on years of observation, knowledge acquired through reading, and training (table 7.1). He's skeptical of predictions made on speculative and wishful thinking. He knows that his predictions and the resulting plan are only as good as the information he uses to generate them.

Table 7.1. A learning plan to develop sound IPM practices

What Steps	Who?	When?
1. Learn about predicting infestations from salespersons, literature, researchers, and growers. Recommend equipment specifications.	Jim	November
2. Learn about leaf-litter control. Implement practice as soon as practical.	Jim	November
3. Learn about least-spray IPM practices at the university workshop. Identify other growers using IPM.	Jim, Bill, Warren	December 5–9
4. Talk to other orchardists to find out shortcuts and pitfalls.	to be assigned after workshop	January–February

Now Warren plans to implement a package of unfamiliar pest-management practices. He has a general idea of what is involved, but he isn't certain of all the specific steps and techniques required. He doesn't have all the information he will need, and he knows it. Rather than planning implementation based on what could be flimsy assumptions, he systematically plans how he will learn what he needs to know to improve his predictions. He plans as far as his present information will take him. He will reduce the risk of trial-and-error learning by acquiring as much information from as many sources as possible, integrating and making sense out of the information he acquires before he develops implementation plans. Where immediate action is required—burning leaf litter and applying nitrogen fertilizer to kill overwintering spores—he proceeds with the information he has.

Warren plans to gather information from several perspectives and several sources for each perspective. He'll look at extension's applied theoretical information; he'll get product-specific information from the suppliers of sulphur-based sprays and scab predictor equipment as well as experience-based information from growers who are using IPM. With this information, he'll learn how the technologies are supposed to work under ideal conditions, how specific products are supposed to work when used according to the manufacturer's recommendations, and how they actually work for practitioners using them in the orchards.

Comparing information from all three sources will give him greater confidence in his predictions. Inaccurate predictions of cause and effect are probably the most common reason well-executed action plans don't achieve the intended result. In Warren's case, the consequences of not achieving his objective could be extreme. While he can handle short-term productivity losses, secondary leaf infestation can denude and kill trees, drastically reducing apple production for several years. Of course, Warren wouldn't allow this to happen. Confronted with a primary infestation, he likely will fall back on his old every-other-week spraying program.

There is no right amount of information. Someone less cautious than Warren might have been willing to plan with less information in hand. How much is enough is an individual choice that depends on how much risk he or she (or the group) is willing to take. However, the desire for more information, which is really a desire for more confidence, can become insatiable, paralyzing the will to take action. Groups are particularly prone to this malady. At some point, the individual or group needs to recognize that change is inherently risky and accept the risk to solve the problem, or accept the situation as it is.

Warren intentionally makes planning an iterative process, building in regular meetings to monitor, take corrective action, and move forward. He schedules meetings at key points to share information, reevaluate objectives, and revise or add detail to their plans. By doing so, he will avoid planning paralysis and reduce his risk of failure.

Refining steps

Once no one has anything to add to the list of steps, the group can begin to refine the list they have. Discussion can be made more productive through facilitation. The facilitator can guide the discussion by asking

- Can some fine-tuned steps be grouped under one heading?
- Should some broadly stated steps be divided into smaller steps?

These questions help the group list steps of comparable detail. If the plan is likely to be very complex, the steps may be listed broadly on the first pass. Then these broad steps can be put into sequence, target completion dates set, and broad assignments of responsibility made. Then each broad step may be broken down into smaller steps. If necessary, each step can be broken down into even finer levels of detail in subsequent passes. Group members are more likely to retain a common sense of purpose if they start with a general plan and gradually move to more detailed plans.

1. *What is the sequence of steps? When does each need to be completed?* Sequence and timing are closely related but separate issues. A plan's quality depends on appropriate sequencing and careful timing of steps. There is no right or wrong sequence and timing of steps. The sequence varies depending on the relationship among steps and the relative importance the group

attaches to each step. The following questions help define the sequence and timing of steps:

- *What steps are critical to the steps that precede or follow?* Some steps must be completed before others can be started. The quality of the plan hinges on identifying these critical steps and the steps linked to them. In many cases, the sequence may be dictated by biophysical relationships, social norms, organizational procedures, or some other standard. For example, it is obvious that Warren cannot begin monitoring scab infestations without first purchasing the scab predictor equipment.

    Often, sequence is a matter of judgment. Warren wants to get as much information as possible before he talks to orchardists with IPM experience because he expects to learn more from these people than anyone else. He wants to ask the questions that will elicit the most information possible, and phrasing good questions requires a good understanding of what is involved. Someone else might not think it important when they talk to the orchardists.

- *What steps can/must be done simultaneously?* Some steps are not sequential but parallel. While not related, they must be completed by roughly the same time. If you are building a house, you first pour the foundation. Then you frame in the walls and roof. Next a whole group of related steps must take place more or less simultaneously. An electrician, plumber, and several general laborers may be working on different parts of the house at the same time, but they all must complete their work before the wallboard people arrive.

    Whether these steps can take place simultaneously depends on the answers to several questions. Is there enough labor, managerial capacity, equipment, and other resources to do these tasks simultaneously and complete them on time? Construction often takes longer than anticipated because skilled workers aren't available at the same time; or the materials are not on site when they are available.

- *Who controls the timing? On what steps do we control timing? On what steps is timing controlled externally?* Answers to these questions indicate how much flexibility there is in scheduling. Many steps are not time sensitive. They can be completed far in advance. Plans are improved when these steps are scheduled so as not to conflict with tasks that are highly time sensitive and linked to other steps.

    Often a group has broad flexibility about when to make a change, but once the decision to change is made, the timing of many steps is externally controlled. Whether Warren begins using IPM this year or next is completely within his control. But once he decides to make the change this year, the timing of many steps is beyond his control. Spores in leaf litter must be controlled after leaf fall and before the first snow. He must allow six to eight weeks for delivery of a scab predictor.

* *On what events does the sequence of steps depend?* While the company that sells the scab predictor promises delivery in six to eight weeks, delivery could take longer. Warren can't predict delivery time with any real confidence, so he will allow plenty of time. While there is a pattern to leaf fall and first snow, he can't be sure about them either. He will have to maintain some flexibility in his plan. He feels comfortable dealing with these kinds of variables because they are familiar; he schedules harvest crews weeks in advance, not knowing exactly when the fruit will ripen and crews will be needed.

* *On what steps is timing critical?* Timing is critical for some steps and not for others. The two-week course offered by the state university is only offered once a year. If Warren misses the application deadline, they cannot attend the course. Whether or not this step is critical to subsequent steps depends on how Warren perceives it. If he thinks the training is essential, he would consider postponing implementation for another year. If he sees the training as helpful but not essential, he might proceed without it.

* *On what steps are timing and sequence critical?* If timing *and* the step are critical, then the step becomes an anchor for sequencing the rest of the plan. Planning the time frame will work forward or backward from this step. For example, when Warren plans the harvest each year, he estimates the date the harvest will begin in earnest, perhaps August 20. That is the date the temporary crews will begin picking the main crop. In planning, he works backward from that date. Equipment must be ready to go, contracts signed with local pickers and contract crews, housing arranged for contract crews, ladders and bags available for every picker who won't bring his or her own, and so on.

2. *Who is responsible for each step?* Even the best-laid plans won't get carried out unless someone is made responsible. All too often, everybody thinks somebody else will follow through. Especially when anybody could, inevitably nobody does unless each task is specifically assigned to an

individual by name. The following questions will help you assign responsibility. First ask

- *Who is best suited to carry out the task,* given the nature of the task and the time available, the skills and experience of people available, and competing demands on their time?

When all tasks have been assigned, review the tentative assignments, asking

- *Have critical steps been assigned to reliable and competent individuals?* Critical steps are those in which inattention to timing and/or sequence will create critical bottlenecks to timely, purposeful, effective action.

- *Are assignments appropriate to each individual's authority and responsibility?*

- *Is anyone assigned more than he or she can reasonably complete on time?* (Have you created any bottlenecks?)

Where there are problems, reevaluate both the timing and sequence of steps as well as the assignments. Continue juggling the pieces of the plan until you have a workable plan.

4. Gain commitment to the plan.

```
                    Process for Action Planning

PLAN:       1.  Decide who to include in planning.
            2.  Translate decision into a series of targets.
            3.  Identify the steps necessary to achieve the target.

        ┌──────────────────────────────────────────────┐
        │   4.  Gain commitment to the plan.            │
        │       Confirm that everyone understands the   │
        │       plan.                                   │
        │       Confirm willingness to commit.          │
        └──────────────────────────────────────────────┘

            5.  Consider closely related targets.

ACT:        6.  Implement the plan.

CONTROL
RESULTS:    7.  Monitor progress.
            8.  Take corrective action.
```

When Warren, Bill, and Jim finish planning the learning phase of their implementation plan, Warren asks, "Are we all agreed?" Jim and Bill nod. Commitment to a plan is important, particularly where close coordination is required to achieve the objective. Individual commitment is most readily offered when those who will have to carry out the plan are involved, one way or another, in the planning. It is relatively easy for Warren to get Bill's and Jim's commitment to implementing his decision to use an integrated pest management approach to scab infestations. The next chapter, where we look at implementing a group decision, will consider commitment in more detail.

Bill returns to the issue of marketing. "Before we quit, we need to do the same thing on the marketing side. If we separate the two, we could run into problems selling our crop in the fall."

5. Consider closely related targets.

Process for Action Planning

PLAN: 1. Decide who to include in planning.
           2. Translate decision into a series of targets.
           3. Identify the steps necessary to achieve the targets.
           4. Gain commitment to the plan.

> **5. Consider closely related targets.**

ACT: 6. Implement the plan.

CONTROL
RESULTS: 7. Monitor progress.
           8. Take corrective action.

Some simple plans require only that we lay out the steps to achieve a single target. However, most plans include multiple and closely related targets. To make progress towards our broad goals, we must achieve all of our targets simultaneously or in sequence.

When we are reaching out for new and better ways of doing things, we rarely have the ability to anticipate all of the interactions and consequences change may bring; consequently, it may be difficult to anticipate the chain of objectives and plans required over time. However, progress toward our broadest goals can be accelerated by anticipating and planning for as many interactions as possible. This generally involves setting multiple, but closely linked, targets.

Warren, Bill, and Jim have the beginning of a working plan for implementing IPM. Their current plan involves clearly specified steps directed at learning more about the technology and equipment as well as dates by which they need to decide on specific sprays and equipment. They will refine their plan as they learn more about IPM. They also will need to plan for the remaining two targets: marketing and pressing cider.

Production and marketing targets are interrelated. Warren realized from the beginning that shifting to IPM and organic sprays would have marketing implications. Especially in the first few years, he can expect to produce more blemished apples than he had using Benomyl. On the other hand, consumers are willing to pay a premium price for apples, cider, and sauce produced without chemical fertilizers, Alar, hormones, or highly toxic pesticides. A savvy businessman, Warren decided to shift marketing strategies to take advantage of the marketing opportunities IPM provides. This part of the plan is represented in Warren's second target. To minimize the added risk of overproducing low-grade apples, Warren also plans to press more cider during the transition years, as stated in his third target. As you recall, these targets were

- To create in the minds of local consumers the image of a health-conscious, environmentally responsible Olson's Orchard by year 3. This will potentially increase retail sales of premium priced apple at the farm from 20 percent to 50 percent, thus reducing reliance on the wholesale market and improving income by the year 5.

- To develop cider press capacity to process 40 percent of the coming year's apple crop into cider. Currently, the orchard can process no more than 5–10 percent of a year's harvest.

Jim raises a question, "*How* are we going to press more apples into cider this year? We don't have enough capacity to press many more apples than we did last year. Are we going to add another press?"

Warren answers, "I'm not convinced we should add another press here on the farm. Several local orchard owners are producing more seconds than they can press. I've been talking to Gordon Thomas at Northfield Orchards and Dave Stowe of New Era Farms about buying a large press together and forming a cooperative. It's a pretty novel idea. I've never heard of a cooperative cider press. But I think it has potential.

"We made a tentative decision to go ahead, and we will meet Friday to figure out how to proceed. Would either of you like to join me? The meeting's at Stowe's place." Jim answers, "I would. I've always thought we should expand our press capacity."

Warren's decision to join Gordon and Dave in forming a cooperative cider press is interrelated to the decision to switch to IPM. But planning for the cooperative cider press will be a different sort of plan because Warren's targets won't be the only ones that matter. The next chapter will look at how the three orchard owners make an action plan together. Meanwhile, Warren needs to begin planning how he will increase farm-gate sales of his premium apples from 20 percent to 50 percent.

Targets that are realistic but challenging

Bill looks over the marketing targets.

"Pretty ambitious, isn't it?" he asks. "Do you think we can develop a local health-conscious market that quickly? I know we're in a good place to do it. Our closest competitors will be Gordon Thomas and Dave Stowe. They are still using Benomyl, but both are talking about shifting to IPM and organic sprays." Warren interrupts, "That's why we have to move quickly. If we don't develop the local market, they will."

Bill continues, "We're not talking about trying to get certified as an organic producer are we? Certification takes three years of production without chemicals. If we aren't certified—and even if we are—we'll have to do a lot of promotion to develop a health-conscious market for cosmetically blemished apples that can still command a premium price. And nearly all the promotion has to be done just before and during harvest, our busiest ten weeks of the year." Warren answers, "That's true, but I think we can have most of the promotional work ready to go early in the summer if we're organized."

Bill agrees to defer the issue. "If we're realistic in our planning, the process will reveal whether the time frame is reasonable or not. If it isn't, we can adjust the target later. So let's get on with it."

Warren's IPM and marketing targets are related and complementary. Together, when achieved, they will lead Olson's Orchard closer to Warren's broad goals: improving productivity and profitability over the long haul; leaving the orchard in better shape for his son Bill; doing something about his long-standing concern for the environment; and preserving his independence and lifestyle. His targets describe concrete accomplishments. They are measurable and state completion dates. The targets provide benchmarks to measure progress. They are realistic yet challenging.

List necessary steps without discussion.

Warren is more willing to make assumptions about the steps required to promote and sell apples than he was about IPM. Although he doesn't have any more confidence in the accuracy of his assumptions, he thinks of promotion as hocus-pocus, so he doesn't expect to be confident. He tries something; and if it works, fine. If it doesn't, he tries something else. That's not to say he doesn't try to anticipate the effects; he just doesn't expect the same degree of certainty as he does in production. A marketing professional might insist on more analysis in support of a marketing plan. One is not right, and the other wrong. Rather, Warren and the marketing professional require different levels of confidence in different plans.

Warren, Jim, and Bill begin listing steps. The promotional possibilities seem endless. Their excitement grows as the list grows. As they brainstorm, they don't consider priorities or the resources required. They put all of their creative energy into developing the most complete list possible. When they know what the possibilities are, they will link tasks, eliminate the least productive tasks, and evaluate the resources required.

- Develop a slogan to differentiate Olson's apples from other apples (e.g., "Apples with a Healthful Difference").

- Write a brochure describing the orchard and the benefits of IPM on consumer health and the environment.

- Send a brochure to every health food store in a 50-mile radius.

- Write a news release for the local paper describing the major change at Olson's Orchards. Talk to the publisher about placing it in the food section just as harvest begins.

- Identify an advertising agency to develop a new logo, cider label, and bags for the on-farm market.

- Develop a newspaper ad for the "new" products—natural cider and healthy premium apples.

- Produce a 20-second radio advertisement for the new products.

- Buy radio time during hourly news update six times a day from mid-July through mid-November on the local station only.

- Place a newspaper ad in the food section of the Sunday edition of the local paper and nearest big city daily, mid-July through mid-November.

- Develop and print a leaflet explaining the benefits of IPM to hand out at the on-farm stand.

- Compile and print a booklet providing healthful apple recipes, including recipes for home-canned applesauce and other foods that encourage bulk purchases of lesser-grade apples.

- Redesign and repaint the farm stand using the new logo.

- Contract with a local sign company to build and install a new sign for the orchard gate using the new logo.

- Place directional signs pointing to the orchard on all major highways with easy access to the orchard.

- Arrange a guest interview with the host of the local TV station's noon food show to promote the orchard and the benefits of "naturally" produced healthy apples.

Refining the list

Jim comments as they look over the list.

"I hope you're not planning to do all of this before harvest. There's no way we'll be able to afford to do everything even if we have the time."

Warren answers, "We have a wish list. We have to revise it and decide what we're actually going to do. First, let's group steps that go together into broad activities. Then, we'll tackle each category separately, evaluating cost and time requirements. Finally, we'll decide what marketing activities to do this year, sequence the steps necessary to carry them out, set deadlines, and assign each task. OK?"

Bill begins the discussion. "I think we can group all the steps we've listed under five broad categories." He writes five general headings on the flip chart and organizes the related steps underneath each heading. As he finishes writing one step, Warren or Jim call out the next. When they finish, they look over their effort (table 7.2).

Bill asks, "How much do you have budgeted for promotion and advertising, Dad?" Warren answers, "I figure we'll need to spend about 2 percent of our gross on advertising and promotion this year and next year. But I hope to bring that down once Olson's Orchards new image is established in people's minds." Bill responds, "Then, here's what I suggest. Let's plan on doing everything this year except the radio advertising. That's the most expensive item on the list. I think we need a detailed advertising and promotion budget along with the plan."

Continuing, Bill insists, "When we start implementing the plan, we are going to have to monitor our progress closely and evaluate the effectiveness of our advertising dollars. We want to learn from this year so that next year we can get more for our time and effort. Otherwise, this trial-and-error approach doesn't make much sense!"

Warren says, "Maybe we need to add another step to our list. What about developing a survey to determine how effective our advertising is? We can ask customers at the roadside stand where they heard about Olson's Orchards and what was most important in their decision to buy apple products from Olson's."

Jim answers, "I like that. Then maybe you'll figure out that this advertising stuff is a waste of money. Guess I liked the business better when all we did was grow apples. This marketing stuff isn't my cup of tea."

Table 7.2. Group tasks

General promotion
- Develop a slogan to differentiate Olson's apples from other apples (e.g., "Apples with a Healthful Difference").
- Contract with an advertising agency to develop a new logo for cider label, bags, farm market signs, advertising, etc.
- Write a brochure aimed at health food stores describing the orchard and the benefits of IPM for consumer health and the environment.
- Send a brochure to every health food store in a 50-mile radius.
- Write a news release for the local paper describing the major change at Olson's Orchard. Talk to the publisher about placing it in the food section just as harvest begins.
- Arrange a guest interview with the host of the local TV station's noon food show to promote the orchard and the benefits of "naturally" produced apples.

Consumer education
- Develop and print a one-page flyer explaining the benefits of IPM to consumers and the environment to hand out at the on-farm stand.
- Compile and print a booklet providing healthful apple recipes, including a recipe for home-canned applesauce.

Facilities
- Redesign and repaint farm stand using new logo.
- Contract with a local sign company to build and install a new sign for the orchard gate using the new logo.
- Place directional signs pointing to the orchard on all major highways with easy access to the orchard.

Advertising—newspaper
- Develop a series of newspaper ads for the "new" products—natural cider and premium apples.
- Place newspaper ads in Sunday and Wednesday food sections of the local paper and nearest big city daily mid-July through mid-November.

Advertising—radio
- Produce a 20-second radio advertisement for the "new" products.
- Buy radio time during hourly news update six times a day from mid-July through mid-November on the local station only.

Put steps in sequence, set deadlines, assign tasks. Once all the steps are identified, the group talks about the sequence of steps and deadlines. It quickly becomes apparent that many steps can be done simultaneously. The more critical issue is the quality of the promotional pieces developed. A sloppy brochure won't sell apples; poorly written news releases won't get printed in the paper; and poorly conceived print ads won't draw people to the orchard.

■   Warren says, "Maybe we had better figure out who is going to do each task first. Then we can set deadlines based on that person's availability." Jim says, "Well, I'm sure not the right person to do this stuff. I say we let Bill handle it from beginning to end."

Bill replies, "You know, Dad, this is the end of the business that I really enjoy. I'd like the chance to make this work. How about it? Are you willing to turn it over to me? I'll develop a detailed plan from what we've done here. You and Jim can look it over. We can discuss it next week. OK?"

Warren agrees, adding, "I wish you were as interested in growing apples as you are in selling them." Bill laughs, "C'mon, Dad, you have to sell them somewhere. Might as well get the best return you can. Right?" Warren laughs too.

Which matters most—when it's done or who does it? What comes first—the chicken or the egg? Deadlines or assignments? It depends. Set the deadlines first if timing is the most critical factor. Assign responsibility first if quality of work is most important and specialized skills are needed to do the work. When both are equally important, you have to go back and forth. Start with those pieces of the plan that are out of your control. Put these dates (or people) into the plan as a given. Identify the critical factor that limits your flexibility most. Plug it into the plan. Then move to the next most limiting factor, and so on.

In this case, quality is essential. Bill is the only one of the three with the skills to produce the quality of promotional items required. So deadlines are set around his school schedule. Bill can produce the materials whenever it is convenient between now and early summer as long as he allows enough time for Warren to review them, the printers to print them, and so forth. However, steps will have to be sequenced and scheduled carefully during the busy harvest season when the promotion plan will be implemented.

What's in a deadline? Even though timing isn't critical until just before harvest, Warren encourages Bill to set deadlines and stick by them.

Warren gives Bill one of his fatherly talks about time, explaining, "Don't lose track of time. You lose a minute here and an hour there, and before you know it there's not enough time to get everything done. Then you either have to give up something you had planned to do or sacrifice quality to get the job done on time."

Warren explains, "I know that from experience, Bill. After harvest, I have the whole winter ahead of me to get the equipment ready for spring. It seems like an eternity. 'No rush,' I say to myself. 'Take a little time off, Warren, you deserve it.' And you know what happens, don't you? Every spring, we rush around at the last minute. I have to wait in line at the equipment dealers with everybody else who waited until the last minute. Every part I need is on back order because somebody just bought the last one. I go to bed at night exhausted and worried whether everything will get done on time."

Bill laughs, "Dad, you're not like that and you know it! You don't put the equipment away in the fall until it's all repaired and ready to go for the spring." Warren smiles, "Yeah, but it makes a good story. And I mean what I say. I'm going to hold you to those deadlines. So make sure they're realistic."

Getting commitment

Warren, Jim, and Bill complete their plan.

Warren asks, "Where do we stand? Are you comfortable with what we've done? What remains to be done? Have we left anything out? Does everyone know what he needs to do?" Jim and Bill look over the plans.

Jim says, "I'm comfortable with the IPM plan as far as it goes. There are a lot of gaps to fill in. I'll defer to your judgment on the marketing stuff."

Bill replies, "I think this is a good starting point. I want both of you to review the draft marketing plan before I start producing materials. When do you want to meet to finalize the marketing plan?" They agree on a date. Warren adds the meeting to the plan and writes the date on his calendar.

6. Act! Implement the plan.

	Process for Action Planning
PLAN:	1. Decide who to include in planning. 2. Translate decision into a series of targets. 3. Identify the steps necessary to achieve the target. 4. Gain commitment to the plan. 5. Consider closely related targets.

ACT:	**6. Implement the plan.**
	   Confirm that everyone understands the plan.
	   Confirm willingness to commit.

CONTROL
RESULTS:
	7. Monitor progress.
	   Have you followed the steps planned?
	   Have the steps taken achieved your target?
	   Did achieving the target move you toward
	      your broad goals?
	8. Take corrective action.

Planning is a wasted effort unless effective action follows. The plan helps ensure that action is purposeful and timely. Monitoring and controlling results help ensure that action is effective.

When the marketing plans are finalized, Warren rewrites the skeleton of the IPM plan and the more well developed marketing plans on poster board. He tacks them on the office wall where all three can see them. As each step is completed, Warren records the date it was completed and evaluates whether or not it had the expected effect. Warren also adds more detailed steps to the plans as they are identified.

7. Monitor progress.

As discussed earlier, each step in the plan implies an if-then statement. "If I do this, that will result." As each step is completed, Warren asks whether it accomplished the expected result. If it did, he moves to the next step with confidence. If it doesn't, he asks why and takes corrective action.

He asks, "Were related steps completed on time? Did related steps have the intended effect? How can we get back on track?"

8. Take corrective action.

If corrective action is taken immediately and succeeds, little more than a slight deviation from the plan may be required. If corrective action is delayed, the problem may compound itself, requiring major effort later. Some apple growers use an alternate row spraying program, spraying every other row on a rigid 10–14 day schedule. While this approach reduces cost and has environmental benefits, an infestation may occur on the seventh or eighth day. If the grower sticks to the plan without taking corrective action, the infestation can get quite serious by the scheduled spraying day. The risk of a secondary infestation increases later in the summer, making it necessary to continue spraying throughout the summer season and erasing any cost savings.

Sometimes succeeding steps may be difficult or impossible to complete until early steps are completed. Bill can't have the barn repainted with the new logo until the logo is designed. Jim can't monitor scab indicators until the scab predictor has been selected, ordered, received, set up, set out, and is in working order.

The ability to predict the effects of each task often improves as the plan is implemented and time passes. The plan often starts out as a broad list of tasks, each implying a series of smaller tasks. As implementation proceeds, Warren fills in detail—adding and refining steps, juggling responsibilities, and adjusting deadlines. Warren knows that action planning isn't a recipe. It's a tool. What he gets out of it depends on how skillfully he uses it.

Monitoring a results-oriented plan

In addition to calling attention to problems before they become unmanageable, monitoring keeps our attention focused on the *results* of what we do. All too often, plans take on more importance than they deserve, becoming an end in people's minds instead of a means. Carrying out the plan becomes more important than getting the desired result. There is a subtle but important difference between being task oriented and results oriented. A task-oriented person carries out the plan. As long as each step is done well, the individual can take pride in a task well done. A results-oriented person is more concerned about the outcome than the plan—the results more than the task. The plan is a means to achieve the desired results. As such, it is an evolutionary document that incorporates new information as it becomes available.

Accumulation of actions and broad goals

After ten years, Warren finds himself looking back and evaluating the shift to IPM. While production declined more than they had hoped initially, they have gained experience using integrated pest management. The percentage of second-grade apples they produce has decreased, and quality has returned to previous levels. They expanded the orchard, planting scab-resistant 'Liberty' cultivar. Production will increase substantially when these trees begin producing. While they didn't establish Olson's Orchards in the organic market, they were able to create an image of Olson's Orchards as health conscious and environmentally sound. Over five years, on-farm sales actually increased more than they expected. They now sell most of the crop at the farm. Bill, who came into the business full time two years after the change, handles marketing. Advertising is a routine part of the annual budget.

Overall, Bill and Warren are pleased, particularly Warren. Now if Bill desires, he too can enjoy the lifestyle Warren has treasured so much. At the same time, Warren has maintained the orchard's profitability in a highly competitive market. With integrated pest management, organic sprays, and resistant trees, he's doing his part to protect the environment for his grandchildren and the whole community.

Objectives and change of direction

When Bill and Warren achieved their objectives, they were pleased. They had moved closer to their long-term goals. It isn't always so. You may achieve your immediate targets and objectives only to realize that they haven't moved you closer to your broad goals. Or you may achieve your immediate objectives and make progress toward your broad goals, only to find that your broad goals don't reflect what is truly important—your values. In either case, change is required, not minor adjustments, but major shifts in direction.

■   Consider again the 52-year-old man who wakes up one morning, wondering what he's done with his life. He has done everything right. He went to the right schools, earned good grades, and got a good job when he graduated. Wherever he has worked, there have been regular promotions. He is a senior manager. He married, bought a house, and has three grown children. They've all done well. Despite all of his successes, he is unhappy. He has achieved his objectives and has made progress toward his broadest goals, but something is missing. His goals are not consistent with his values. His children grew up with a father who was always at work. His marriage is not bad, but it could be better. His only friends are business associates. Accepting his dissatisfaction, he begins to question his most closely held assumptions.

Questioning closely held assumptions

Shifting direction almost always requires a willingness to question assumptions. We make assumptions all the time—some little, some big. Our erroneous assumptions about factors we think we understand and don't lead us astray. We make erroneous assumptions about fact—things that we could measure but don't because there is not time, measurement is too costly, or practical means of measuring are lacking.

We also make cultural assumptions. We assume we should behave in a certain way because that is the cultural norm. We don't realize that cultural norms are little more than shared assumptions. They are not right or wrong. They may make sense at one point in time, but over time, changing conditions may make them nonsensical. Some cultural assumptions that influence our actions as individuals and the actions of businesses and institutions are the following:

- Bigger is better—bigger cars, bigger houses, bigger farms, bigger businesses.

- Consumption is good.

- Time is our most precious resource; conserving time and improving convenience are more important than conserving other resources.

- Success is measured in the size of our house and the amount we consume.

- Successful people earn a lot of money.

- We are each responsible for ourselves; other people can take care of themselves.

- The present is more important than the future.

- Short-term profits are more important than long-term productivity.

- Preserving individual freedom is more important than all other goals.

We are generally unwilling to question our cultural assumptions—and for good reason: They organize our collective behavior so that we know what to expect; without cultural assumptions, there would be anarchy. However, many of the assumptions that impede progress toward sustainability fall in this category. Most of us are unwilling to question assumptions about lifestyle, convenience, efficiency, income, and productivity because they are so deeply ingrained in our culture.

It is not easy for individuals to question these most closely held assumptions. It is even more difficult for businesses, organizations, and a pluralistic nation like ours to question them. Nevertheless, we can address cultural assumptions at all levels of social organization: in decision making because of the nature of criteria, in problem definition because assumptions underlie problem framing, and in monitoring and controlling because we have the opportunity to ask if we have achieved our broadest goals.

8

■ Taking Action When No One Is in Charge

Ensuring timely, purposeful, and effective action can be difficult in an ad hoc group. You will recall an ad hoc group is one that comes together voluntarily to solve a problem. The group's leader has no clearly defined authority. Each person cooperates voluntarily, and each person's decision to take action is based on personal commitment.

In ad hoc groups, commitment is required at two levels. Each individual has to be committed to the broad purposes implied in the decision to be implemented as well as to carrying out his or her assigned tasks. Frequently, individuals are committed to the broad purposes of the group but not to the specific tasks assigned to them. Perhaps they are overcommitted or don't feel qualified to do an assigned task. As a result, they follow through halfheartedly or not at all. Conversely, individuals can be fully committed to carry out their assigned tasks and harbor misgivings about the overall purposes. If their misgivings gnaw at them enough, they may fail to follow through effectively, on time, or at all.

The Action Framework and Process Steps

The action framework and process steps presented in chapter 7 help ensure that all of an ad hoc group's members understand and are committed fully to a common plan. When an ad hoc group uses the framework and process skillfully, each one of the group's members will understand what is expected and when. They will know who depends on them and on whom they depend.

Every group, even an ad hoc group, needs a leader. When all of the members are peers, the leader's responsibility is to keep track of what has to be done, to remind members of their commitments, and to bring any unexpected deviations from the plan to the group's attention. The leader's authority comes from the group. In dealing with members, the leader represents the group's commitment to the plan rather than his or her own interests.

The action-planning framework and process give the group's leader a tool to motivate, remind, or twist members' arms to follow through with their assigned tasks. The structure helps create realistic expectations. The completed plan provides an objective standard against which the group can measure progress toward the desired results. The plan helps point out when progress is lacking so that the group can see the need for and take corrective action.

Make a decision.

Warren Olson, Dave Stowe, and Gordon Thomas have decided to set up a cooperative cider press. While they compete for customers, they have cooperated many times over the years. Warren loaned Dave a sprayer when his was broken, and Warren and Gordon shared machinery to establish controlled atmospheric conditions in their cold storage units. Both Dave and Warren helped Gordon deliver apples once when Gordon's truck skidded off an ice-covered road.

Coincidentally, they all need to expand their cider operations at the same time. Warren expects to produce more second grade apples while he learns to use integrated pest management effectively. Dave has expanded his apple production in recent years and is outgrowing his present press. Gordon's operation is small, and he has relied on Dave to press his apples for many years. But last year Gordon had to find another orchard to press his crop because Dave needed all of the press time available for his own crop.

When the three made the decision to set up the cooperative, they decided to locate the press at Dave's orchard because of his central location. They also agreed to rotate press time on a weekly basis with each orchard providing its own bottles. Each member is to pay a small fee for each gallon of cider pressed. Costs will be subtracted from the fees, and any surplus will be divided among the member orchards in proportion to the amount they process. They tentatively agreed on the wording for their objectives expressed as a target:

> Purchase and operate a cooperative cider press that will handle Dave Stowe's and Warren Olson's volume in excess of what their existing presses can handle and Gordon Thomas's entire press. At present, these are roughly equal needs.

At 3:00 on Friday, Dave opens the meeting and introduces Andy Shutsman, his orchard manager. Warren introduces Jim and Ron Brown, the attorney who handles the local farm supply co-op's legal matters. Gordon arrives alone.

Translate the decision into targets.

Gordon suggests that they begin by formally adopting the target proposed at the last meeting.

Dave Stowe has some concerns. "What if my production increases? Are we going to build in any expansion capacity?" Warren adds, "And what about costs? The cooperative won't do any of us any good if our costs per gallon pressed go up."

Ron suggests changing the target to purchase and operate a cooperative cider press that will be large enough to handle Dave's and Warren's excess volume, Gordon's entire press, plus 20 percent expansion capacity. Costs should be kept at or lower than the cost of pressing on farm.

"Suits me," Dave says. "Me, too," Gordon agrees.

List but do not evaluate steps.

Dave describes his plan to the group.

Dave begins, "First thing we have to do is get price quotes for a press and build a shed to house it."

Gordon laughs, "If it were that simple, I wouldn't have so many reservations. We have to open a bank account, decide which cider press to buy, and get price quotes. Then we'll have to decide how to manage the operation."

As Gordon takes a breath, Warren starts, "We have to agree on press fees and a schedule. Someone has to handle the finances, and we all have to feel comfortable with how they're handled. We'll probably need written guidelines." Gordon adds, "Ditto the written guidelines for fees and schedules. Not that I don't trust you guys, but we have to be careful with these things. We don't want to be defending what we think we agreed to in court."

"That's right," Ron adds. "You want everything in writing. You'll also need articles of incorporation and bylaws."

"We'll have to develop a maintenance schedule and decide who will be responsible for it," Dave says. "Someone will have to arrange for state and local inspections," Jim adds. "We'll have to get food-processing licenses. Are there different license requirements for cooperative presses?"

Dave continues, "A lot of tasks are involved in building the shed. Should we list those as well?" Warren answers, "Let's leave that for later, OK? Let's get a general list of what we need to do for organization, setting up operations, preparing equipment and facilities, and beginning operations. I think we should meet every two or three weeks to monitor progress and revise the list. Otherwise, we're sure to leave out something important." Gordon responds, "I agree. I'll be more comfortable if we meet regularly."

Brainstorming, the six men generate an impressive collection of tasks. Warren writes them on a flip chart.

Revise the list.

After some discussion, the group organizes the steps into groups of related tasks. They revise the steps as they go along, adding some and combining others. They identify questions they will have to answer, especially regarding special regulations for cooperatives.

Schedule steps and assign responsibilities.

First, the group members identify linked activities. Then they put these activities in sequence. To schedule activities, they fix a point of reference—the critical date (or dates) on which everything else rests. Harvesttime is the fixed point of reference, give or take a couple of weeks for variances in the weather.

Then they identify activities in which timing is controlled by others. For example, the supplier controls the length of time from equipment order to delivery. The licensing board determines how much time elapses between the application and issuance of a food-processing license while the contractor determines how quickly or slowly the shed to house the press is constructed. An attorney will write the articles of incorporation and bylaws.

The group works backward from harvest, scheduling each activity. They allow plenty of time for activities they cannot directly control. Equipment suppliers recommend allowing six to eight weeks for delivery, so they allow twelve weeks just to be sure. Contractors say construction will take four weeks, so they allow eight.

While the group members could schedule activities over which they exercise control closer together, each one recognizes that this is a voluntary effort. Moreover, each has other responsibilities and must juggle priorities. As a group, they would rather have it take a little longer than expected than be overburdened with more responsibility than each one can deliver. On the other hand, they agree that it would be best to get as much as possible done before the busy spring and summer months.

The group schedules and assigns responsibility for each task. Members will monitor each other's progress at their every-other-week meetings. Dave writes the steps out in a list as the group discusses the finished plan.

Choose a leader.

The group finishes the agenda.

Warren says, "Something's bothering me, and I can't quite put my finger on it. This plan will work if each of us follows through. But what happens if one of us falls behind? Or worse, if someone just plain doesn't do the job? Who's going to see to it that everything gets done right and on time?"

"That's been bothering me too," Dave says. "We're all used to being in charge. I'm not sure how any one of us would feel about answering to someone else on this. On the other hand, I don't like feeling like everybody's in charge. That just creates chaos. Let's face it, guys. There's going to be times when we don't agree, and someone's going to have to decide one way or the other. We can't always be waiting for the next meeting to make critical decisions."

"I agree," Gordon adds, "but who? And how are we going to decide?"

Warren answers, "One thing is sure. We're not going to hire a manager at this point. That would defeat the purpose of organizing a cooperative. If we agree on that, then it's one of us. Right?"

"Right," Dave remarks, "but who?"

After going around in circles for awhile, Gordon declares, "Enough is enough, guys. This can't be that hard. What if we rotate the job? This year is a critical year. Warren, you have as much as you can handle switching to IPM. I'm snowed under with other things. Dave, because we're building the shed on your property, I think you should take the job this year. Next year, it's your turn, Warren. The year after, I'll take my turn. After three years, we can reevaluate. What do you think?"

Warren states, "I like it, and you're right. Dave's the right man for the job this year. Dave, what do you think?"

Dave ponders for a moment then speaks slowly, "You know, I've been looking for a new challenge. I've expanded my orchard all I'm going to for a while. Everything is going well for Helen and me. Yes, I think I would enjoy doing this right now. OK, let's get on with it."

They add several tasks to the plan under monitor and evaluate to show Dave's leadership role during the next year.

When does leadership become an issue? Different groups address the leadership issue at different points in their evolution. In the Powder River group, the group's diversity and size made leadership a critical issue from the start. Most larger groups have leadership in place as they move from decision making to action planning and implementing the plan. The Powder River group could not have agreed on an approach without skillful leadership.

> **Steps to Show Dave's Leadership Role**
>
> Monitor and evaluate—group
>
> Manage/coordinate—Dave
>
> - Schedule monthly management meetings.
> - Facilitate meetings.
> - Monitor progress against plans and toward objectives.
> - Recommend corrective action as needed.

In contrast, the cooperative cider press group is small and relatively homogeneous. While each member's reasons for wanting a co-op cider press differ, they are all apple growers who face similar costs and competitive pressures. The group's smallness makes it easier for them to agree in principle to organize a co-op without any one person providing leadership. Indeed, if someone had taken leadership early on, the others might even have become skeptical of his motives and withdrawn their support for the co-op.

Few ad hoc groups can take effective action without some kind of leadership. But the issue arises at different points in the formation of each group. It is nearly always a sensitive issue, but not one to be avoided when it surfaces. On the other hand, the leadership issue should not be forced before its time. Lack of leadership and overbearing leadership are, perhaps, two of the most common reasons ad hoc groups fail to take purposeful, effective, and timely action.

Strengthen commitment and follow-through.

In voluntary groups, the strength of each person's commitment to the group's objectives differs. Similarly, each person's willingness to accept responsibility and reliability differs. These are very personal characteristics that no amount of planning can completely control. However, several factors will strengthen commitment, increase willingness to accept responsibility, and improve reliability.

Clearly state objectives and share the plan with everyone.

Commitment is much more likely when everyone understands the plan's targets, why they are important, and how they will help the group achieve its broad goals. When group members understand the link between their goals and targets as well as the plan to achieve them, they are more likely to follow through.

Facilitate effectively.

The group adopts the targets and plans as a collective, but each member commits to the plan as an individual. Effective facilitation during the group planning process can promote individuals' sense of ownership, making sure each member's ideas have been fully considered. Effective facilitation gives each person an opportunity to speak freely and be heard and understood by encouraging all group members to participate, by affirming all contributions, and by clarifying the points raised.

Build on small accomplishments.

Building on small accomplishments fosters the mutual trust that grows over time in an action group. Trust is founded on predictability, and predictability is based on experience. When people follow through as they promised, trust grows. When they fail to follow through, trust diminishes.

Without a history of trustworthiness, most people are willing to trust the group and the process when the stakes are low—when it doesn't matter too much whether or not the targets are achieved. When the stakes are high, few people will place their trust in someone they don't know is trustworthy. As a result, voluntary groups are most likely to succeed in carrying out large-scale plans when they have a history of small accomplishments to build on.

Warren, Gordon, and Dave trust each other to follow through because they have worked together on small projects for many years. Similarly, an ad hoc group may have to successfully achieve a series of small, incremental objectives before addressing their overriding concern—simply to build a foundation of trust.

Set realistic deadlines.

Take into account group members' other responsibilities when setting deadlines. It is better to allow more time than necessary and set a slower pace, than to set unrealistic deadlines that cannot be met. When the sequence and timing of activities are critical, a missed deadline can throw the entire schedule off, diminishing trust and commitment.

If each person follows through on time, trust and commitment grow. Skeptical members begin to think, "Maybe we can accomplish our goals. I don't want to be the one who lets the group down." If someone fails to do a promised task because of unrealistic deadlines, trust breaks down. There is a snowball effect. Other members take their commitments less seriously. Members think, "If the group fails, it won't be because I didn't do my part. He didn't do his either."

Assign each task to a single individual.

All too often groups talk about the need for a task without deciding who will follow through. Inevitably, no one takes responsibility and nothing is done. At the next meeting, everyone ducks responsibility, each pointing the finger at the others. Members lose focus on the group's objectives and get defensive.

If this happens repeatedly, defensiveness becomes a habit. The tone of group meetings shifts from being positive and goal directed to defensiveness and turf protection. Eventually some members will get impatient and quit; others will separate themselves emotionally from the group. To avoid this common pitfall, assign each task to one person.

Frequently, the situation demands shared responsibility—a committee is assigned responsibility to do a task. Shared responsibility does not preclude assigning specific tasks to individuals. It simply shifts the burden for assigning tasks from the larger group to the smaller committee. A statewide membership organization was planning a resource fair. The event coordinator, a volunteer, appointed two committees: exhibits and promotion. The exhibit committee immediately decided on a chairperson, who assigned specific tasks to individual members. In the promotion committee, two individuals wanted to chair the committee. Unable to decide who would assign tasks, none were assigned. The day of the event the hall was filled with exciting exhibits but was empty of people. The next year both committees were effective. However, fearing a repeat of the prior year, many exhibitors were hesitant to invest their time. The people came but there was little to see. Afterwards the membership organization decided not to hold a resource fair the next year.

Assign tasks to willing volunteers.

In ad hoc groups, no one has authority to require group members to act on time, to ensure that the action taken is effective, or to force quality standards on the group. Individuals volunteer. A person may volunteer out of commitment, a sense of obligation, because their arms were twisted, or a combination of these. Volunteers are more likely to follow through on a timely basis when they commit to the task willingly.

When no one volunteers, group leaders have two choices: they can reassess whether the task is necessary at this time or they can recruit someone. Recruiting volunteers is a tricky business. There is a fine line between recruiting willing volunteers and shaming unwilling volunteers into reluctantly saying "yes" in a moment of weakness.

It is tempting to recruit volunteers from people who are likely to say "yes," or who have "time on their hands," or who haven't volunteered for anything else. Those who always say "yes" are probably committed to do more than their share already or more than they can complete in the time available. Those we think have time on their hands often don't and may resent the assumption that they do. Those who haven't volunteered for anything may not have the time or skills; or they may not be fully committed to the group's plan.

A more positive approach to recruiting volunteers is preferable. It is easier to "sell" prospective volunteers on a responsibility if both the volunteer and the group appreciate the contribution of the task to the successful achievement of the group's goals. The benefits of volunteering are satisfaction and recognition, both of which depend on clearly knowing the importance of your contribution.

Ask for volunteers whenever possible.

Group cohesion and individual trustworthiness are enhanced when members feel needed. People feel needed when they are asked to contribute ideas and labor. Trustworthiness is improved when group members believe that the job will not get done if they don't do it.

Fearing that others can't be relied upon, some group leaders assume all of the responsibility themselves, denying others the opportunity to participate. This leads group members to assume that someone else will do the job. Over time, more and more of the responsibility falls on a smaller and smaller group of people. Eventually the majority may cease to feel a sense of ownership in the group's objectives, dropping out entirely or providing only token support.

Match tasks with appropriate skills and experience.

Some tasks call for specific skills and experience. It is not enough simply to do them; they must be done right. Group leaders balance the need to promote group cohesion by issuing open calls for volunteers against the need for specialized skills and training. When specialized skills are required, the group leader may turn to one or two people who have the necessary background for a given task. For example, Dave might turn to Ron, an attorney, and ask, "Ron, can you take care of this legal matter?"

Make sure everyone involved understands the plan.

All group members need to understand how their assignments link to other tasks. They need to know on whom they depend and who depends on them. It also helps when they know which tasks must be done right and when good-enough-to-get-by is adequate.

Ask group members to go the distance.

Group members should agree that if they can't follow through, they will find someone to fill in for them. Inevitably situations will arise when members cannot reasonably complete their assigned tasks, no matter how much they want to. If group members agree that they will find someone to carry out their task, two things happen. First, the group reduces the possibility that one person's inability to finish a task affects the group's ability to achieve its objectives. Second, there is greater willingness among group members to cover for each other when each one knows that they may have to ask someone to fill in for them at some point.

Celebrate progress.

Demonstrable progress motivates people to keep going. Lack of visible progress is debilitating. Members should be aware of progress towards the objectives. Celebrating progress gets to be a habit and creates a positive, results-oriented attitude among group members. When a plan will be implemented over a long period of time, set intermediate objectives so that progress can be demonstrated. The group should celebrate milestones along the way. This keeps members motivated and keeps the vision before them.

These celebrations also reduce the inevitable tensions that arise when people are focused on their small piece of the plan. It is hard to remember why you're doing what you're doing when you're the janitor cleaning up after everyone else. Celebrating milestones is an opportunity to acknowledge everyone's part in the group's progress.

Make sure someone is responsible for the big picture.

In ad hoc groups, implementation depends on all members doing their part voluntarily. There is no one with the authority to demand, bully, or coerce people to follow through. Nevertheless, leadership is needed to execute the plan. Giving someone responsibility to shepherd group members at each step along the way could be described in many ways: to nurture the faint-hearted; to encourage the skeptics; to coordinate people, processes, and resources; to monitor progress; to solicit ideas on alternative approaches to point out accomplishments; to keep a vision before the group. Leadership is essential to effective action. Without leadership, voluntary action groups fail to meet their objectives.

Let the group take action.

Over the winter, Warren, Dave, and Gordon each follow through with the tasks they agreed to do with help from Andy and Jim. Gordon and Warren take care of the financial pieces while Andy and Jim focus on operations. Andy lines up the contractor to build the shed. Warren works with Ron, the attorney, to draft the bylaws, and Dave provides overall leadership to the group.

The group meets every other week to monitor progress, coordinate small details, and discuss what needs to be done next. They talk about what they have learned, reevaluate the context, survey where the last steps left them, and consider the next steps. At each meeting, Warren, Dave, and Gordon look at the plan. Dave asks

- Have we followed the steps planned?
- Are the completed steps leading us toward our objective?
- Has anything changed?
- Are the assumptions we made in planning still reasonable?
- What steps need to be added to the plan?
- What steps are unnecessary?
- Does the sequence of steps make sense? If not, what adjustments are necessary?

- Do the assignments still make sense? If not, how should they be adjusted?
- Do our objectives still make sense given what we know now?

The initial plan gives them a sense of direction and continuity, but each knows they are breaking new ground. They don't know anyone else who has organized a cooperative cider press. They are learning what is needed as they progress toward their objective. As they learn, they revise their plan to reflect their new understanding.

Monitor progress.

Monitoring is the prerequisite to taking corrective action. Without conscious monitoring, groups or individual members may fail to take timely corrective action even when they realize that a plan is going awry.

This is not as surprising as it might seem. When a group invests time and emotional energy into a plan, the last thing group members want to hear is that the plan is not working. No one wants to be the bearer of bad news. Raising difficult questions carries with it the responsibility to address the questions. Without a groundswell of concern, only a few courageous individuals will raise the difficult questions and lead the group through the process of finding answers. Even when there are obvious distress signals, many groups continue until some crisis forces them to deal with the situation.

In part, the unwillingness to take corrective action midstream results from unrealistic expectations. Most of us assume that planning is a once-and-for-all, step-by-step guide to get the group from where it is to where it wants to be. It is not. A plan is a neverending process of asking and answering questions:

- Where are we?
- Where do we want to go?
- What is the first step?
- What is the next step?
- And the next? And the next?

Each additional step in a plan introduces more uncertainty. Our ability to predict the outcome decreases because more and more factors enter into the picture. In the cider press illustration, the group will be ready for operations in August—*if* Warren opens the bank account, *if* each member puts up his share of the investment, *if* Dave orders the equipment on time, *if* Gordon finds a contractor, *if* the contractor builds the shed, *if* the plumbing and electrical subcontractors do their part on time, *if* Dave hires a press crew, and *if*. . . . If something goes wrong along the way, the whole plan could fail.

At the same time, the context is always changing. People come and go. Halfway through the winter, Jim could resign, leaving Warren shorthanded and unable to make all the changes he planned. Their financial situation could change. A rich uncle could die and leave Gordon better off financially causing him to set up his own press rather than cooperate with Warren and Dave. Deadlines are changed. A subcontractor could go bankrupt, putting construction a month behind schedule.

Take corrective action.

By February, it becomes clear that the cooperative will need a small bank loan to finance the press and shed. About the same time, they realize that they can't wait until March to line up a contractor. But the contractor won't make a commitment until the loan is approved. For a couple of weeks, Dave goes to bed at night worrying whether or not everything will come together in time.

Dave wishes they had focused on the finances more when they started planning, but all he can do now is take corrective action. He can't do over what has been done. Fortunately, everyone accepts that they have to do whatever is necessary or their effort will be wasted.

Throughout those trying weeks, Dave is thankful for the group's bi-weekly management meetings. The group has put a lot of trust in Dave, and he wants to keep it that way. The meetings give them an opportunity to iron out inevitable differences and maintain trust in each other. In addition, regular meetings encourage the group to incorporate new understanding into the plans. They are a constant reminder that "planning" is a neverending, circular process of setting targets, mapping out a course, taking action, evaluating results, and setting new targets.

Make contingency plans.

Contingency planning answers these questions: What could go wrong with this plan? What events could interfere with the plan? What opportunities might require modification of the plan? What symptoms would suggest that the plan is not working? How could the plan be modified to minimize the impact of unpredicted problems? To maximize the benefits of unpredicted opportunities? What will I do if the plan gets off track?

For the three apple growers, the most significant contingency is the possibility that they will not have a press in place in time for the fall.

████ Warren went home from the November organizational meeting satisfied that the group had made progress. Yet, he's realistic. There is a good chance that the cooperative cider press will fail to get off the ground in time for the fall cider pressing. There's a chance it won't ever get off the ground.

He thinks, "What would I do with all those apples if the co-op isn't ready?" Staggered by the implications, he makes alternative arrangements—contingency plans.

He arranges to lease press time at an orchard 100 miles to the south. He doesn't mind paying the nonrefundable deposit. The peace of mind is worth it. The distance would mean a big inconvenience and additional transport cost. Even this he doesn't mind because the arrangement assures him that he will be able to press his surplus crop no matter what. With his contingency plans in place, he feels free to throw himself into the work ahead. He feels confident the cooperative will be ready on time.

Predict what could go wrong.

In Warren's case, what could go wrong is fairly obvious. Warren can predict with some certainty what will happen if someone fails to follow through on his piece of the plan. He can plan for that possibility, and he does. He arranges a back-up cider press.

In other situations, answers to this question are not so clear. Consider the Powder River group. The interrelationships between the pieces of the plan are so closely intertwined that predicting the chain of consequences of any single failure to follow through is nearly impossible. No one knows for sure whether all of the little efforts each group member undertakes to reduce soil erosion will bring down the river's sedimentation to acceptable levels. Of course, they believe the plan will work; otherwise, they wouldn't have agreed to it. Conversely, no one knows for sure how much tolerance there is in the plan. Making contingency plans is problematic. The best they can do is monitor sedimentation closely. When sedimentation levels rise, they will have to work backward from the symptoms to discover what is causing the rise, using the causal analysis framework described in the next chapter.

Continue the process after the first critical year.

The process will not stop when the group achieves its target—operating a cooperative cider press. At the end of the harvest, they will evaluate the results. Based on their evaluations, they are likely to revise their operating plans. With several years experience, their end-of-harvest evaluation may result in fine-tuning or no changes at all. Yet, they would be remiss to abandon the routine monitoring. What if the context changes? Operating costs could increase substantially. Without a built-in monitoring process, the group might not notice until after the harvest is completed. After the fact, they may resent paying the added cost, whereas hard feelings might have been avoided if the rising costs had been brought to their attention early on.

Periodically, Warren and the others have to consider their broad goals and determine whether achieving the immediate objective of operating a cooperative cider press has moved them closer to achieving them. For Warren, if the cooperative cider press reduces his costs and assures him that he will have sufficient capacity to press all of his second-grade apples, it meets his goals.

ırgets, Goals, and Values—A Reprise

Groups, like individuals, may find that achieving their targets, and even successfully reaching their long-range goals, is not as satisfying as they had expected. But the goals are assumed to reflect the basic values that the group shares. When achieving the goals doesn't bring success, the group is forced to reexamine basic assumptions. Warren, Dave, and Gordon have narrow, well-defined goals for the cider cooperative, goals that represent productivity values; and success of the cooperative will not disappoint or disillusion them. But groups formed to pursue goals that represent sustainability and equity values more frequently find that achieving their goals does not result in solving the problems they set out to address.

During the 1960s and 1970s, the civil rights movement was extraordinarily successful in achieving important and difficult goals, including integration of schools, voting rights, and equal opportunity guidelines for housing and employment. After achieving success in the courts and legislative bodies, many groups dissipated their energies in divisive internal conflicts as they sought to reevaluate their values and redefine their goals. Many of their members simply lost the feeling that they were making an important contribution and turned to other aspects of their lives.

By the 1980s, many were surprised and disappointed to find that integration and legal protection had not eradicated racism. Racial justice seemed as elusive as ever as racism continued to dominate American culture. Reexamining their goals, many groups realized that economic justice was fundamental to racial justice. Today the fight against racism has shifted to community-based groups seeking to create jobs and improve the welfare of low-income African Americans.

Americans have also been extraordinarily successful in working toward economic goals. The gross national product has grown steadily this century. Our standard of living is among the highest in the world. As our wealth increased, national concern focused on environmental protection. Through the courts and legislation, environmental groups have gained standing in management of public lands, and regulations have been developed to protect water and air.

Just as the civil rights movement reexamined its goals after achieving success, environmental groups are just beginning to understand that advocacy and legislation can only accomplish so much. A growing number of environmental groups are beginning to develop and carry out community-based projects that balance people's need for a job with the need to protect the environment. It is likely that this shift will cause some members of the environmental movement to become disheartened. Seeking balance among productivity, sustainability, and equity requires giving up cultural assumptions about winners and losers in order to find solutions that meet multiple objectives.

The next chapter presents causal analysis—a framework that enables an individual or group to accumulate and organize all that can be observed about a problem and work backward from what is known to figure out what might have caused the problem. Through this process we will accumulate the body of facts linking cause and effect that can prompt us to question the cultural assumptions that conflict with our values.

9

■ Understanding Cause and Effect

n the Powder River illustration, Sid understood cause and effect. His understanding was based on concrete research results. He knew that excessive runoff leads to high turbidity, which limits salmon runs, thus reducing the salmon population. Frequently, however, we are concerned about a disturbing symptom but do not understand the cause-and-effect relationships behind it. We may see increased rates of morbidity, a decline in fish populations, or a deterioration of range conditions, but we don't know what is causing these symptoms. We don't know what the problem is. The causal analysis framework and process presented in this chapter help us find out.

ʹhy Is This Happening?

In the illustration below we meet Ellen Dichter, the air quality section head in a state agency responsible for enforcing environmental regulations. We will go back a few years in time and observe the process Ellen and her agency went through as they became aware of acid rain. We will watch them move from awareness to problem recognition to problem definition with an imperfect understanding of the cause-and-effect relationships involved.

Ellen Dichter's job is largely administrative, but she tries to keep up with the professional literature. One night a few years ago, she ran across an article on the effects of acid rain on conifers in the Northeast. She had read a little about acid rain in Sweden and Canada, but not much. This was the first article she had seen that linked acid rain to U.S. forests, and it piqued her interest.

The next day, she asks some of her colleagues what they know about acid rain. Most don't know much more than Ellen, but one fellow who has been with the agency for years became interested in the issue when it was first raised. Ellen sits in his office talking for almost an hour.

Over the next few months, Ellen's interest in acid rain grows. She reads all the journal articles she can find on the issue. She talks to the agency's director, Walt Smith, about attending an acid rain workshop. He isn't very enthusiastic about the idea, so she pays her own way.

The more she learns about acid rain, the more convinced she is that this is an issue her unit will eventually address. Several of her colleagues agree, but they argue that if regulation is necessary, it is a job for the federal government, not the state. When the Environmental Protection Agency announces a conference on acid rain, Ellen approaches Walt again. This time he supports the idea, reluctantly acknowledging that Ellen could be right. "Mark my words," he says, "if the Feds weasel out of this and we end up with it, it will be a regulatory nightmare."

During this period, Ellen looked for ways to define the acid rain problem that would clarify her agency's involvement. In spite of everything she knows, she can't identify any specific problem the agency could or should take action to solve. The problem just doesn't seem to be defined on the state level. The state doesn't have authority to regulate or tax industries outside the state. And the political support isn't there.

Recently, however, the state legislature announced a series of public hearings on acid rain. One hearing was scheduled for Forrest City in the northern part of the state where pine forests have recently shown damage that many local people attribute to acid rain. People in the northern counties want legislative action to save the forests. Two hearings are scheduled for the southern, more densely populated area of the state where residents rely heavily on industry for jobs and where the business and industry lobby is powerful. They want nothing to do with controlling acid rain, stronger air quality standards, or anything else that might increase costs or reduce operating flexibility.

Ellen was asked to prepare testimony supporting the agency's official policy that existing air quality standards are adequate. Ellen and several others have been pushing for months to get the agency to reevaluate the standards. While the agency has finally decided to set up an internal task force, it isn't yet prepared to recommend any changes.

Walt points out to her that the hearings couldn't have come at a worse time. The agency will look foolish testifying that air quality standards are adequate and then proposing changes a short time later. Ellen recommends that the testimony describe existing standards, the task force, and its charge. But Walt Smith balks because he doesn't want to commit the agency to anything. Ellen is disappointed because she believes the standards are inadequate, but she is a professional and will respect agency policy.

Ellen has another concern. She isn't convinced that the yellowing of pines in the northern part of the state is caused by acid rain—the evidence just isn't sufficient. She needs a better understanding of what is causing the problem. It would be politically and economically costly if the legislature took action on acid rain because of these yellowing pines only to find out that the yellowing was caused by something other than acid rain.

Ellen hasn't time for a long-term study. She needs the information before the hearing in Forrest City next week. But she wants more information before she testifies. She calls the extension specialist who alerted her to the problem, and they schedule a field trip to Forrest City for tomorrow.

Defining Ellen's problem as a need to know why

Almost as soon as she became aware of the acid rain issue, Ellen recognized a potential problem. Without a solid understanding of cause-and-effect relationships, she couldn't circumscribe the problem sufficiently to phrase a question that called for action at her own level of authority—state air quality regulation. There was no precipitating event that called for action. She was stuck in the problem-definition stage.

She and her colleagues were aware that their understanding was inadequate. Yet they anticipated that some day the agency would be called on to act on the acid rain problem. They pushed for reevaluation of air quality standards, hoping that the process would help clarify their thoughts and define the acid rain problem in the context of the agency's responsibilities. Meanwhile, the state legislature scheduled its hearings. This precipitating event helped Ellen narrow the problem so that she could take action.

■   Ellen is concerned. "Suppose," she thinks, "the legislature responds to concern about the Forrest City pines with air quality regulation, and acid rain is *not* the cause of the yellowing pines? Then the legislation won't achieve the legislative intent, but the regulations will still create economic losses in the industrial areas of the state. Misdirected legislation at this time might fail to solve the problem of the pines while making it more difficult to take appropriate action in response to acid rain later."

Ellen is concerned with the broad problem of acid rain, but it isn't clear how that problem falls within her purview. She can, however, deal with the narrow problem of her responsibility to advise the legislature. She says, "I have a problem. The state legislature may take action on acid rain based on erroneous assumptions about cause and effect. Why are the pines yellowing and dying in the Forrest City area?"

In the next few days, she will use all the information at hand to identify the cause of the yellowing pines in and around Forrest City. She will answer the question—why?

Going from symptoms to action

We recognize a problem through its symptoms. A symptom is an observed deviation from the expected or desired situation. For example, gullied fields are a symptom of soil erosion; endangered species are a symptom of habitat destruction; and smog is a symptom of auto emissions. Yellowing pines are a symptom—but of what cause?

There is an important distinction between a problem and its symptoms. Problems call for action; symptoms merely point to problems. Problems are solved by removing or changing the problem behavior or condition. When we try to remove or change a problem's symptoms, leaving the problem intact, we may achieve a temporary respite or we may have no effect whatsoever. In either case, the underlying problem will continue to manifest itself one way or another until the problem—the behavior or condition that caused the symptom to occur—is changed. The farmer can fill in the gully, but it will begin to form again with the next heavy rain unless he takes measures to reduce soil erosion.

Every problem-solving effort is precipitated by some person or group recognizing a symptom. Solving the problem hinges to one degree or another on understanding what caused the symptom to occur and what action(s) will result in the desired change in the symptom. We can see problem solving as having four distinct parts (figure 9.1). We move from symptoms to action by asking questions. We may begin problem solving at any point. For example, we begin with planning if the cause of the problem and its solution are obvious. But no matter where in the process we start, a clear understanding of cause-and-effect relationships is required. If this understanding is lacking, the causal analysis framework and process developed in this chapter are needed.

Causal analysis is not a particular stage in problem solving. Rather, assumptions of cause and effect underlie all problem solving. A situation

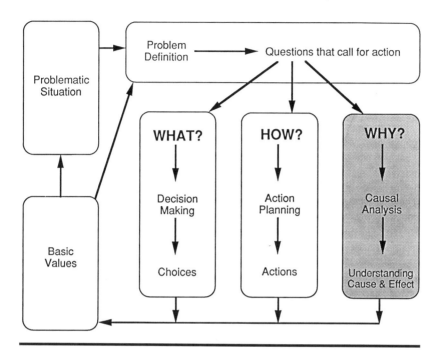

Figure 9.1. Problem-solving framework—understanding of cause and effect.

presents us with a symptom or set of symptoms. We work backward, objectively evaluating the pattern of symptoms to identify plausible explanations for the problem's cause, answering the question "*Why* is this happening?" In chapter 2, Sid Riedel found elevated turbidity levels at the Red Ridge water treatment intake. He implicitly used causal analysis to diagnose the causes of increased sedimentation: recent rains, runoff from cultivated bottomlands, a washed-out road, and land-management practices on commercial and public forestlands.

Suppose we can relate the disturbing symptoms to a complex bundle of causes. We need to separate the bundle of causes into related, but separate problems that call for action. We are defining the problem in a question that calls for action. Doing this hinges on disentangling the problem bundle into simple cause-and-effect relationships that relate the symptoms to problems.

In chapter 2, Sid used his understanding of social and biophysical cause and effect to define the Powder River problem. He related the disturbing symptom—increased turbidity, forward to a threatened consequence, declining salmon runs—forward and backward to a diverse group of actors, using what he knew about the cause-and-effect relationships between state regulations, landowners' economic needs, soil erosion, turbidity, and salmon.

Once we recognize that we have a problem that calls for action, we need to know "*What effect* will alternative responses have on the problem and thus on the disturbing symptoms?" In chapter 5, Paul Hartner and his department used their understanding of cause and effect to predict how alternative ways of reducing soil erosion on a logging road would affect their ability to meet state regulations, cost, public relations, soil erosion, and other criteria.

We also use our understanding of cause and effect to choose among alternative responses to a problem. We answer the question "*What* should we do?" selecting the course of action that will lead to the most desirable outcome. Paul and his staff chose the best alternative given their understanding.

In chapter 6, the Powder River group used its understanding of cause and effect to choose a package of small efforts that together will likely reduce soil erosion, reduce turbidity, and protect salmon runs.

Having decided what to do, we face the question "*How* shall we achieve the desired outcome?" In action planning, we use our knowledge of cause-and-effect relationships to design a sequence of steps that is likely to lead us to the desired outcome. Each successive step is based on the assumption that the previous step had the intended effect and did not have negative unintended effects that might outweigh the benefit gained. Our understanding lets us take small incremental steps, confident that the accumulation of steps will lead us to achieve our immediate targets and move us closer to accomplishing our broadest goals.

Warren Olson's action plan for changing his pest-management approach was based on what he knew about the causes of scab infestation and about the effects of integrated pest management. This knowledge enabled him to take timely and effective actions to discourage spore reproduction (e.g., removing leaf litter) and to apply organic fungicides at the optimum time to prevent primary infestation in the early spring.

In Ellen Dichter's case, there is a disturbing symptom, but what is the cause? *Why* are the pines around Forrest City yellowing? The causal analysis framework is a set of questions and a process designed to help us sort through what we observe and know about a problem's symptoms systematically to identify possible explanations. Understanding a problem's causes equips us to predict the consequences of alternative solutions and to prescribe a solution (or package of solutions) to remedy or improve the situation.

Studying the yellowing pines situation

The people of Forrest City noticed two years ago that the area's majestic white pines were yellowing. They are an important part of the community's aesthetic appeal, adding color to the bleak winter landscape and variety to the dominant hardwoods.

After hearing news reports of trees damaged by acid rain, many Forrest City residents blame yellowing of the pines on coal-burning power plants and auto emissions in the populous cities to the south and west. Concern has become widespread; property owners worry that clean-up bills will be high and property values could plummet if many of the pines die.

A few people are particularly incensed. They see the yellowing pines as one more example of a callous disregard for nature by the southern urban half of the state's population. People in the Forrest City area have organized their friends and neighbors to put pressure on state legislators to do something about the acid rain problem. In response, the chairperson of the state senate's natural resources committee has announced a series of public hearings to gather information and to diffuse the growing resentment.

The committee chairperson asked Ellen's agency to prepare expert testimony for the hearing. The agency, in the beginning stages of reviewing the state's air quality standards, wants to forestall piecemeal legislation. Walt Smith directs Ellen to drop everything and concentrate on preparing testimony for the Forrest City hearing.

Ellen isn't convinced that the yellowing of pines is necessarily caused by acid rain. She knows that other factors can cause pines to yellow as well. Smog in the Los Angeles basin has caused a conifer blight. Other New England communities have reported symptoms that mimic disease seemingly related to road salt. Northern European nations are reporting other disease and growth problems that are associated with industrial pollution.

Ellen calls Bob Bowles, the extension forestry specialist who brought the yellowing pines to her attention. They agree to meet in Forrest City tomorrow with Joe Berwick, the Forrest County agent. Joe works with owners of small woodlots, encouraging them to manage their woodlots for cash, firewood, and bird habitat. A significant loss of white pine will affect many of these woodlot owners adversely, discouraging their interest in forest management. It was Joe who told Bob Bowles at the state agricultural university about the Forrest County situation. Bob's research focuses on plant pathology, and he develops disease- and pest-management programs for county agents. In recent years, he has become increasingly interested in air pollution, toxic wastes, and other human interventions that cause physiological problems for trees.

The Causal Analysis Framework

Ellen, Bob, and Joe will use the causal analysis framework to answer this question: Why are the pines yellowing? Four pairs of questions help them describe the symptom systematically. A fifth set of questions helps them identify the pattern of symptoms.

1. What are the symptoms? What are not symptoms?

2. Where are the symptoms observed? Where aren't they observed?

3. When are the symptoms observed? When aren't they observed?

4. How often and how severely are the symptoms observed? How often and how severely aren't they observed?

5. *What* are the differences? *Where* are they? *When* are there differences? *How often* are there differences? *How much* are the differences?

Answers to these objective questions can be recorded in the following manner (figure 9.2).

The framework's objective questions call for factual answers. Ellen, Bob, and Joe will observe the yellowing pines as systematically as they can

Causal Analysis Framework			
	are the symptoms?	are not symptoms?	are the differences?
What			
Where			
When			
How often			
How much			
How severe			

Figure 9.2. Causal analysis framework before it is filled in.

in the time available. Organizing their observations will help them compare differences between affected and unaffected trees. They hope to find a pattern in the differences. Patterns make it possible to generalize about which trees are affected and which are not. Then they will draw on their theoretical knowledge and experience to develop plausible explanations that account for the pattern of symptoms observed.

While time constraints make it impossible to apply rigid scientific controls, there is still real value in systematic observation and organization of data. The framework encourages systematic observation and gives the group a tool to record and organize responses so that more information can be incorporated into the comparisons that will be made. They use the framework with confidence that the reliability of their initial observations can be tested later using random sampling techniques or controlled experiments.

Basing the framework's assumptions on scientific enquiry

The framework is based on four assumptions:

- Some identifiable factor or combination of factors is causing the symptoms.

- The causal factor affects the trees predictably, causing the symptoms to manifest in a pattern.

- The pattern can be identified by comparing similarities and differences between symptomatic and asymptomatic trees and the context in which they are present.

- Plausible hypotheses can be developed to explain the pattern of symptoms. Hypotheses that do not plausibly explain the pattern of symptoms can be ruled out.

Nearly all major advances in scientific understanding of the biophysical and social worlds have resulted from asking these basic comparative questions either explicitly or implicitly. Charles Darwin explicitly used comparative questions to identify differences among and within species. The hypotheses he generated to explain the differences he observed are the basis for his theory of evolution. This logic also underpins the scientific methods we rely on today—experimental control, random sampling techniques, and comparative analysis.

Questioning as a thinking process

Like the turbidity in the Powder River, yellowing pines are symptomatic of some underlying condition. Yellowing pines are not a problem; they signal a problem. Yellowing is a symptom that describes a deviation from the desired situation—healthy pines. However, "yellowing pines" is a vague description. It signals a problem but doesn't isolate possible causes. Ellen, Bob, and Joe will need to know a lot more about the yellowing pines before they will be able to talk about possible causes.

The causal analysis framework provides a guide to formulate a set of questions that covers all possible avenues of enquiry: What? Where? When? How much? How often? When problems have a social dimension, a sixth line of questioning may be required as well: Who?

The specific questions will flow out of the particular set of symptoms observed. The Forrest City group asks an initial set of questions guided by the framework based on what they know about trees, tree physiology, plant pathology, and the context. This knowledge helps them to frame questions that yield the most useful information possible. For example, if they didn't know the difference between a white and a red pine, their questions would produce lower-quality information. However, they must take care to avoid assuming too much based on their prior knowledge.

Answers to the initial screening questions point to areas where more specific, probing questions may be productive. Answers to these probing questions may point to more specific questions that yield additional detail. A line of questioning is productive as long as the answers continue to differentiate affected and unaffected trees. We continue pursuing the productive lines of questioning until either a pattern becomes apparent, no further information is available, or time and/or money run out. Inevitably, we will pursue some lines of questioning that seem productive only to find that the information gained does not help specify the symptoms' pattern. If we knew the answer to begin with, we would not need to do causal analysis.

■   Using the framework as a guide, Ellen, Joe, and Bob talk about their specific questions on the drive to Forrest City. They also talk about what avenues of further enquiry may be required. "Are other pines affected?" Bob asks. "Is it only the white pine? How about deciduous trees?" Joe responds, "We'll have to check those out. I'd also like to isolate what part of the pine is yellowing," he adds, "Is it the whole tree or only part of the tree? And if only part, which part?" Bob continues. "And which trees? Are they concentrated in certain places, or is the yellowing spread over the whole white pine population?" Ellen wonders, "When did this begin? Was it sudden or gradual? Is it getting worse over time?"

They make notes about the avenues they will pursue. They realize, however, that it is impossible to plan all of their questions in advance. They will need to respond to each new piece of information with increasingly specific questions, refining their observations about the lines of questioning that seem to differentiate affected trees from others. They will continue to ask questions until a pattern emerges. Only when a pattern emerges can they begin to isolate the likely causal factors.

Examining the yellowing pines

Whenever a question provides information that seems to point to a pattern, the group will probe more deeply, asking increasingly detailed questions and filling in as many observations as they can. Each one makes a list of questions that will require additional information for follow-up.

Ellen, Bob, and Joe begin their day by driving around Forrest City. They quickly realize that the yellowing isn't evenly distributed. In some areas, nearly every tree seems to be affected; in others, the trees appear healthy. They stop at a diner to discuss strategies. They agree to separate, each focusing on a different line of questioning. Bob will examine the trees themselves for clues to the symptoms' cause. Ellen will talk to people living near affected trees to find out when the symptoms began to appear. Joe will divide the town into four areas and systematically plot the location of affected trees.

On close examination, Bob finds that the needles are turning yellow from the inner needles to the tips. The older needles seem to be more affected than the younger needles. White pines retain their needles for three to five years. Lower limbs appear to be more frequently affected than upper limbs. He takes soil samples to test for nutrient levels, acidity, and salts. He also takes samples of the affected needles to study in the laboratory. He wants to rule out possible disease and insect-caused problems. He notes that the soil around many of the affected trees is compacted, dry, and rocky.

Nearly everyone Ellen talks to recalls first noticing the symptoms about two years ago. Ellen gets excited by this piece of information. It suggests that some event or dramatic change in the underlying conditions might have triggered the yellowing—perhaps the drought that is still affecting the area. She probes more deeply trying to pinpoint the timing more precisely. Few respondents can remember the details. One person recalls a front page newspaper article calling attention to the yellowing.

Ellen goes to the local newspaper and gets the article. She shows the article to several of the people she had talked to earlier. Ellen realizes the article may have caused people to notice the yellowing pines. As a result, there may not be anything significant about when people first noticed the symptoms. She decides that this line of questioning is probably a blind alley.

Before abandoning this line of questioning, however, she talks to the reporter who wrote the article. She asks what prompted him to write the story. He answers, "I live up here because I love the woods and spend a lot of time there. I noticed the pines yellowing about five years ago. Two years ago, a lot more pines began to yellow all at once. The community seemed oblivious so I wrote the article to draw attention to the symptoms and the potential effects on the community."

The fact that nearly everyone recalled noticing the symptoms about the same time seemed significant. Ellen pursued this line of questioning as long as it produced useful information. As more information became available, Ellen realized it was leading her nowhere.

We tend to cling to a line of questioning once we begin to probe it, unwilling to abandon it even when it ceases to produce new and useful information. As a result, we lose sight of alternative approaches. This tendency can lead us to jump to a cause before we have exhausted other productive lines of questioning.

As Joe moves through the town, he finds clusters of affected pines. He doesn't find many affected trees in the middle of woodlots, neither does he see any variance in trees at different elevations. Most affected trees are along roadways. He's puzzled because not all roads have affected trees. This looks like a productive line of questioning, so he pursues it, probing with more specific questions to find out what is different about the locations where affected trees are more prevalent. He plots the roads with a high proportion of affected trees on a map. He notices that the soil along roadways tends to be compacted and rocky. Some areas are much more severely affected than others. He finds dead and nearly dead trees in two locations. As he looks at the dead trees, a passing woman tells him that's where the plows pile snow in the winter.

Some questions provide more information than others. The *where* questions seem to discriminate between affected and unaffected trees more than other questions. Affected trees are clustered along roads. There are fewer affected trees on lawns and woodlots. What is different about the trees along roads? Some roads have a greater proportion of affected trees than others. The group asks, "How do roads and woodlots differ? What is different about roads with a higher proportion of affected trees and roads with few affected trees?" This is a line that they will continue to probe.

Process steps and improving the framework's usefulness

When Bob, Ellen, and Joe get back together, they share the information they have gathered. Ellen organizes the information in the form of figure 9.2. She suggests using the following process steps to guide their discussion:

1. Collect objective facts.
   - Let's first list answers to the framework questions without discussion, until we've completed the first four pairs of questions.
   - Then we can discuss and refine observations to make sure our observations are as accurate as possible. We should avoid trying to identify the cause at this point. Focus on the facts.

2. Compare similarities and differences.
   - With the facts in hand, we can proceed to identify similarities and differences category by category, collecting a list of generalizations about the patterns of yellowing.

3. Generate alternative hypotheses.
   - Once we've identified some patterns, we can list all of the possible causes that might explain why some trees are affected and others aren't. At this stage we should keep an open mind and consider every possibility, not discussing or rejecting any hypothesis yet.
   - With the full list of possibilities in hand, we can further discuss and refine the set of hypotheses.

4. Test the plausibility of alternative hypotheses.
   - For each hypothesis, we can ask these questions: Does this hypothesis explain all of the symptoms observed? What symptoms doesn't it explain? What symptoms does it explain?
   - Then we can look for which hypothesis explains the most symptoms. It may be that there are multiple causal factors working in combinations. Would a combination of hypotheses explain more symptoms?

The logic of the process

Like the process steps used with other frameworks, this one separates objective fact finding from exploration of subjective opinions as well as critical thinking from the creative generation of ideas. This separation gives the group objective and critical standards by which it can judge its own performance while making room for subjective information and creative idea generating and thus improving the quality of the product that results.

In the noncritical "brainstorming" process steps, the facilitator's role is to support expansive listing of all facts, distinctions, and possible hypotheses.

In the critical, analytic steps, the facilitator can ask, "Have we stuck to the facts? Do the facts support the similarities and differences we have identified? Have we applied what we know to create reasonable explanations of what caused the symptoms to occur? Are the explanations plausible? Do they account for the similarities and differences observed?"

The facts → patterns → hypotheses structure of the process also discourages jumping to a cause. Just as we have a tendency to jump to solutions before we have defined a problem, we also tend to assume we understand the chain of events that led to the problem situation without considering the facts of the situation. This tendency to assume we understand the cause often leads us to skip key steps in the problem-solving process. Skipping steps may not be costly—we could arrive at an effective solution through a lucky break. On the other hand, we may miss information and wind up with an inefficient response or select a misdirected action with regrettable consequences. It is much safer to explore alternative explanations before we develop a response than to introduce omitted information after we have already implemented a response.

1. Collect objective facts.

Answering the first four pairs of questions calls for objective fact finding. Ellen, Joe, and Bob have observed the symptoms as systematically as possible, gathering quantitative and qualitative data to answer the framework's paired questions. When a question yields answers that suggest a pattern, they probe more deeply, asking increasingly specific questions.

In theory, everyone who observes the symptoms will answer the questions in the same way. In reality, group members often disagree about the facts of a situation. Frequently, definitions and measures are at issue—*yellowing* may mean different things to different people. Yellowing and other qualitative descriptors do not have to be defined absolutely. However, it is important that everyone involved visualize the same thing when they use qualitative descriptors and that they use the word consistently each time.

Other factors also affect people's perceptions of the facts. People's powers of observation differ. A skilled observer may see nuances of detail where others cannot. Some people base their observations on measurements, others on impression; some measure precisely, others use broad measures; some observe casually, others more systematically. Which of the following gives you greater confidence?

- A commuter drives a stretch of road every day at 55 mph. After several months, he reports yellowing pines.

- A dozen vacationers drive the same stretch of road. Independently, they report the same pattern of yellowing pines at a tourist information center.

- After exploring the county's highways and backroads during a weekend holiday, a forester reports unusual yellowing of white pines along some roads.

- An extension agent trained in agriculture systematically drives up and down the county roads marking areas with affected pines on a map.

- A forest specialist trained in biological sampling divides the county into sectors, selects a random sample of roads, drives along each road selected, and systematically stops every 200 feet to count the number of affected trees and assess the degree of yellowing.

We have different degrees of confidence in these assessments for different reasons. Those with technical training give us greater confidence than the layperson's reports. Despite repeated observation, the commuter sees a blur of trees at 55 mph. The untrained eye will make many feel uncomfortable with those observations. For tourists who come to the area for its aesthetic appeal, a very prominent yellowing tree at the entrance to a stately old resort calls attention to all yellowing, encouraging exaggeration. A forester on vacation may be a reliable observer, but the methods used probably are not very systematic. An extension agent's systematic approach gives confidence. However, the lack of forestry training may raise questions in some people's minds. A specialist trained in biological sampling may give us great confidence, but we may feel more comfortable with someone who is more "down to earth."

Ellen has confidence in the reporter's recollection of when he first observed the yellowing pines. As a reporter, he is a trained observer. As an avid woodsman, he is likely to notice subtle changes over time. She has less confidence in the information provided by many of the people she interviewed because she has no way of knowing how much their observations are influenced by the newspaper article.

Personality influences our observation powers as well. Some people quickly jump to explanations of cause, so that in later observations they unconsciously look for symptoms that support that explanation. Others are quick to generalize. They observe a symptom once or twice and immediately see a pattern. In later observations they are likely to perceive facts that fit the pattern. Perspective also plays a role. Engineers tend to see symptoms from an engineer's perspective, economists from an economist's perspective, hydrologists from a hydrologist's perspective, and so on.

In principle, a fact can be shown to be true or not true. However, practical considerations often limit our ability to verify facts. Costs may be prohibitive; the parties may not agree on the validity of measures and measurements; time constraints may make timely data collection impossible.

As a result, we often have to decide how much reliance to place on the observations in hand and whether to search more widely for missing information. These are separate questions. To evaluate the reliability of the observations in hand, we consider the source and how the data were collected. If we feel comfortable, we proceed to the next steps. If we don't feel comfortable, we ask different people to observe the same symptoms and note whether or not their observations match. Alternatively, we move to a different location or time, noting whether or not the same pattern of symptoms is observed. If we have confidence in the observations we have but there are gaps in the data, we may proceed to the next steps anyhow. The existing data may allow us to eliminate several alternative hypotheses and focus the search for missing data.

Ellen, Joe, and Bob organize their observations in the causal analysis framework (figure 9.3). They stick to the facts. Each one is trained in a technical field. While they would feel more comfortable with more systematic measurements, they don't have time to make more precise measurements now. Their technical training makes them aware of both the strengths and limitations of what they are doing. Ellen will present her testimony carefully, emphasizing that it is based on preliminary, not conclusive, analysis.

2. Compare similarities and differences.

Comparing observations to find similarities and differences depends on critical thinking. Ellen, Bob, and Joe compare affected and unaffected trees in like categories for specific similarities and differences. The paired questions provide the like categories: What are the symptoms and what are not symptoms? Where are the symptoms observed and where not? and so on. The comparison is systematic. They compare category by category, always comparing like conditions of affected and unaffected trees. Their comparison

	are the symptoms?	are not symptoms?	are the differences?
Observations about Yellowing Pines **Motivating Symptom: Pine Trees Are Yellowing**			
What	Yellowing from inner needles to tips; only white pines affected	Younger needles less affected; higher branches less affected	
Where	Near some highways and streets where soil is compacted and rocky; pines where snow piled most affected	Not in middle of woodlots; not on lawns	
When	First noticed about five years ago; became more severe two years ago(?)	Not previous to five years ago(?)	
How often	Enough pine trees to be easily noticed.	Most trees are unaffected	
How much	NA	NA	
How severe	Highly variable; slightly affected to dying trees		

Figure 9.3. Observations by Ellen, Joe, and Bob.

yields a detailed accounting of similarities and differences between affected and unaffected trees. As they talk, Ellen completes the framework (figure 9.4).

Critical thinking enables the group to discover patterns in the symptoms. Analyzing the similarities and differences, the group looks for patterns that enable the group to make generalizations about which trees are affected and which are not. Ellen, Joe, and Bob find the following generalizations:

Differences between Affected and Unaffected Pines Motivating Symptom: Pine Trees Are Yellowing			
	are the symptoms?	are not symptoms?	are the differences?
What	Yellowing from inner needles to tips; only white pines affected	Younger needles less affected; higher branches less affected	Older needles on lower branches are affected; symptom is not universal
Where	Near some highways and streets where soil is compacted and rocky; pines where snow piled most affected	Not in middle of woodlots; not on lawns	Proximity to some (but not all) roads
When	First noticed about five years ago; became more severe two years ago(?)	Not previous to five years ago(?)	Something changed five years ago? Another change two years ago?
How often	Enough pine trees to be easily noticed	Most trees are unaffected	Number seems to be rising each year.
How much	NA	NA	
How severe	Highly variable; slightly affected to dying trees		

Figure 9.4. The completed framework.

- Only white pines are affected. Other conifers seem unaffected.

- Affected trees are more prevalent along some roads. Trees in lawns and woodlots are less affected or unaffected.

- Some roads are more affected than others.

- Soil around affected trees tends to be more compacted and dry than that around unaffected trees.

- Older needles are affected more frequently than younger needles. Lower branches are more affected than upper branches.

- The affected needles are distinctly yellow, not bright red. No black spots are present. Affected trees do not appear to be diseased and infested with insects. (Laboratory evaluation will confirm this observation.)

- Individuals in the community first noticed yellowing trees about five years ago. They report that the number and severity of symptoms began increasing about two years ago. There is a question about the reliability of these observations.

With these patterns in hand, the group proceeds to the next step—a search for possible causes.

3. Generate alternative hypotheses.

At this step, the question is what might cause the patterns of symptoms observed? Answers to this question are subjective and creative. Answers require no objective foundation. The critical objective step is *hypothesis testing*, where we confront the hypothesis with the facts to see if it explains what we observe.

There is no inherent superiority of the hypotheses of scientific enquiry over thoughtful explanations of cause offered by reflective practitioners. While scientists have the advantage of rigorous training in hypothesis testing, they may be limited by the boundaries of their disciplines, institutions, or professions. The reflective practitioner draws on theory, experience, and observations of the symptoms at hand to create alternative explanations of cause. Most of us, scientists and practitioners alike, have a natural tendency to consider familiar explanations and exclude plausible but unfamiliar ones.

Stepping outside familiar ways of explaining patterns to explore plausible but unfamiliar explanations is a creative act. Thinking in unfamiliar ways about cause and effect is risky; we may generate ideas that make little sense upon closer examination. Few of us are willing to risk ridicule to be creative. Separating the creative process from critical thinking (generation of alternative hypotheses from hypothesis testing) gives group members the freedom to brainstorm without an immediate responsibility to making sense. Brainstormers are free to create alternative explanations. They can offer even the wildest explanations with confidence that the group will evaluate their worth without judging their talent.

Ellen, Bob, and Joe list the following hypotheses:

- Acid rain is causing the yellowing.
- Local auto emissions are causing the yellowing.
- Salt used to melt ice and snow from paved roads is causing the yellowing.
- Moisture stress resulting from prolonged drought is causing premature needle drop, including some first-year needles.
- Effects of road salt are being exacerbated by moisture stress.
- Moisture stress, road salt, and auto emissions in combination are causing the yellowing.

4. Test the plausibility of alternative hypotheses.

Revising and testing hypotheses call for critical thinking. If we skip this step and rely solely on subjective opinion about causal mechanisms, we are likely to misunderstand the situation and undertake misdirected action. Sticking closely to empirical reality increases the likelihood that the hypotheses chosen to explain cause and effect will explain the observed symptoms accurately.

The group "tries on" alternative hypotheses as you would try on new suits of clothes. When you buy a new suit, you check the overall fit. Then you check the fit in specific categories—shoulders, sleeve length, inseam, and so on. Ellen, Joe, and Bob use a similar process to determine whether or not a hypothesis fits the observed data. They look for hypotheses that have the best fit overall. Then, they evaluate how well each hypothesis fits the observed data in specific categories—What symptoms? When? Where? How much? How often?

For each hypothesis, the group asks three key questions:

1. Does the explanation fit the symptoms observed? (Does it explain the differences between affected and unaffected trees?)
2. Is it plausible?
3. Can we reject the hypothesis? (What observed data would disprove the hypothesis?)

Ellen knows from her reading that acid rain deposits affect younger needles first and tend to blanket large sectors downwind from the source along the path of the prevailing winds. It is unlikely that acid rain would affect trees in groups along roads. Also, the yellowing they have observed affects older needles first—the opposite of what you would expect from acid rain. They reject the acid rain hypothesis.

Bob questions the auto emissions hypothesis, saying "If this were a densely populated area with a lot of commuters, I would feel more comfortable with the auto emissions hypothesis. But this is a small town. If white pines are that sensitive to auto emissions, then the problem should be well-documented in urban areas." While auto emissions seem an improbable cause, the group doesn't have any observations that lead them to reject the auto emissions hypothesis outright so they leave it in.

The road salt hypothesis seems to explain the group's observations. Joe says, "There's an easy way to check out this hypothesis. Call the Forrest City Superintendent of Public Works and find out whether or not they use road salt. If they don't, we will have to reject the hypothesis."

Joe notes that drought would affect all pines, not just pines along roads. Bob cautions against rejecting drought stress too quickly. The soil along roads is highly compacted, and its moisture-holding capacity is impaired. While no one would argue that drought stress is the sole cause, it may be a contributing factor.

Joe looks over their work. "I guess we can rule out acid rain. Your boss will be happy about that, Ellen. But I don't think the people of Forrest City will be satisfied until we can tell them what is causing the yellowing pines. Where do we go from here?"

Deciding what is next

Unable to construct a plausible hypothesis to explain the patterns of symptoms, the group decides what to do next.

Bob says, "I'll send the soil samples to the state lab by overnight mail. We should get the results back by tomorrow afternoon. Maybe we'll learn something from the chemical analysis." Ellen smiles, "You must have some pull with the state lab. It takes me more than a week to get results back." Bob responds, "It helps to know people."

He proceeds, "In the meantime, I suggest we spend tomorrow at Peterstown. The extension agent at Peterstown has reported a similar problem. Maybe if we see the same problem in a different context, the pattern will become clearer."

"I like that idea." Ellen responds. "Before we quit for the day, let's decide what additional information would help us narrow the list of hypotheses."

"I'd like to see rainfall data for the area," Bob continues. "I'd be willing to bet that whatever the problem is, moisture stress is exacerbating it. This area has had below normal rainfall for three years in a row." Joe answers, "I'm sure you're right, but we can't do anything about rainfall. I'd like to figure out what we can do besides hope for rain."

Bob adds, "I've worked with a plant physiologist at the university who has been doing some research on road salts and their effects on conifers. I'll give him a call tonight and see if he can give us some clues to look for."

Joe offers to call the Forrest City Superintendent of Public Works and find out if the city uses salt. The superintendent says, "No, we quit using salt three or four years back." Joe looks puzzled as he replaces the receiver, "Now, where do we look? I would have bet good money it was road salt causing the yellowing.

"I'm grabbing at straws," Joe continues, "but it seems to me that if auto emissions are the cause there would be a predictable pattern to the distribution of affected trees. I would expect to see the most severely affected trees along the roads and at low elevations in the valleys where the particles settle." Ellen responds, "I don't know, Joe. Auto emissions are airborne. It doesn't make much sense to me to assume such a predictable pattern."

Expanding the picture

Sometimes initial observations do not provide enough information to generate a plausible hypothesis or even narrow the field of alternatives. In this case, there are several options. We can

- *Observe a similar set of symptoms at a different time or place.* Ask the same framework questions to find the differences between affected and unaffected populations. Comparison of the symptoms and underlying factors in two different situations increases the chance that a piece of key information will pop out. It also expands the amount of information you have to evaluate, and may make it easier to eliminate implausible explanations of cause.

- *Perform more extensive diagnostic tests on the same set of symptoms.* Support or eliminate alternative explanations. This is what doctors do when they have a patient with an unexplained lump in the neck. The doctor will probably do thyroid function tests and a biopsy, seeking evidence to support or eliminate the alternative explanations—hyperthyroidism and cancer.

- *Take limited action to solve the problem.* Assume one cause and then another, treating the problem until the symptoms respond. For example, symptoms for rheumatoid arthritis differ from patient to patient, and present diagnostic tests are imperfect. When efforts to diagnose the patient's symptoms fail, a doctor may treat the patient on the assumption that he or she has some type of rheumatoid arthritis. If the symptoms diminish in response to the treatment, the doctor assumes the diagnosis was correct. If the symptoms do not diminish, the doctor prescribes a different treatment. He or she continues this process until the symptoms respond, there are no more alternative treatments to try, or there are none that do not have serious side effects.

- *Wait until something changes.* The symptoms can improve spontaneously or worsen. New information or technology may become available. The context may change. At times, waiting is the only viable option, but at others, inaction worsens the problem.

Expanding the search for understanding

Ellen, Joe, and Bill have decided to expand their information-gathering efforts to Peterstown to see what symptoms are similar and dissimilar with what they now know about yellowing pines in Forrest City. In Peterstown, they see a similar pattern of affected and unaffected trees. Affected trees are grouped along the roads. But a lower percentage of trees seems to be affected overall.

They show the city manager a map with the affected areas highlighted. Ellen asks, "Is there anything different about these roads that might account for yellowing pines?" After studying the map, the city manager speaks slowly, "Looks to me like you've marked the emergency school bus routes. Those are the roads we salt during ice and snow storms so that the school buses can get through. Costs a lot of money to close the schools for a day. Salting is the only way we can protect the safety of our youngsters and keep the schools open."

"Now that's really strange," Joe says. "That's what I would have guessed if I hadn't talked to the Forrest City Public Works Superintendent myself. But they don't use salt over there."

The city manager turns to Joe, "What question did you ask?" Joe answers, "I asked whether they use salt, and he said 'no.'" The city manager says, "That's not what Ellen asked me. She asked, 'What is different about the highlighted roads?' If she had asked me, 'Does the city use salt?' I would have said 'no' too. We don't apply salt to town roads. The county takes care of the emergency snow routes and primary roads. They apply the salt." Looking sheepish, Joe offers to call the Forrest City Superintendent of Public Works again. This time he will phrase the question differently.

Joe begins by explaining to the superintendent what they are doing and why. He rephrases the question. The superintendent is hesitant to generalize over the phone. He wants to look at the map with the highlighted roads first, so they set up an appointment in the afternoon.

At that moment, Bob comes in with the preliminary results of the soil samples. Salt concentrations are higher than normal and consistent with what Bob's friend, the plant physiologist, said he would find in an area with salt-damaged trees.

Ellen has rainfall data for Peterstown and Forrest City faxes in from her office. Bob is right about below normal rainfall. There was a 35-inch cumulative rainfall deficit over the last three years. Bob comments, "My friend, the plant physiologist, said frequent rains wash the soil, leaching the salts out. When it's dry, the salts accumulate near the soil surface, and salt damage is more severe."

Back in Forrest City, Joe meets with the superintendent. After studying the map, the superintendent says, "All of the highlighted roads are primary roads maintained by the county. The phone's over there if you want to call the county maintenance supervisor. He can tell you whether or not they use salt in their road mix."

Joe dials the county maintenance supervisor and explains why he's calling and asks about road salt. The supervisor answers, "Yeah, we use salt in all of our road mixes. And I'm not going to apologize for it."

Joe asks, "Have there been complaints?" "Yeah," the supervisor answers. "The Forrest City Town Council has been fussing with us for some time trying to get us to cut back on the salt. They've had complaints from a few troublemakers about contaminated wells. But salting helps us hold down the cost of snow removal. You can't close everything down every time it snows a little. We have to keep the roads open and taxes down. They can just keep on fussing."

Phrasing the question

How we ask questions matters. The quality of our questions will determine the usefulness of the information we get back. The following are guidelines for asking useful questions that will help us uncover the information we need to

- *Ask broad questions first, probing for additional detail.* Overly detailed questions at the outset may give us misleading and incomplete information that leads us down a blind alley.

- *Complete one line of questioning before pursuing another.* All too often a questioner jumps haphazardly from one line of questioning to another. As a result, valuable information may be inadvertently overlooked. We need to write our questions and answers down and then ask these questions: What additional questions does this answer raise? How does this piece of information differentiate symptomatic and asymptomatic trees?

- *To the extent practical, pursue a line of questioning until the readily available information is exhausted.* Questions start with the general and move to the specific. Typically, patterns are revealed in the nuance of detail. We tend to identify patterns and stop probing too quickly, possibly overlooking the nuance of a pattern's detail that points to causal mechanisms.

- *Ask neutral questions.* If we ask a leading question, we are likely to get misleading information.

Avoiding a particularly hazardous pitfall

Joe asks the superintendent of public works if the town uses road salt. It is a question any of us might ask. But as we see, the question doesn't elicit the information Joe needs. Often our probing questions single out one causal mechanism and exclude others. Joe's question assumes that the problem is road salt. The respondent can answer with a simple yes or no. The superintendent isn't thinking about why the question is being asked or what the interviewer is trying to determine. Ellen's question, "What is different about the affected and unaffected roads?" forces the Peterstown city manager to think critically. The question involves the city manager in the causal analysis process without leading him to a premature conclusion.

Joe's question carries another assumption—that all roads are town roads. This unconscious assumption generates accurate but incomplete information. Forrest City does not use road salt. With this piece of incomplete information, Joe prematurely eliminates the road salt hypothesis.

Conversely, Joe would have been ready to accept the hypothesis if the superintendent had said, "Yes, the town salts snow-covered roads." In either case, incomplete information could prove detrimental. What if the county uses more salt than the town and the affected trees are concentrated along county roads? Even if the town quit salting roads, the problem would go unsolved because the county was not identified as a contributor to the problem.

Ellen's more open-ended phrasing of the question produces information that will be useful in solving the problem as well. In Peterstown, the primary factor that differentiates roads with affected trees from roads without affected trees isn't salt—it is emergency school bus routes. To resolve the yellowing pines problem, Peterstown will have to find an alternative to salt to keep the emergency school bus routes open—a social and political concern.

When Joe asks the Forrest County maintenance supervisor about road salt—another leading question—the supervisor gets defensive. Because the supervisor has been criticized about the county's use of road salt on several occasions, he feels accused, even though Joe is just looking for information. Joe might avoid the supervisor's defensiveness by explaining what he is doing and why, showing the county supervisor the map, and asking if the marked roads have any special characteristics. By becoming involved in the causal analysis process, the county supervisor might discover for himself the negative side effects of road salt.

Reconsidering the hypotheses

The group discusses the pattern of symptoms they have observed. Ellen, Joe, and Bob feel confident that they've figured out the cause of the yellowing pines. But they decide to go through the remaining hypotheses one more time—just to be sure that they are not overlooking something important.

Local auto emissions are causing the yellowing. Auto emissions still cannot be ruled out. However, the low population density makes auto emissions an unlikely cause.

Road salt applied to aid snow removal is causing the yellowing. Several observations point to road salt; however, no conclusive evidence is available. Affected trees in both Forrest City and Peterstown seem to be grouped along roads where road salt is applied. In Forrest City, where more road salt is used, there appears to be a higher proportion of affected trees. Selected soil tests confirm the presence of higher-than-normal salt concentrations. Severely affected trees at one site are located where salt-contaminated snow is piled during the winter months. Some households in Forrest County report salt-contaminated wells.

Moisture stress caused by prolonged drought is exacerbating the effects of road salt. This hypothesis cannot be rejected. It was noted that soil around affected trees tends to be compacted and dry. Rainfall data show a cumulative deficit of 35 inches below average over the last three years. The newspaper writer reports a substantial jump in affected trees about two years ago, an observation that suggests moisture stress may play a role. Research shows that salts tend to leach out of the soil more quickly when rainfall is high. Soil tests demonstrate higher-than-expected levels of salt around some affected trees. A number of Forrest City residents first noticed yellowing two years ago, one year after the drought began.

Road salt, moisture stress, and auto emissions are interacting to cause yellowing. While there is no evidence to reject this hypothesis, little is gained by assuming it is true. Of the three factors, road salt is the easiest cause to address. Reducing auto emissions is a long-term and difficult task. Rainfall cannot be controlled.

Realizing that action is always based on incomplete understanding

Whether corrective action is undertaken will depend on how confident problem solvers are that their hypothesis is correct and on their willingness to take the action. These two factors are related: Problem solvers are unlikely to incur high costs when there is a low probability of the measure actually correcting a problem situation. However, when the political climate is highly charged, as it is with the yellowing pines, corrective action may be implemented if there is *any* chance that it will be effective. In most cases, some reasonable degree of confidence is needed.

Ellen writes her testimony based on her understanding at this point. Though she believes acid rain may be an issue that will one day affect the pines of Forrest City and Peterstown, she feels confident that other, more localized factors are causing the yellowing pines observed now. In her testimony, she notes that preliminary analysis suggests accumulated road salts are the primary cause of the yellowing pines. She also concludes that the current drought seems to be accelerating the trees' physiological response to the salts, making the problem worse. She recommends further testing to confirm the group's preliminary observations, followed by appropriate corrective action.

We can test the significance level of our hypotheses statistically by collecting and analyzing data. However, as practitioners, we may not have time or resources to develop statistical tests of significance. Often we must take timely action based on what we know now, continually reevaluating our choices as new relationships are identified.

No hypothesis can be proven: The best we can do is fail to disprove a hypothesis under increasingly stringent tests. In actual resource-use decisions, data are often incomplete or unreliable. The assumptions we are forced to make in order to perform statistical significance tests may not reflect reality (e.g., the independence and form of variables). Statistical problems, such as multicollinearity, may limit the usefulness of results. Consequently, our ability to predict the chain of multiple effects that results from any action is inevitably limited.

Back-of-the-envelope analysis yielding real benefits

Good quality, productive research requires valuable time, money, and expertise. Very often these resources are unavailable to answer critical questions of cause and effect. Action-oriented practitioners often cannot wait.

They must act. The quick analysis employed by Ellen and her colleagues can fill the knowledge gap temporarily by

- Eliminating conventional wisdom that is clearly wrong
- Identifying what additional information is needed
- Structuring what we know in a way that encourages systematic comparison
- Grounding our understanding of cause and effect in the context of the specific problem
- Enabling us to make decisions and act with confidence that we have diagnosed the problem as accurately as possible given the time and information available

Quick analysis can substantially improve our understanding. As a result, actions taken based on causal analysis are more likely to improve the situation than actions based on intuition alone. We are more likely to define problems appropriately, to make effective decisions, and to take timely and purposeful action. If we are decision makers, we are likely to be better clients for consultants, extension personnel, and researchers who want to help us; conversely, if we are technicians, the causal analysis framework can make us more effective consultants, extension personnel, and researchers. Even when the causal relationships are complex and beyond our ability to appreciate fully, the improved understanding that causal analysis yields can help us avoid the traps of bias and ignorance.

Complex Causal Relationships

The practitioner's problems with imperfect data and a world that does not conform to statistical assumptions are compounded when we try to use our knowledge of cause and effect to make predictions. We may be able to predict the immediate effects of a particular alternative with some confidence; but our ability to predict the effects on subsequent generations is more problematic as we reach further through time.

Our knowledge will always be limited and to some degree inadequate to solve the problems at hand. Choosing to wait until we have a better understanding of cause and effect before we take action can have deleterious consequences. We have known for several years about the build up of so-called "greenhouse gases." As a matter of policy, we have chosen to wait for more convincing evidence of the greenhouse effect before taking action. Our inaction has resulted in increasingly higher concentrations of atmospheric carbon dioxide.

On the other hand, misdirected action based on misunderstood cause-and-effect relationships can have negative consequences as well. Burning fossil fuels is the primary cause of the greenhouse effect. Suppose the response were a requirement that fossil fuel use be reduced by, for example, 25 percent. Without alternative energy sources, a worldwide effort to reduce the use of fossil fuels will reduce the energy available for industrial production, resulting in declining economic growth rates, factory closings, lost jobs, and recession. Economic decline affects society's poor more heavily than the rich. In developing nations, economic decline combines with population pressures to force ever-larger numbers of unemployed people to farm ever-more-marginal lands, thus eroding soils, reducing soil fertility, destroying fragile ecosystems, and eventually creating new wastelands. In addition, restrictions on fossil fuels in these regions means more reliance on wood as a source of energy. Forested areas then would be thinned out, reducing the forest's capacity to transform carbon dioxide to oxygen and hastening the greenhouse effect.

Depending on how it is implemented, the solution—reducing the use of fossil fuels—could hasten the very greenhouse effect it is intended to eliminate, leaving us no closer to a sustainable alternative than before. The difficulty is compounded by the likelihood that the solution would have a disproportionate and inequitable effect on the poor.

Here, too, quick analysis can at least alert us to possible cause-and-effect relationships that may create unanticipated consequences. The simplest of these relationships are as straightforward as "If I take action A, then outcome B results." In many situations, cause and effect is not so simple (figure 9.5).

Applying the causal webs

The causal web relates multiple influences on a symptom or symptoms that can be used at any level of knowledge and information, though it is, of course, a better tool with good information than it is with poor information. First, in a brainstorming mode, all factors that influence the symptom(s) of interest are identified and listed. Then, those relationships that are sequential (i.e., acid rain → acid runoff → increased acidity of soils and lakes → dying fish and trees) are arrayed in order, as are those that are interactive (i.e., nitrous oxide emissions and sulphur dioxide releases combine creating acid rain). The influences that are subject to corrective action (points of intervention) can then be identified, as well as the side effects of corrective changes in these influences. Figure 9.6 represents a causal web actually used

From Simple Cause and Effect to Causal Webs

Simple cause and effect:

Ray Green plows his bottomlands and plants seed → Corn and green beans grow

Simple causal chain:

Farm and forest production → food, fuel, and fiber → jobs, income, and profit

Multiple effects:

Farm and forest production ↗ food, fuel, and fiber → jobs, income, and profit

↘ soil erosion → runoff → increased turbidity → decreased salmon runs → decreased income for Native American fishers

Multiple causes:

Driving to work → nitrous oxide emissions ↘

acid rain → acid runoff → increased acidity of soils and lakes → dying fish and trees

Producing electricity in coal-fired plants → sulphur dioxide releases ↗

Multiple causes and effects:

Driving to work ↗ income → food, housing, and other consumer goods

↘ nitrous oxide emissions ↘

acid rain → fish kills / dying forests

sulphur dioxide releases ↗

Producing electricity in coal-fired plants ↗

↘ electricity ↗ jobs, income, and profits

↘ convenience

Figure 9.5. An example of information for a causal web.

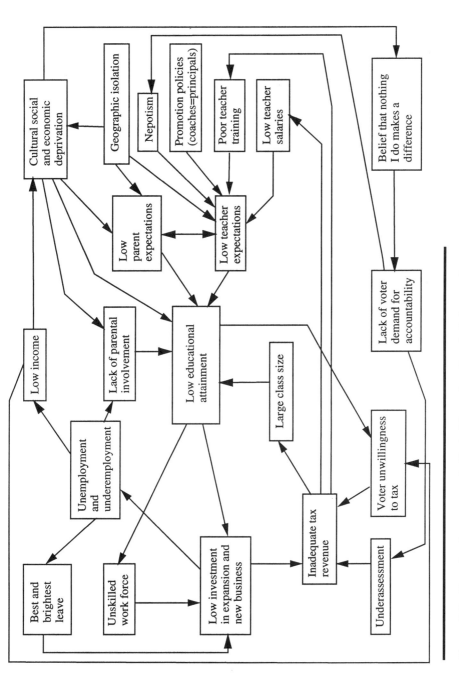

Figure 9.6. Causal web—cause and effect of low educational attainment in Appalachian Kentucky.

to develop an intervention strategy to improve the percentage of students graduating from high school in 26 Kentucky counties in Appalachia.

When causal relationships are complex, effective action depends on identifying points in the casual web where your intervention will make a positive difference given who you are and your particular context.

1. Identify points of intervention.

The web of cause-and-effect relationships highlights points of intervention—places where the individual or group has the authority and responsibility to make changes that will yield the desired outcome. In figure 9.6, which shows a causal web developed by a group of citizens concerned about the high proportion of students who fail to graduate in Appalachian schools, the initial point of intervention identified was "low teacher expectations." The group instituted a multifaceted program to recognize and reward teachers. The program encouraged teachers to challenge their own low expectations of student performance. Their intervention resulted in improvement of attendance at all grade levels and graduation rates.

Points of intervention may be several steps removed from the symptoms that precipitated the recognition of a problem. Low educational attainment itself was seen as supporting voter unwillingness to tax, which in turn caused inadequate tax revenues, large class sizes, low salaries, and poor teacher training, all of which were seen as reinforcing high rates of school dropout. The Kentucky group, a loose-knit coalition of businesspeople, parents, and educators, decided that a direct attack on voter unwillingness to tax through campaigns in support of bond issues had little prospect for success, given who they were and the political forces lined up against tax increases of any kind.

2. Intervene given who you are and the context.

In earlier chapters, we focused on identifying objectives that are broad enough to represent movement toward our goals and narrow enough to motivate specific actions. Here causal analysis helps us to identify cause-and-effect relationships that are narrow enough to identify specific points of intervention yet broad enough to account for important interactions.

Intervention to solve a problem is neither easy nor risk free. If our focus is too narrow, it may be easy to identify a corrective action, but the action is more likely to be misdirected. In the Appalachian education example, a narrow focus on the relationship between lack of parental involvement and low educational attainment might lead the Kentucky group to concentrate on a drive to organize parents to participate in the schools. If there is no change in classroom size, school resources, or teacher expectations, the result is likely to be a flurry of parental activities, the investment of parents' scarce time, but little actual change in education. Parents might easily be left more discouraged than before, compounding rather than relieving the problem. In the approach actually taken, once parents found that the reward program was actually changing their children's performance in school, a focus on parental involvement was more productive, with real changes reinforcing parental investment.

Basing action on a snapshot of reality

The piece of the bigger picture that we usually address is like a snapshot. Causal analysis can freeze motion in time, with dynamic relationships appearing static. We can, however, focus on "when" questions to reach backwards in time to capture the historic dynamics. Sometimes we can even reach to the future with "what if" questions. Incorporating cause and effect through time helps make our snapshot into a movie. It is still important to keep in mind that representing causal relationships is a subjective activity: We are the photographer who takes the snapshot, the director who makes the movie. What actions we record will depend on our creative choices as photographer and director. The cause-and-effect snapshot or movie that we choose influences

- How we define a problem that calls for action
- How we define our objectives and phrase the decision question
- How widely or narrowly we search for alternatives
- How we predict the consequences of our alternatives
- The choices we make
- The effectiveness of our actions

The causal analysis framework helps us make sense of symptoms that we can observe. The nature of resource degradation, pollution, and depletion problems makes it difficult, however, to observe many factors in the causal chain. For example, root mass, organic content, and microorganisms decline before surface soil erosion becomes obvious on degrading lands. Build-up of nitrates in groundwater occurs long before birth defects are observed.

More critically, it is impossible to understand and anticipate the full consequences of changing social, demographic, and production patterns. By necessity, we take action without knowing what all the consequences will be. The unintended side effects of our actions become apparent as unwanted symptoms. We responded to the problem of mosquito-borne malaria with a vigorous DDT campaign of mosquito control. The campaign was successful in the United States—malaria has been effectively eradicated. However, the food chain was seriously threatened as a result—DDT residues are still present in the food chain many years after the chemical has been banned.

Southwestern urban populations mushroomed during the 1970s and 1980s as an immediate result of the energy crisis and a long-term result of the shift in the economic nexus from the heavy-industry centers of the northeast to the Sunbelt's financial and communications/information industries. The pressure placed on scarce water resources and fragile desertlands has given rise to a whole spectrum of new symptoms, emerging as an important new problem. In many areas the response to the need to provide water to Sunbelt cities has been to shift water from low-value range crops. However, drying up western farmlands to provide water for the growing Sunbelt cities in turn creates unintended consequences for the rural communities from which water is taken, resulting in still more problems.

Problems as a call to action

At one level, Sid's and Ellen's problems were very different. Sid understood cause and effect. The Powder River problem could be circumscribed. Sid's role and authority were defined. He could identify the people involved. The legal and political context was fixed. He had official standards against which to measure performance. The Forest Practices Act provided him with an alternative approach to address the problem that was creative, participatory, and had the potential to generate long-lasting solutions. And he had time.

Ellen recognizes that acid rain is a problem, but she cannot circumscribe it in a way that calls for action. As she contemplates testifying on acid rain and the yellowing pines, she does not fully understand cause and effect. The agency's role and authority to address the acid rain problem are not defined. As a result, Ellen's responsibility for acid rain is not established. Policies and standards addressing the problem don't exist. The legal and political context is just beginning to evolve. When the legislature scheduled its hearings, they only gave her one week to prepare. The close-at-hand deadline seriously limits her options to act.

At another level, Sid and Ellen have something important in common. Both are professionals. As professionals, they are action-oriented. Both realize that regardless of the pitfalls they cannot always wait to make decisions and plans. In spite of the risk, they must take action now based on what they know.

The tools presented in this book help us systematize our understanding. These tools also help us step away from the immediate problem and think strategically about the big picture: Where are we? Where are we going? What do we need to do to get there? In the final chapter, we consider a community's solid waste problem where group formation, social and biophysical interactions, and uncertainty of consequences make thought and action yet more difficult. In this chapter, we take a step back and consider the strategic nature of defining and acting on problems.

10

■ Challenging Ourselves to Action

Rural Resource Management begins and ends with a water quality problem. In this chapter, we return to problem definition to focus on how short-run problems can be redefined in long-run terms of sustainability. We will join the Fredricksburg landfill site selection committee, which is grappling with a changing political, legal, and economic reality as it tries to provide the Fredricksburg community with safe waste disposal facilities.

This chapter's solid waste problem differs from the Powder River situation in important ways. The biophysical relationships are different—the Powder River issue was watershed management, while the Fredricksburg problem involves groundwater protection. The Powder River problem dealt with soil erosion and its effects on salmon runs, while in this chapter the problem is solid waste disposal and its effects on drinking water. In the Powder River situation, many people had different stakes in the outcome. The citizens of Fredricksburg, a town of 25,000 people in a south central state, have a more or less common stake.

The two situations have many similarities, however. In both, the legal or regulatory context has changed recently, directly and indirectly affecting many people. More importantly, both situations illustrate how an immediate threat presents an opportunity to seek forward-looking solutions that meet both our immediate objectives and our long-run goals.

Changing Landfill Regulations

In six to nine months, Fredricksburg's present landfill will be full. Twenty years ago, the town would have bulldozed over the saturated landfill and opened another at a new or adjacent site. But today it is not so simple.

A problem for Fredricksburg officials

The EPA has proposed new, tougher rules that will be phased into effect beginning January 1 of the coming year. Each state is required to establish regulations that meet the standards even before the final language in the EPA rules is approved. The south central state where Fredricksburg is located has been slow to respond with rules of its own. Six months before the January 1 deadline, it still has not announced its regulations.

Early this year, Fredricksburg's mayor, Alan Johnson, appointed a committee to evaluate potential sites for a new town landfill. The committee was unaware of the impending change in the state's regulations during its search for a new landfill site. When the town submitted a preliminary site plan to the state for conditional approval in April, the state informed town officials that the proposed site will have to meet the new standards, even though they are incomplete.

On June 1, Darryl Stevens, a specialist in municipal solid waste disposal with the state's department of pollution control, notified Johnson that the preliminary site plan does not come close to meeting the expected regulations. While Darryl can't give Johnson the final regulations, he can tell him that the landfill plan will have to have a double lining system (clay and plastic), a leachate-collection system, and environmental monitoring capabilities, none of which are included in the Fredricksburg plan. In addition, the plan will have to include financial assurances to cover the costs of environmental monitoring and maintenance for 30 years after the site is closed.

Finally, Darryl is concerned that the Fredricksburg plan only briefly mentions the waste from the local poultry-processing plant. "Where the plan mentions poultry offal," Darryl says, "I assume you mean carcasses, feathers, and the like. The solid waste from processing chickens contains high levels of disease-causing bacteria and chemicals. That combined with the karst geology in your area could result in contaminated private wells adjacent to the proposed landfill, or possibly even the city's water supply. I assume the potential risk to public health from this kind of waste will put Fredricksburg's proposed landfill site into the 'higher-than-normal' risk category, which means there may be more requirements to satisfy."

Alan questions Darryl about the expected regulations. Darryl answers as specifically as he can. The more he explains, the more confused Alan gets. After a while, Alan quits trying to understand. "I think I'm a reasonable person, Darryl. I understand why the regulations are needed, but I have to tell you I'm really frustrated. How can a small town like Fredricksburg possibly *understand* the regulations, much less pay for everything that's required? How can we proceed when we don't even know what we have to do?"

Darryl slows his pace as he responds. "I have a lot of sympathy for you and the other towns in the same situation. Over the next five years nearly a quarter of the municipal solid waste facilities in the state will run out of permitted landfill space. Each one will have to deal with these same regulations. Even existing facilities will have to comply with most of these requirements. It's not going to be easy, and it's not going to be cheap.

"We've all taken adequate landfill space for granted. We haven't been overly concerned with air and water quality. Municipalities have taken pride in their ability to handle waste, and we've encouraged the ordinary citizen to assume waste disposal was problem free. Now the time has come to 'pay the piper.' Everyone is going to have to face the fact that it costs money to dispose of solid waste safely. If it is any consolation, the department and I will work with you on this. All of us have a stake in making the regulations work. And none of us know for sure what impact these regulations will have."

"You can be sure," Alan replies testily, "I will be asking for your help often. The first thing you can do is come down here and explain the situation to my landfill site selection committee—and the sooner the better." Darryl answers, "Is tomorrow night convenient?"

Making sense out of the rules

Alan figures he might as well break the news to his committee sooner rather than later. A few phone calls are enough to set up a meeting for the next night.

After Alan introduces Darryl to the committee, Darryl explains the regulations: "The federal government has set a 'risk-based performance' standard for the expansion of old facilities and design of new facilities. This standard gives us—the state, I mean—flexibility to determine the 'allowable risk level' and the 'point of compliance' within the federal guidelines."

Preston McCrossen, a local contractor on the site selection committee, interrupts. "Sounds like bureaucratic mumbo-jumbo to me. Just what do 'allowable risk' and 'point of compliance' mean?"

"You're right," Darryl answers. "The rules are intentionally ambiguous to give each state a say in the regulations."

"You still haven't answered my questions," Preston demands. "What risk are we taking? How much risk? What do we have to do to comply?"

Darryl nods, "We're talking about the risk of getting cancer as a result of the chemicals that are likely to leach from the proposed landfill into the groundwater. The feds leave it up to each state to decide how much risk of cancer they are willing to accept. The state can decide whether it will accept one cancer case in 10,000 people or one in a million people."

Preston isn't mollified. "That sounds like more mumbo-jumbo. How can you figure out in advance who is going to get cancer and who isn't?"

"We don't," Darryl answers. "But we can make a prediction about how many people out of any given population will get cancer based on historical studies that demonstrate a link between groundwater contamination and the incidence of cancer. When we evaluate the cancer risk, we account for the hydrogeologic characteristics of the site region, climatic factors, volume and physical characteristics of the leachate, the proximity of groundwater uses, and, of course, groundwater quality."

Preston asks, "What's leachate?" Darryl answers, "As rainwater moves through the landfill it picks up whatever chemicals and bacteria are in the waste material. The leachate is the watery substance carrying cancer-causing chemicals and bacteria that leaches into the subsoil and groundwater."

Darryl continues, "The federal regulations are intentionally ambiguous in other areas too. Once the state sets a risk level, we also have to decide how to enforce the standards. The federal government gives us three options: We can establish a mathematical formula to evaluate the risk; we can take a categorical approach and specify design requirements; or we can monitor groundwater quality and fine you if you don't meet the standards.

"Our department is still fine-tuning the details, but we have the basic outline. The state has decided to permit the highest risk level allowable under the federal standards. Meeting these regulations is going to be economically difficult. We're a poorer-than-average state, so this decision was economically motivated. To meet these standards, we will specify minimum design standards. Then we will evaluate site-specific risk factors. When the site-specific risk is higher than normal, we will specify additional precautionary design requirements."

"I take it," Alan adds, "that Fredricksburg's proposed site falls into the higher-than-normal risk category." Darryl responds cautiously, "Yes. With the chicken-processing plant tipping its waste at the municipal landfill, the karst geology of the area, and your city water supply not far from the proposed site, Fredricksburg will be required to meet more than the minimum design requirements." Alan responds, "Keep in mind, Darryl, the poultry plant doesn't create nearly as much waste as they once did. We may not have as high a risk as you think."

What will it cost?

Alan groans as he thinks about expenses and turns to Darryl.

"How much is it going to cost to meet these regulations?" Darryl answers, "I'm not a design engineer, and I don't have a lot of experience with these cost figures yet. But I can give you some ball-park figures.

"You can expect to spend something over a half-million dollars on engineering design, mapping, site selection, permit applications, legal work, public hearings, land purchase, brokerage fees, and the like. A 200-ton per day facility will cost about $2 million for initial construction. This size facility will serve about 80,000 people. The $2 million includes access roads, site excavation, erosion and sediment control, a liner and liner-cushion systems, leachate collection and landfill gas venting systems, and leachate treatment systems. This figure does *not* include a double lining system or a leachate detection system, which may be required in your case. Nor does it include upgrading the local sewer service to accept additional discharge."

Alan objects, "We don't need a landfill that will handle 200 tons per day. We only handle 40 to 50 tons per day."

Darryl replies, "I don't know how much a smaller facility will cost, but the design requirements are the same regardless of size so there are economic benefits to constructing a facility that can handle larger volumes."

Preston asks, "Is that it?" Shaking his head, Darryl continues, "Operating costs will increase as well. Operating a landfill of this size will run just under $1 million per year. That includes $50,000 a year set aside to cover closure and postclosure requirements."

Alan puts his head in his hands. "There's no way we can pay those costs. Fredricksburg is a town of 25,000 people!"

Cooperation as part of the solution

Darryl, Alan, and Preston continue the discussion.

"There is a way," Darryl replies, "but it will take planning and hard work. The year before last, the state legislature authorized the organization of regional waste management districts. Like rural water districts or school districts, a waste management district provides services across traditional municipal and county boundaries."

Alan responds, "We're pretty independent folks, and we'd rather not get involved with a lot of other towns, never mind counties. But it seems like we're between a rock and a hard place. We could resist these new rules, go kicking and screaming the whole way—and we'll likely end up contracting with another municipality until their site fills up. That way we move from one makeshift solution to the next until we're finally forced to address the problem directly. Or we could take these regulations as a challenge to plan a solid waste disposal facility that will serve our community over the long run. That's going to mean enlisting the cooperation of our neighbors. What does the committee think?"

Preston is the first to respond. "Alan, you know as well as I do that even if we could talk two or three counties into forming a regional waste management district, we could never convince the public to approve the tax increases to pay for a dump. Get real, Alan. We have a hard enough time convincing voters to approve tax increases to educate our kids."

Before Alan can speak, Darryl answers, "Preston, no community can afford to pay these costs out of general tax revenues. The time has come when everybody is going to have to pay to dispose of the waste they produce. With a $2 million facility serving 80,000 people, you can cover capital and operating costs one of two ways: You can charge tipping fees, or you can charge households a monthly fee for disposal and more for businesses that produce more waste, or both."

Fredricksburg's Problem Confronting Us All

Fredricksburg is in a predicament. The town's present landfill will soon be full. The traditional solution—a new landfill, designed and operated as they have been for years—is not a legal option. The site selection committee finds itself confronted with unfamiliar problems and forced to think in unfamiliar ways.

Many communities, businesses, and individuals are finding themselves in Fredricksburg's situation. Public opinion, regulatory change, and the direct effects of degradation, pollution, and depletion have closed the option of taking clean water, clean air, fertile soils, and other resources for granted. One way or another we are being called upon to "pay the piper." As communities, businesses, and individuals, we can either pay for the consequences of degradation, pollution, and depletion indirectly through poor health, reduced productivity, and scarcity, or we can address the problems head on, and pay the direct costs of rehabilitating and sustaining our resources.

How will we respond?

In response to growing public concern, local, state, and federal governments have begun to regulate and tax activities that degrade, pollute, and deplete the resources on which our long-run well-being is based. In the 1990s, we can expect smaller, more widely dispersed producers and consumers to be increasingly regulated: the thousands of farms whose runoff exacerbates the nonpoint source water pollution problem in our rivers and aquifers; the millions of cars whose exhaust makes the air we breathe a health hazard; the American households that are producing 3.5 pounds of solid waste per person every day. Confronted with this situation, we have five alternatives. We can

- Actively resist change
- Ignore the situation and comply grudgingly when forced to
- Anticipate and plan so we are ready when changes come
- Plan and implement in anticipation of regulatory changes
- Actively work for change

A few individuals, communities, and corporations are taking action now. Cities as small as Champaign, Illinois, and as large as Seattle, Washington, are recycling solid waste as a matter of course. Los Angeles, America's smog capital, has recycled solid waste since the 1920s and now has the most stringent air quality standards in the world. DuPont will phase out production of the CFCs (chlorofluorocarbons) that cause ozone depletion even before a complete ban is negotiated. Most forest products companies convert wood waste into electrical energy rather than burying or burning it.

The willingness to anticipate, plan, and take forward-looking action involves certain costs in the present. These are balanced by the possibility of substantial long-run benefits. On the other hand, fighting change may guarantee benefits in the short run in the form of lower expenditures, but the long-run costs may be devastating to individuals, businesses, and communities.

How individuals and communities weigh the tradeoff between these long- and short-run benefits and costs depends on many factors. Ultimately, all of them can be reduced to two:

- What results we expect from the choices we make today—our understanding of cause and effect;
- What we think is important—our values.

What consequences can we expect?

Few people argue that our present resource management practices are without harmful side effects, but there is widespread disagreement about how severe these side effects are. Many believe the long-run consequences of maintaining our present course are negligible, that our declining natural resource base will not limit economic growth, and that environmental degradation is not so severe as to impair our physical health and safety or threaten our quality of life in the foreseeable future.

In contrast, a growing body of evidence suggests that our present natural resource management practices are not sustainable. That is, these practices *will* impair the ability of future generations to meet their needs and may pose a threat to the present generation as well.

There is evidence to support both notions. Lake Erie, once pronounced dead, has been rejuvenated. The Cayahoga River, about which Randy Newman sang "Burn on, great River, burn on," no longer catches fire. On the other hand, the complex ecology of the enormous Chesapeake Bay is threatened by farm runoff. Soil losses in the Midwest exceed those of the dust bowl days. Many once-pure groundwater resources that supply major cities with drinking water are becoming polluted. These essential aquifers lack the self-cleansing properties of the polluted rivers with which we have had success in the past, and clean-up projects are more costly and are less likely to succeed.

In the long run, experience will prove or disprove one of these viewpoints. Meanwhile, we make decisions based on what we believe to be true. If we believe that our present course is not sustainable, continuing on it is like borrowing money to buy groceries. Once you begin, the debts keep adding up and there's no easy way out.

What is important to us?

Recent opinion polls show that most Americans think of themselves as "environmentalists." We say that taking care of the environment is important to us. However, there are conflicts among alternative things that we say are important. Consider the working mother who says that caring for the environment is important to her and her family. Having time to spend with her children is also important to her. These values may come into conflict when she has to choose between disposable and cloth diapers. She has to decide which value is more important. When she makes this choice, she reveals the ranking of her values.

As we confront the consequences of taking our natural resources for granted, we are driven to rethink the way we rank alternative values. Simply caring about the environment is not enough to change our behavior. Changes in our actions can only happen if we allow our stated values to shape our questions and guide our search for answers. Growing awareness of the consequences of environmental degradation may shift our concern from the present, where actions that strain the environmental capacity are easy and inexpensive, to the future, where the eventual cost of today's exploitation of the natural world may be very high. As we experience this shift in concern, the questions we ask must also change. Where we once asked, "How can I dispose of my community's waste cheaply and efficiently?" we may now ask, "How can I dispose of waste safely and distribute the cost fairly?" If we don't change the questions, we will find ourselves still coming up with old status quo answers.

If we value future generations' well-being, we will ask ourselves searching questions that lead us to more sustainable ways of managing our resources now. We must be willing to question our assumptions (i.e., "The public will never be willing to pay for waste disposal") and reassess our goals and objectives. Then we must broaden our search for answers, searching not only for scientific and technological innovation but also for more effective rules and regulations, improved institutions, restructured economic markets, expanded cooperation, and other people-oriented solutions.

How will Fredricksburg respond?

When the discussion slows, Alan poses a question to the committee.

"There's no one here who likes the predicament we're in, but there's nothing we can do now except to move forward. The question before us is, 'How will we respond?' I'm ready to entertain a motion."

"I think this whole thing stinks," Andy Garcia, a local realtor, declares. "Don't take this personally, Darryl. We appreciate you coming to Fredricksburg and explaining this to us. But waste disposal has always been a local issue. Now you come in here as a patsy for those Washington bureaucrats telling us what we can and can't do. I say ignore the whole thing and keep piling our waste on the present site. What are you going to do if we thumb our noses at you?"

Before Darryl can answer, Alan responds, "We could probably get away with that for a while—but at what cost? The people of Fredricksburg expect clean water. As you know, Andy, we dealt with this water quality problem not too long ago. Remember the brouhaha when a few families had to start hauling drinking water because our sewer system couldn't handle the poultry plant's effluent? We worked with the poultry plant, and helped them put in a pre-treatment system. Everybody came out ahead.

"The people of Fredricksburg expect us to operate a landfill where they can dispose of their trash. And they don't want the landfill to produce hordes of flies, noxious odors, or acrid smoke hanging over the town. It's time to deal with the issue up front. So I'm asking you again—How will we respond?"

Preston is still uncomfortable with the discussion. The whole problem seems too large and ill defined. He would rather not have to deal with it. He makes a motion: "I move that we table the issue pending further study." Though Alan is disappointed at the direction the meeting is taking, he calls for discussion of Preston's motion.

Arethra Price, the administrator of the county hospital, hasn't spoken during the discussion so far. She responds to Preston's motion, "That doesn't help us at all, Preston. I'm not going to support any open-ended study. At some point we've got to make some hard decisions, and I don't want to put that moment off indefinitely while you or somebody else goes off studying the thing. I say, if we need more studying, let's decide what we're going to study, who's going to do the studying, and when the study is going to be completed."

"Are you amending the motion?" Alan asks. "Not right now, no. Just making a comment," Arethra answers. "Is there further discussion?" Alan asks the group.

Rueben Snow, who operates the local Wings n' Things take-out chicken franchise, comes into the discussion. "Frankly, I'm not sure what there is to study at this point. If we're willing to consider a regional landfill, then we need to contact municipalities and counties in the area to see whether they even want to talk about the possibility. If not, then somebody had better start contacting private and municipal landfills we might be able to contract with."

Arethra adds, "If we decide to consider a regional landfill, we haven't committed ourselves to it. We've just narrowed the focus of our study. I move that we amend Paul's motion and study the feasibility of a regional landfill."

"Is there a second?" Alan asks.

Darryl interjects, "If you decide to consider a regional landfill, the state has two publications that can help you. We have guidelines for conducting a regional needs assessment. I can also get you guidelines for developing a regional solid waste management plan. You'll have to do the assessment and the plan before you can get approval for a regional waste management district. The guidelines are self-explanatory and your group should be able to pull together and analyze the needed information."

Preston asks suspiciously, "Can we really do it, or will we need to hire an expensive consultant?"

Darryl answers, "These publications were written to help communities like Fredricksburg avoid the cost of a consultant. Don't get me wrong. If you go through with this thing, you will need consultants and they will be expensive. But you shouldn't need one at this stage."

"In that case," Preston responds, "I withdraw my motion and second Arethra's." Surveying the group, Alan asks, "Is there further discussion?"

Andy Garcia answers, "I don't know about anyone else, but I don't think we ought to be taking such a big step so quickly. I've got a sick feeling in my stomach. We're talking about a lot of money and a lot of change. Where are we going to get the money? How will people react to having to pay more for waste disposal? More importantly, how will the executives at the chicken-processing plant feel about the increased fees? The folks here in Fredricksburg rely on the plant for jobs. What if the plant pulls out on account of us charging them more to dispose of their waste? They could, you know. Then where would we be?"

"I'd like to respond to your last question," Darryl says. "Your concern about the town's major employer is shared by virtually every community in this situation. But with the new regulations, this plant is going to have to pay more for waste disposal, wherever it locates. If they don't pay the town, they will have to pay someone else or build their own landfill that passes state scrutiny." Darryl continues, "But I think your concern goes deeper than that. Sometimes our fears of what might happen are practical and well founded. But sometimes specific fears are just masking a more general fear of change. Sure, the chicken plant could pull out of Fredricksburg and move somewhere else. But what's the likelihood of that really happening? They have several million dollars invested in this plant. They've trained the people here to do the job. When their operations were contaminating wells, they put in a pretreatment plant to reduce the load on the city sewer system. No matter where they go, they're going to have to pay for waste disposal sooner or later. Do you really think they'll leave? And if you do, why not talk to them instead of assuming the worst?

"If you let 'what might happen' set the limits on what you're willing to consider, you become a slave to the status quo—not just on this issue, but on lots of other important issues as well. I hope you don't do that. No matter what you do or don't do tonight, change is going to happen—it's already happened, the regulations have changed. These regulations aren't going to be easy for small communities to comply with, and that's a fact. That's why it's important that you explore every promising alternative. I guarantee you every person living in Fredricksburg will be better off if you look for lasting rather than makeshift solutions." Darryl stops, a little embarrassed. "I didn't mean to preach. I know how hard this is."

Waste disposal or waste management?

Alex Fourche, president of the local bank, stands up to speak.

"I really don't like to talk off the cuff so I usually stay quiet in these meetings, but this is too important to remain silent. Darryl is right. If we give in to our negative fantasies about the worst that could happen, we abdicate our responsibility to Fredricksburg. Our fears can keep us from addressing the problem meaningfully.

"And I agree with Arethra. We need to consider a regional landfill seriously. But I think we need to go farther. Disposing of our waste is only part of the problem. We also need to think about how we can reduce the amount of solid waste we produce and dispose of.

"When our creditors are having difficulty repaying their loans, I always tell them there are two elements of cash flow: You can increase what comes in or you can decrease what goes out—increase your sales or decrease your costs. The solution probably involves some of both. It's the same here, but opposite: We can expand our disposal capacity *or* reduce the amount we have to dispose of. We'd be fools not to do the best we can at both.

"We're talking about building a $2 million landfill that will last 20 years at the present rate we produce trash. If we could find ways to reduce the stream of waste, we might be able to extend the life of that landfill to 25 or 30 years or more. I don't know what those ways might be right now. And I don't really know if it's practical to talk about extending the life of the site that long.

"But I guarantee you that if we expand our definition of the problem, we will find ourselves looking at recycling options, public education, incentives for home recycling, and some things I can't even imagine now. We have to focus on *waste management* not *waste disposal.*"

Pausing to collect his thoughts, Alex concludes, "Mr. Mayor, I would like to amend the motion on the table: I would like to propose that we contact the regional planning group and the county administrators of all adjacent counties and set up a meeting to discuss forming a regional waste management district as a first step. If they are willing to consider the idea, the group's first task should be to develop a comprehensive, long-run strategic plan for solid waste *management* in the region. And Mr. Stevens, I hope you and your agency will assist in this effort."

Arethra Price turns to Alex and says, "Mr. Fourche, you surprise me. I always think that bankers are unimaginative. I guess I need to think again. I withdraw my motion and second yours." Order breaks down as everyone tries to make themselves heard above the rest.

Alan pounds the gavel to regain order. "Everyone will have a chance to talk if you will just be patient." Moving around the table, Alan encourages each group member to respond to Alex's motion. After discussing the idea, everyone except Andy Garcia seems comfortable with the approach. "If there is no further discussion," Alan declares, "I'll ask the question. All those in favor? Opposed? Motion carried. Do we have any other business?"

Prudence Snow, Rueben's wife, who recently retired as Fredricksburg High School's senior civics teacher, raises her hand. "Alan, if you don't mind. I'm not a member of the committee. I just came to see what was going on, so I've kept quiet till now. But I'd like to say something about what you all are doing here, if no one objects."

"We always appreciate hearing from you, Pru," Alan responds deferentially. Like most other members of the committee, he had been a student in Mrs. Snow's civics class quite a few years ago.

Prudence stands up. "You have taken a very important step tonight. You have committed yourselves to look for long-lasting solutions to the broad issue of waste management. And you have decided to explore the potential of working with other municipalities and counties to find cooperative solutions." As she walks to the chalkboard several faces around the table smile. "These commitments are the first steps in a long process." While she draws (figure 10.1), Prudence explains the process.

"The work you've done tonight is to define the waste-management problem as a long-run problem of producing and disposing of waste. The causal relationship between how we dispose of waste and the quality of our water made it necessary for you to think about waste management differently than you used

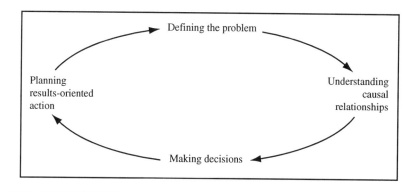

Figure 10.1. Iterative problem-solving process.

to—helped along by some changes in federal and state regulations." Prudence nods at Darryl and goes on. "The high cost of dealing with this harder waste-management problem forced you to consider a different kind of action—regional cooperation. You've made a decision to explore this new type of arrangement." By now the whole picture was drawn, with arrows leading around the circle.

"What I wanted to point out is that these are the first steps in a long process. That's what makes Andy nervous, I think, and he's right to feel that this is a major undertaking. You will spend a great deal of time building consensus in Fredricksburg and in all the other villages, towns, and counties in the region. They will have to define the problem for themselves. You will have to find out more about cause and effect, both with regard to waste flow, as Alex pointed out, and to find the best disposal approach for this new, larger region. You'll have many more decisions to make, some on your own, and others with the other participants in the regional waste management district. And you'll need to make a step-by-step action plan for implementing these decisions. Every stage in this process is related to every other stage, and sometimes you will feel that you're just going round in circles like my picture."

"What you've done tonight is the first step to long-term change. You've decided you want a long-range plan that will let Fredricksburg manage its waste and protect its water. Progress from one step to the next depends on your ability to focus on each task while keeping in mind what you want to achieve. There's no question in my mind that you can do it. I'm proud of you all."

There is a brief silence after Prudence sits down. Alan stands up, grinning. "Class dismissed, I guess."

Openness to Change

When the Fredricksburg committee was appointed, they viewed the problem as a straightforward site selection problem. The question that called for action was, "Where should we build the new landfill?" Consistent with this definition of the problem, the committee identified a site and submitted a preliminary plan to the state agency responsible for reviewing landfill permits.

When the state rejected their initial site plan, the committee broadened the question that calls for action. They asked, "What should we do to dispose of Fredricksburg's solid waste and meet state regulations?" They viewed the problem as a waste disposal problem. When the cost of complying with the new regulations caused them to rethink their definition of the problem yet again, they broadened the geographic scope of the question, asking, "How can we cooperate with neighboring communities to dispose of our waste and meet state regulations?"

Alex Fourche, the banker, was even skeptical about whether this broader question could yield long-lasting solutions. After some discussion, the committee again broadened the nature of the problem, defining the problem as a waste-management rather than a waste-disposal problem. This shift led them to ask questions they might not have asked otherwise: How can we slow the stream of waste produced now and in the future? How can we utilize the waste we produce through recycling or other means now and in the future? How can we dispose of the waste we produce efficiently and safely now and in the future? Answers to these questions are likely to produce a broader range of potential alternatives.

Going from narrow to broad questions

Moving from a narrow question to a broad question is critical to addressing natural resource management problems effectively. Narrow questions often exclude all but the old familiar and all-too-often unsustainable choice. When the question is where to site a city landfill, the answer is a point on the map. The question excludes regional cooperation, waste reduction, recycling, and other waste management alternatives. If we want to find more long-lasting and sustainable answers, we have to ask questions broad enough to allow for innovation and change.

Some groups never take this critical step. They ask questions that are too narrow. Many, like Andy Garcia and Preston McCrossen, are fearful of change. They fear that change may lead to conflict and affect the town adversely. They may exaggerate potential obstacles. Ultimately their fears may lead them to abdicate responsibility for seeking the "best" alternative.

Those groups willing to ask questions that allow for innovation and change have the potential to find more long-lasting and sustainable ways to manage natural resources. However, this step is just the first of many required to move from problem recognition to positive action.

Making progress in a neverending process

In the weeks and months ahead, the Fredricksburg group will take a sequence of small steps that together can lead to more sustainable waste management. But there will be times when even the people most committed to the group's goals feel overwhelmed by the size of the task ahead.

At each step along the way, progress depends on being able to focus on what needs to be done right now—while keeping in mind how today's step relates to all of the other small steps that have been and will be taken. The frameworks and group process steps presented in this book can help.

As long as the Fredricksburg group is open to questions that allow for innovation and change, there will always be some improvements that can be made. Ultimately, the process of asking and answering questions that leads to longer-lasting, more sustainable solutions is neverending. It is a way of thinking and acting that could fundamentally change the way we manage natural resources.

Suggested Readings

Ackoff, Russell L. 1978. *The Art of Problem Solving*. John Wiley and Sons: New York. 214 p.

Adams, James. 1976. *Conceptual Blockbusting*. San Francisco Book Co.: San Francisco.

American Academy of Arts and Sciences. Fall 1967. Special Issue: "America's Changing Environment." Deadalus.

Argyris, Chris, and Donald A. Schon. 1978. *Organizational Learning: A Theory of Action Perspective*. Addison-Wesley: Reading, Mass.

Beach, Lee Roy. 1990. *Image Theory*. John Wiley and Sons: London.

Behn, Robert D., and James W. Vaupel. 1982. *Quick Analysis for Busy Decision Makers*. Basic Books, Inc.: New York. 415 p.

Bentley, W. R., J. Marketta, and D. W. Countryman. 1984. "Management of People." *Forestry Handbook,* 2d ed. (K. F. Wenger, ed.). John Wiley and Sons: New York.

Berger, Peter L., and Richard John Neuhaus. 1977. "To Empower People: The Role of Mediating Structures in Public Policy." American Enterprise Institute for Public Policy Research: Washington, D.C. 45 p.

Braybrooke, David, and Charles E. Lindbolm. 1970. *A Strategy of Decision: Policy Evaluation as a Social Process*. Free Press: New York. 268 p.

Bryson, John M. 1988. *Strategic Planning for Public and Nonprofit Organizations*. Jossey-Bass Publishers: San Francisco. 311 p.

Chambers, R. A., Pacey, Thrupp, and L. A. Thrupp. 1989. *Farmer First*. The Bootstrap Press: New York. 238 p.

Delbecq, Andre L., Andrew H. Van de Ven, and David H. Gustafson. 1975. *Group Techniques for Program Planning: A Guide to Nominal Group Techniques and Delphi Process*. Scott, Foresman and Company: Glenview, Ill.

Dewey, John. 1933. *How We Think*. Henery Regnery Co.: Chicago.

Dover, M., and L. M. Talbot. 1987. "To Feed the Earth: Agroecology for Sustainable Development." World Resource Institute: Washington, D.C.

Drucker, Peter I. 1974. *Management: Tasks, Responsibilities, Practices*. Harper & Row: New York. 839 p.

Goffman, Erving. 1974. *Frame Analysis*. Harvard University Press: Cambridge, Mass.

Gordon, Thomas. 1980. *Leader Effectiveness Training: L.E.T.* Bantam Books, Inc: New York. 278 p.

Gordon, William. 1962. *Synectics.* Harper & Row: New York.

Gross, Edward, and Amitai Etzioni. 1985. *Organizations in Society.* Prentice-Hall, Inc.: Englewood Cliffs, N.J. 232 p.

Harrison, Michael I. 1987. *Diagnosing Organizations: Methods, Models, and Processes.* Sage: Newbury Park, Calif. 159 p.

Harwood, Richard R. 1989. "A History of Sustainable Agriculture." *Sustainable Agricultural Systems* (C. A. Edwards, et al., eds.). Soil and Water Conservation Society: Ankeny, Ia.

Huber, George P. 1980. *Managerial Decision Making.* Scott, Foresman and Company: Glenview, Ill. 225 p.

Janis, I. L., and L. Mann. 1977. *Decision Making.* Free Press: New York.

Jay, Anthony. 1976. "How to Run a Meeting." *Harvard Business Review,* March–April 1976. pp. 43–57.

Kahneman, D., P. Slovic, and A. Tversky. 1982. *Judgment under Uncertainty: Heuristics and Biases.* Cambridge University Press: London.

Kanter, Rosabeth Moss. 1983. *The Change Masters.* Simon and Schuster: New York. 432 p.

Kaufman, Herbert. 1960. *The Forest Ranger.* Johns Hopkins Press: Baltimore.

Kepner, Charles H., and Benjamin B. Tregoe. 1965. *The Rational Manager: A Systematic Approach to Problem Solving and Decision Making.* McGraw Hill Book Company: New York.

Kolb, David A. 1984. *Experiential Learning: Experience as the Source of Learning and Development.* Prentice-Hall: Englewood Cliffs, N.J.

Kuhn, Thomas S. 1959. "The Essential Tension." *Third University of Utah Research Conference on the Identification of Creative Scientific Talent* (C. W. Taylor, ed.). University of Utah Press: Salt Lake City.

Lee, Robert G., Donald R. Field, and William R. Burch, Jr., eds. 1990. *Community and Forestry: Continuities in the Sociology of Natural Resources.* Westview Press: Boulder, Colo. 289 p.

Le Master, Dennis C., and John H. Beuter, eds. 1989. *Community Stability in Forest-based Economies.* Timber Press: Portland, Ore. 191 p.

Leopold, Aldo. 1970. *A Sand County Almanac.* Oxford University Press: New York. 226 p.

Lindblom, Charles I. 1959. "The Science of Muddling Through." *Public Administration Review* 19:78–88.

Locke, Edwin A., and Gary P. Latham. 1984. *Goal Setting: A Motivational Technique that Works!* Prentice-Hall: Englewood Cliffs, N.J.

McGregor, Douglas. 1960. *The Human Side of Enterprise.* McGraw-Hill: New York.

McKenna, Christopher K. 1980. *Quantitative Methods for Public Decision Making.* McGraw-Hill Book Company: New York. 425 p.

March, James. 1988. *Decisions and Organizations.* Basil Blackwell: New York. 458 p.

Mintzberg, Henry. 1980. *The Nature of Managerial Work.* Prentice-Hall: Englewood Cliffs, N.J.

Mintzberg, Henry. 1983. *Structure in Fives: Designing Effective Organizations.* Prentice-Hall, Inc.: Englewood Cliffs, N.J. 312 p.

Morgan, Gareth. 1986. *Images of Organizations.* Sage Publications: Newbury Park, Calif. 423 p.

Morgan, Gareth. 1988. *Riding the Waves of Change.* Jossey-Bass: San Francisco.

Okun, Arthur M. 1975. *Equality and Efficiency: The Big Tradeoff.* The Brookings Institution: Washington, D.C.

Osborn, Alex. 1949. *Your Creative Power.* Charles Scribner's Sons: New York.

Ouchi, William. 1981. *Theory Z.* Addison-Wesley: Reading, Mass.

Piaget, Jean. 1974. *Understanding Causality.* W. W. North: New York.

Sauer, Carl Ortwin. 1963. *Land and Life.* University of California Press: Berkeley. 435 p.

Schein, Edgar. 1985. *Organizational Culture and Leadership.* Jossey-Bass: San Francisco. 358 p.

Schon, Donald A. 1983. *The Reflective Practicioners.* Basic Books: New York. 374 p.

Selznick, Philip. 1957. *Leadership in Administration.* Harper & Row: New York. 162 p. University of California Press, 1984.

Senge, Peter M. 1990. *The Fifth Discipline: The Art and Practice of the Learning Organization.* Doubleday Currency: New York. 424 p.

Simon, Herbert A. 1976. *Administrative Behavior: A Study of Decision-making Processes in Administrative Organizations,* 3d ed. Free Press: New York. 364 p.

Thompson, James D. 1967. *Organizations in Action.* McGraw-Hill: New York.

Von Winterfeldt, Detlof, and Ward Edwards. 1986. *Decision Analysis and Behavioral Research.* Cambridge University Press: New York. 604 p.

Whetten, David A., and Kim S. Cameron. 1984. *Developing Managerial Skills.* Scott, Foresman and Company: Glenview, Ill.

Wilkins, Alan L., and William G. Ouchi. 1983. "Efficient Cultures: Exploring the Relationship between Culture and Organizational Performance." *Administrative Science Quarterly* 23:468-481.

Wilson, Gerald L., and Michael S. Hanna. 1986. *Groups in Context: Leadership and Participation in Small Groups.* Random House: New York. 349 p.

World Commission on Environment and Development. 1987. *Our Common Future.* Oxford University Press: New York. 383 p.

Yukl, Gary A. 1987. *Leadership in Organizations,* 2d ed. Prentice-Hall: Englewood Cliffs, N.J. 340 p.